REPACKAGING THE WELFARE STATE

Pranab Chatterjee

NASW PRESS

National Association of Social Workers
Washington, DC

Paula L. Delo, Publications Manager
Linda Dziobek, Senior Editor, Books
Marcia D. Roman, Production Editor
Caroline Polk, Copy Editor
Susan J. Harris, Proofreader
Bernice Eisen, Indexer

Library of Congress Cataloging-in-Publication Data

Chatterjee, Pranab, 1936–
Repackaging the welfare state / by Pranab Chatterjee.
p. cm.
Includes bibliographical references and index.
ISBN 0-87101-304-5
1. Welfare state.
JC479.C535 1999
361.6'5—DC21 98-43521
CIP

Printed in the United States of America

To Sraboni

Also by Pranab Chatterjee

Approaches to the Welfare State. (1996). NASW Press.

Dialogue

[The aft-deck of a large ocean-going boat, as it is steaming away. A father and his six-year-old daughter are standing side by side, overlooking the waves.]

Daughter: Daddy, you like those waves?

Father: [Eyes on the waves] Yes, honey.

Daughter: What was that you said, we just left what?

Father: Over there, we just left an international border.

Daughter: Dad, I don't see any borders!

Father: Well, borders don't exist out there. We humans keep putting in make-believe borders on the sea. We call them international borders.

[A few minutes of silence.]

Daughter: Those waves are pretty, aren't they?

Father: Yes, honey. Each one of them is like a lesson to be learned. One of them is like an economics lesson, and another one is like a psychology lesson. . .

Daughter: Like, each wave is a lesson?

Father: Yes!

Daughter: Oh, each wave is a lesson!

[Some more minutes of silence.]

Father: Come, we have things to do in our cabin. [Stands up, and starts walking to the cabin.]

Daughter: [In an irritated voice] Dad, those waves keep bothering each other, and they don't *obey* any borders!

CONTENTS

A Storyline: Danielle's Dilemmas

Danielle is getting a strange form of heartburn. The dean of a prominent American social work school, she is beginning to realize that the positions and values she learned as a social work student in the 1960s, as a caseworker in a family service agency subsequent to her graduation, as a supervisor of social service after that, as a doctoral student in another social work school, and as a faculty member in a school where she is now the dean, meant studying the solutions to human vulnerability in an industrial society. Those solutions included learning that her profession has emerged as one of these solutions, that this profession's reason for being is finding vulnerable populations who are in need of advocacy, that increased redistribution from the state will solve these problems, and that the Scandinavian states are the perfect exemplar of such redistribution.

Even though a dean, she also teaches. She teaches courses in group theory and organizational theory. One principle lesson she teaches is that groups, organizations, and communities develop a culture of their own. Included in this culture are a division of labor, emergent roles related to that division of labor, social behavior of individuals and subgroups according to their own agendas and interest, and modes of social control. As she looks at her social work school as a large group or an organization, she becomes aware of certain problems. According to her perception, she has two types of tenured faculty: the productive ones and the unproductive ones. The productive ones contribute to the school, the unproductive ones do the bare minimum. She would like to see some of the unproductive faculty retire or leave, but now there is no mandatory retirement age, and no other school will hire these people. She feels that what tenure is to a university, entitlement is to a state. Just like governing her organization can cause a heartburn, governing the modern welfare state can cause a headache.

She also feels that she is becoming bicultural. Her culture of identity was the culture of social workers, with its commitment to finding more vulnerable groups and espousing that a better redistribution will solve problems of poverty and marginality. However, the culture of her peer administrators (a culture of the deans and other administrators of the university) is firmly committed to the position that tenure is a serious problem, that faculty should be rewarded only when their productivity is high, that faculty only operate from their own interests and often are totally unconcerned about the survival needs of the school and the university, and governing a school requires a belief in a culture of governance.

When Danielle speaks to her fellow social workers, she affirms the values of social work. When she speaks with her fellow managers, she reluctantly agrees with the values of managers. She is becoming aware that that the two cultures are not quite compatible: This is what is causing her heartburn. Recently she is finding that many agency executives also share her dilemma: Some of the formulas espoused by the profession are not compatible with those needed for managing an agency.

Recently, she has been encouraged to run for a national political office. There is a vacancy in the House of Representatives, and several groups are encouraging her to run for that office. However, in that capacity she needs to develop position papers about what she is going to do for business groups, especially small businesses. She also is becoming aware of the fact that the state's resources are not unlimited, that entitlement-orientation has its own set of problems, and that a visionary representative must offer formulas about balancing needs for equity with needs for efficiency.

She knows cognitively that she has to learn a new set of skills, values, and orientations to manage her school. She definitely needs them if she is to run for Congress. However, these new skills, values, and orientations are affectively alien to her.

She has to manage her heartburn!

INTRODUCTION

The welfare state is a subject of study by social workers, sociologists, political scientists, historians, economists, and moral philosophers. How ever, the approach is different in every discipline. It is the purpose of this book to undertake a study of the welfare state from an **interdisciplinary** perspective. This means that I use constructs from the discipline of social work like social policy; from the disciplines of sociology and anthropology like national cultures, the adaptational styles of national cultures in changing environments, the stratification system within national cultures, and roles developed for key functions within national cultures; from the discipline of economics, concepts like production, distribution, redistribution, and surplus; and from the realm of moral philosophy, concepts like justice, protection, equality, liberty, and rights.

The study of the welfare state is not very common among American social workers. American social workers study what they call social policy, which is the study of how welfare services emerged since the latter part of the 19th century and how they have been shaped by the influence of the "liberals" on one side and "conservatives" on the other (see Karger & Stoesz, 1994). British and European scholars, on the other hand, have approached the subject as of human vulnerability and the efforts of the modern nation-state to manage such vulnerability (Esping-Andersen, 1990; George & Wilding, 1977; Titmuss, 1958; Titmuss 1968). Economists and sociologists in America have also approached the subject as an effort by the state to manage human vulnerability (Rimlinger, 1971; Schumpeter, 1950; Skocpol, 1992; Wilensky, 1975).

Given this background, social policy scholarship sometimes does not present a balanced view of how certain problems of human vulnerability can be solved by the state. Instead, it represents a form of indoctrination that more and more spending by the state on social problems is the only way to solve social problems, that "liberals" who support this point of view are "good" people, and that conservatives who do not necessarily support more state spending as a way to solve social problems are "bad" people. It is important to learn that more spending may not necessarily lead to solutions of social problems; that the state's capacity to spend depends on its ability to tax; that the state creating a series of entitlements for given categories of recipients may lead to serious economic and political problems; and that newer formulas are needed to form and maintain a civil society that will not bankrupt the state, that will work in parity with the changing birth rate and life expectancy, and that will both support vulnerable populations and simultaneously reward those who generate wealth in society.

The problem, then, is how to envision a welfare state that will maintain a civil society (which provides caregiving to the vulnerable) and simultaneously reward wealth-building activities. After all, the former activities (maintaining civil society) are not possible without the latter (wealth building).

Given these assumptions, this book argues that

- The capacity of a society to have a welfare state depends on its productivity.

- The former socialist societies promised a welfare to state its citizens, but were not productive enough to sustain it.

- The capitalist societies, which did not promise any welfare state, are nonetheless the only societies operational with viable welfare states (in all other societies, including Third World societies, most of the welfare functions are performed by the family, the community, or the church and not by the state).

- Even when there is capacity for high productivity, a society's dependency ratio may jeopardize the welfare state.

- Even when there is capacity for high productivity, a society's style of redistribution may jeopardize the welfare state.

One important style of redistribution in a welfare state is a continuum between sharing surplus and marketing surplus; related to that continuum are the following points:

- Sharing surplus leads to what sociologists call "relative deprivation."
- Marketing surplus leads to what economists call "diminishing returns."
- Sharing surplus leads to reduced entrepreneurship.
- Marketing surplus leads to a market of human vulnerability.
- Sharing surplus may lead to relatively decreased commodification.
- Marketing surplus may lead to increased commodification.

To maintain viable civil societies, the following actions are warranted:

- Sharing surplus welfare states need to reduce entitlements.
- Marketing surplus needs what sociologists call "social control" of many types of entrepreneurs.

The mission statement directing such a changed welfare state should read as follows:

> From each, according to his or her productivity, with an ongoing concern for encouraging incentives for further productivity; and
>
> To each, according to his or her basic needs , tested for the recipient's own means and the state's capacity to transfer.

* * * * *

This book also departs from some of the existing "party line" thinking of social workers, policy makers and from the current wisdom of both liberals and conservatives. Some of its points of departures are listed below. In fact, I assert that the ideas of liberals and conservatives are a form of "local knowledge" in the United States, and are not very useful ideas for the analysis of the modern welfare state.

A great deal of Anglo-American social work has been influenced by the thinking of Richard M. Titmuss. It is time to make a shift from the work of Titmuss to that of L. T. Hobhouse. According to Titmuss (1950, 1959, 1968, 1971), massive redistribution is extremely important; welfare is a right, due to community membership and due to citizenship in a modern state; and during times of crisis, able members of a community must altruistically engage in a "gift relationship" to its vulnerable members. According to Hobhouse (1911, 1921), any redistribution must take into consideration the idea of "reciprocity" and the members of a civil society must be committed to this basic idea; all members of a community and the modern state must make attempts to participate in a network of reciprocity; no modern community or society can operate without a fundamental commitment to this concept of reciprocity; and that the modern state cannot depend on mere altruism or gifts for its operation.

Moroney and Krysik (1998) have commented in *Social Policy and Social Work* (1998) that neither the liberals nor the conservatives have what it takes to do a proper analysis of the welfare state, because both of them lack a basic foundation based on a theory of the state. This book attempts to do precisely that by showing the following:

- The modern welfare state is a by-product of industrialization, a point developed already in my earlier book *Approaches to the Welfare State* (1996).
- Capitalist industrial states are the most successful welfare states to date.
- Socialism is a poor idea toward the production of an efficient welfare state.
- The viability of the welfare state depends on its productivity and its dependency ratio.
- The modern state has several functions to perform, like maintain sovereignty, procure resources, provide protection, secure rights, protect liberty, administer justice, promote equality, representation, regulation, and redistribution, and attain full employment (see chapter 3, and especially Table 3-5);
- The modern welfare state is an extension of the protection function (while rights, equality, justice, or such other concepts are mere slogans); and
- The state is continuously impacted on by its redistributionist policies.

References

Esping-Andersen, G. (1990). *The three worlds of welfare capitalism*. Princeton, NJ: Princeton University Press.

George, V., & Wilding, P. (1976). *Ideology and social welfare*. London: Routledge.

Hobhouse, L. T. (1911). *Liberalism*. London: Williams & Norgate.

Hobhouse, L. T. (1922). *The elements of social justice*. London: Allen & Unwin.

Karger, H. J., & Stoesz, D. (1998). *American social welfare policy: A pluralist approach*. New York: Longman.

Moroney, R. M., & Krysik, J. (1998). *Social policy and social work: Critical essays on the welfare state*. New York: Aldine de Gruyter.

Schumpeter, J. (1950). *Capitalism, socialism, and democracy*. New York: Harper & Row.

Skocpol, T. (1992). *Protecting soldiers and mothers*. Cambridge, MA: Harvard University Press.

Titmuss, R. M. (1959). *Essays on the welfare state.* New Haven, CT: Yale University Press.

Titmuss, R. M. (1968). *Commitment to welfare.* New York: Pantheon.

Titmuss, R. M. (1971). *The gift relationship.* New York: Pantheon.

Wilensky, H. (1975). *The welfare state and equality.* Berkeley: University of California Press.

Acknowledgments

An author's debts are many. He or she becomes known as the originator of certain ideas once a book appears in a printed form. However, the debts that a person accrues in the production of those ideas are never really paid. Listed below are the people to whom I am indebted as an author. The contributions of this book to the field, if any, emerged from their participation in the production process of this book and their various forms of reciprocity with me. The limitations of this book are solely mine.

My students: Eileen Abel, Mark Chupp, Susan Cole, Fran Danis, Amy D'Aprix, Sheri Eisengart, Charles Emlet, Ovidiu Gavrolovici, Craig Johnson, Gigi Nordquist, Meeyoung Oho, Yeon-hee Rho, Patricia Sandau-Beckler, John Sinclair, Robert Vander Beek, Sheila Webster, and Phyllis Wharfe.

My colleagues: Darlyne Bailey, Suzy Comerford, Merl C. Hokenstad, Jr., Alice Johnson, Marvin Rosenberg, P.K. Saha, Zoe Breen Wood, and Meyer Zald.

My children: Manu Chatterjee, Sraboni Chatterjee.

Finally, without the tolerance and ongoing support of my wife, Marian, this work would not have been possible.

1

The Welfare State: Promises and Performance

The study of the welfare state has not been based on the same assumptions or developed with the same questions. Different social science disciplines have approached it from very different perspectives that have led to disciplinary tunnel vision. It is important to identify where in a continuum between "equity" and "efficiency" any given scholarly venture lies. Furthermore, the pursuit of only one end of this continuum may lead to partisan advocacy, but not to scholarship.

The term "welfare state" refers to a state that has gone through industrialization and in which, regardless of its ideology, a set of formal and informal social policies have evolved to provide income support, health care, education, and selected other goods and services to vulnerable and potentially vulnerable populations. Those goods and services constitute a form of nonmarket transfer: State policy, taxation, and other devices are used to shift resources from those who are participants in the marketplace to those who are not. Subgroups, such as children and elderly, retired, disabled, ill, mentally handicapped, or unskilled people, often do not participate in the marketplace. In nearly all industrialized states, social policy provides support for these subgroups through nonmarket transfers.

The concept of the welfare state has several intellectual origins. One such origin is Bismarck's Germany in the 19th century (Rimlinger, 1971). Otto von Bismarck (1815–1898) was an aristocrat, who pioneered such welfare programs as protection against old age, illness, and other calamities (Pflanze, 1990). These programs were devices to prevent a working class revolt. A second origin is perhaps in the promise made by socialism: "From each according to his ability, to each according to his need" (as cited in Gould, 1980, p. 178), a motto that guided the formerly communist countries. A third origin, the effects of social democracy in Northern and Western Europe, can be said to have contributed to welfare state development there. A fourth origin, the threat of communism from the outside and the threats of sporadic market failures from within the capitalist countries of Western Europe and North America, pushed welfare state development there (Esping-Andersen, 1990). After World War II, the concept of three parts of the world emerged: the First World, or the capitalist West; the Second World, or the communist North and East; and the Third World, which was the rest of the globe. It seems that the welfare states developed in the First and Second Worlds and not in the Third World (Chatterjee, 1996).

The promise of the welfare state in each region can be summed up in the following manner. In the most powerful country in the First World (the United States), the state promised the moon but not social welfare: "Ask not what your country can do for you; ask what you can do for your country" (John F. Kennedy, as cited in Snowman, 1977, p. 155). In the Second World, the welfare state promised "From each according to his ability, to each according to his need" (Karl Marx, cited in Gould, 1980, p. 178). People in a populous and politically prominent country in the Third World (India), received a forewarning: "Ask not what fruit your labor will bear; for your destiny is to keep on working, regardless of whatever fruit it may bear" (Lord Krishna in *The Gita*, chapter 2, Sloka 47, as produced by Music Today, 1996).

In the First World, Kennedy's admonishment was not only a call for nationalism but also an important statement about capitalism's view of the relationship between the citizen and the state: The state does not necessarily owe the citizen anything. The self-reliance of the citizen is of the utmost importance. In the Second World, the Marxian promise represented socialism's view of the relationship between the citizen and the state: The state owes some degree of support to the citizens for their loyalty and labor, but the independence and individualism of its citizens, if any, should be cause for suspicion. In the Third World countries, Lord Krishna's forewarning is clear: The state (or the monarch) does not owe the citizen (or the subject) anything. It is the duty and destiny of the citizen (or the subject) to engage in labor, which is not a means to an end but an end in itself.

Although the above three axioms metaphorically represent the promises of the modern nation-states in the First, Second, and Third Worlds, the states' performances have been entirely different. In the First World, nearly every country has built a social safety net for its citizens. Within-nation differences in welfare eligibility and types of benefits exist in the First World (Ashford, 1986; Esping-Andersen, 1990; Gould, 1993; Korpi, 1987), but it seems that the capacity to have a welfare state at all is in part a function of a nation's economic position in a world hierarchy (Chatterjee, 1996). Although within-group differences grew during the Second World, after the break-up of the monolithic structure of communism, the welfare states of the Second World are essentially suffering from an economic inability to sustain their cherished welfare states (Dixon & Macarov, 1992). In contrast, only four Pacific Rim countries of the Third World—Singapore, South Korea, Taiwan and, possibly, Malaysia—are contemplating the erection of welfare states because they have only recently developed the economic ability to do so. As we move into the 21st century, the remainder of the Third World is without any social safety net provided by the state; the family and community are the only providers of social welfare in the Third World (Chatterjee, 1996).

One could argue that substantial ideological and technological differences exist within the First, Second, and Third Worlds and that the axioms from Kennedy, Marx, and Lord Krishna consequently are inappropriate. To such arguments, this author—with the support of a large number of scholars (George & Wilding, 1976; Pinker, 1979, Quadagno, 1988; Rimlinger, 1971; Wilensky, 1975)—responds as follows:

- Technological growth is what produces surpluses that make a welfare state possible.
- Ideology is more often a justification than a reason for welfare state development and its allocations.
- Ideology also is more a justification than a reason for the lack of welfare state development in the Third World.

Thus, with the Kennedy axiom as a guide for the First World, the following assumptions apply:

- Adequate technology exists to produce enough for everybody.
- All members of society should participate in some way in this production process.
- Those who have contributed in the past or have the potential to contribute in the future to the production process should be under a social safety net.
- Those who do not participate in the production process should be seen as "deviants." (A hierarchy of deviance may exist within the group of such deviants).

With the Marxian axiom as a guide to the Second World (that is, the former Communist bloc that is now trying to move to a market economy), the following assumptions seem to apply:

- Regardless of technology, all persons have a responsibility to participate in the production process.
- Whatever is produced will be distributed, not by the principle of who contributed most to the production process, but by the principle of who has the most need.
- Those who do not subscribe to the interpretation of this doctrine (usually a dominant political party) are deviants.

Using Krishna's axiom, the following assumptions apply:

- Nature (or God) is always dominant over any technology humans may invent.
- Although at times any production effort may produce very little, humans nonetheless have a duty or obligation (known as "Karma") to participate in the production process.
- It is not a worker's role to ask what return may be forthcoming from participation in the production process.

As the 21st century approaches, welfare states are not promised, but they are nonetheless operational in the capitalist First World. In the Second World, welfare states are promised, but they operate in decreasing capacity. In the Third World, for the most part, there is either no promise and no operational welfare state or lofty aspirations with little capacity to make them real.

Throughout the 20th century, it seems that two types of natural and social experiments have taken place: The first type has sought to determine the kinds of states that can develop and sustain a welfare state, whereas the second type has attempted to ascertain the social policies within welfare states that could solve long-standing social problems of poverty, aging, dependence, ill health, poor mental health, addiction, and other afflictions of human existence. The tentative results of the first type of experiment are that the industrial state was a sufficient condition for welfare state development and that the capitalist industrial state was a sufficient condition for developing as well as sustaining a welfare state. In contrast, although the socialist industrial state also was a sufficient condition for developing a welfare state, it was not necessarily sufficient for sustaining it. Other types of states, including secular, theocratic, pluralist, ethnically homogeneous, and monarchist states (Hall & Ikenberry, 1989), had no relationship with the development of the welfare state, although most of them had some provisions for charity, organized charity, or seasonal charity under the auspices of the state itself. (For a differentiation between organized charity and the welfare state, see Trattner, 1979.)

The main finding from the second type of social experiment of the 20th century is that states in general, and welfare states in particular, may engage in spending behavior to solve certain social problems, but such behavior leads to more demands for spending while leaving the social problems unsolved.

Clarification: Welfare Societies and Welfare States

The distinction between welfare societies and welfare states was first used by Titmuss (see Reisman, 1977). In that distinction, *welfare society* refers to the commitment of the entire society to maintaining its vulnerable and potentially vulnerable populations in a dignified manner, whereas *welfare state* refers to the efforts of the entire infrastructure of that society's central government toward the same ends. Seen in this manner, society is the larger macrosocial unit, and the state is the infrastructure built for the governance of that society. The state is thus a subset of a society.

Another way of looking at the two entities encouraged by Marx (see Gould, 1980, pp. 164–180) is to view the society as an entire people and the state as its managing agent. The people are bound by a set of social institutions, whereas the state is a form of a rational bureaucracy. Any outcome of the way society organizes its caregiving is a result of the culture of the people and the policy of the state. Seen in this way, the two are an interacting pair, and any outcome measure of one is also the outcome measure of the other, since they cannot be seen as separate entities. Most of the discussion in this book springs from this second view of the state and society.

The Foundations of a Welfare Society: Surplus as a Prerequisite

It seems that a basic requirement for a welfare society is the capacity to build a surplus (see Janowitz, 1976). This surplus is built best by a capitalist industrial society (Berger, 1986; Chatterjee, 1996; Schumpeter, 1950). To this idea, Quadagno (1988) adds that although industrialization may lead to the introduction of a welfare society, no uniform timing exists for when such a development may occur. The Third World countries, which are mostly nonindustrial, do not have such surpluses, and the Second World countries, which mostly were planned economies of the former Communist bloc, have insufficient surplus to sustain a welfare society.

Measures of Welfare Societies

No measures exist that are called "measures of the welfare society." The Human Development Index (HDI), however, which the United Nations uses, can serve as an indirect measure of a welfare society. The HDI represents three equally weighted indicators of quality of human life: longevity, as shown by life expectancy at birth; knowledge, as shown by adult literacy and mean years of schooling; and income, as purchasing power parity dollars per capita—income and what it buys (United Nations Development Programme, 1994).

Using an HDI of 0.875 as the threshold (and states rating above it can be called welfare societies), the states listed in Table 1-1 could be called welfare societies in 1992. Using 1993 data (Table 1-2), however, it seems that within a year, the quality of life improved in the market economy countries

Table 1-1. Societies Above 0.875 in the Human Development Index (HDI) Measure, 1992

STATE	HDI	STATE	HDI
Canada	0.932	Belgium	0.916
Switzerland	0.931	Iceland	0.914
Japan	0.929	Denmark	0.912
Sweden	0.928	Finland	0.911
Norway	0.928	Luxembourg	0.908
France	0.927	New Zealand	0.907
Australia	0.926	Israel	0.900
United States	0.925	Barbados	0.894
Netherlands	0.923	Ireland	0.892
United Kingdom	0.919	Italy	0.891
Germany	0.918	Spain	0.888
Austria	0.917	Hong Kong	0.875

FORMER PLANNED ECONOMY SOCIETIES THAT COME CLOSE

STATE	HDI	STATE	HDI
Czechoslovakia	0.872	Belarus	0.847
Lithuania	0.868	Ukraine	0.823
Latvia	0.865	Bulgaria	0.815
Hungary	0.863	Poland	0.815
Russian Federation	0.858		

Source: United Nations Development Programme. (1994). *Human development report 1994.* New York: Oxford University Press.

listed in Table 1-1. Furthermore, 11 other countries that year (Greece, Cyprus, Bahamas, Malta, Republic of Korea, Argentina, Costa Rica, Uruguay, Chile, Singapore, and Portugal) exceeded the threshold of 0.875 and could be added to the list. In contrast, the 10 countries from the former planned economies shown in the tables all had HDIs below the 0.875 threshold. In fact, most of the former planned economy countries seemed downwardly mobile in human development.

The Industrial Society as the Welfare Society

John Kenneth Galbraith (1967) was among the scholars in the 1960s who pointed out that the industrial society can be seen from a bidimensional view. The first dimension is the phase of industrial development, and the second is the ideology of the group that ushers in industrialization. The phase dimension can be divided into early- or late-phase industrialization,

Table 1-2. Societies Above 0.875 in the Human Development Index (HDI) Measure, 1993

MARKET ECONOMY SOCIETIES			
STATE	HDI	STATE	HDI
Canada	0.951	Belgium	0.929
Switzerland	0.926	Iceland	0.919
Japan	0.938	Denmark	0.924
Sweden	0.933	Finland	0.935
Norway	0.937	Luxembourg	0.895
France	0.935	New Zealand	0.927
Australia	0.929	Israel	0.908
United States	0.940	Barbados	0.908
Netherlands	0.938	Ireland	0.919
United Kingdom	0.924	Italy	0.914
Germany	0.920	Spain	0.933
Austria	0.928	Hong Kong	0.909
		Argentina	0.885
Greece	0.909	Costa Rica	0.884
Cyprus	0.909	Uruguay	0.883
Bahamas	0.895	Chile	0.882
South Korea	0.886	Singapore	0.881
Malta	0.886	Portugal	0.878

FORMER PLANNED-ECONOMY SOCIETIES			
STATE	HDI	STATE	HDI
Czech Republic	0.872	Russia	0.804
Slovakia	0.864	Belarus	0.787
Hungary	0.855	Bulgaria	0.773
Latvia	0.820	Ukraine	0.719
Poland	0.819	Lithuania	0.719

SOURCE: United Nations Development Programme (1996). *Human development report 1996.* New York: Oxford University Press.

and the ideology dimension can be categorized as capitalist or socialist. The typologies of the phase dimension have been revised as pre-Fordist, Fordist, and post-Fordist (Clarke, 1990; Ritzer, 1992), which correspond to early industrialization, mass-production industrialization (as it happened in the assembly lines of Henry Ford), and information-dependent industrialization.

The first phase of industrial society—referred to here as pre-Fordist industrial society—developed in the middle of the 19th century, first in England, and then in the United States. It was the beginning of the Industrial Revolution, and the economy was changing from an extractive one to a secondary goods–producing one. The state was relatively small by today's standards, entrepreneurial capitalists rather than big corporations dominated the corporate landscape (Galbraith, 1967), social policy was formulated by what was called organized charity, and no welfare society as we know it today existed. (Skocpol, 1992, however, argues that pension benefits emanating from the Civil War were a major budget item in the United States.) About this time, charitable giving in the United States was made tax deductible, and this policy contributed to the beginning of a nonprofit sector (Weisbrod, 1988). Organized charity was a part of this sector.

The second phase of the industrial society began in the 1930s. Galbraith (1967) called it "the new industrial state," and we will call it the "Fordist" industrial state. Managerial capitalism (as Burnham, 1941, had called it), in which a group of professional managers, rather than the "robber barons" of an earlier time, were making crucial economic decisions, was replacing entrepreneurial capitalism. The state had become quite large and had some new functions, including some forms of regulation of industry and other spheres; new sources of revenue, such as the personal income tax; (often reluctant) mediation in disputes between labor and management; and certain welfare state functions. During and after the second phase of the industrial society, the state engaged in developing social policies to provide income, education and, sometimes, health care to either selected citizens or all citizens; those social policies required a nonmarket distribution. Agents of the state grew concerned that certain vulnerable populations, such as children and disabled and older people, be protected. In effect, the state also became an active agent of distribution, a function that had been previously accomplished only by the market. During this time, organized charity changed, and professional social workers emerged. The upheavals of World War II helped develop state functions, as did the Cold War and other turmoil that followed after 1945. By the 1960s, the state had become more active in nonmarket distribution and was even more engaged in providing protection to vulnerable populations. The nonprofit sector grew substantially (Weisbrod, 1988).

The third phase of the industrial society, the "post-Fordist" phase, began in the 1970s, mostly in America (Clarke, 1990). At the beginning of that decade Kenneth Arrow, in his Nobel Prize–winning work, *Social Choice and Individual Values* (1963), showed that it is not possible for the state to optimize the interests of all its citizens. The social experiments of the earlier years had also proven that the state cannot achieve even democratic participation by all or alleviate relative poverty (see Moynihan, 1969). Those observations, however, did not stop state spending for welfare functions. The economy began to move from a secondary goods–providing economy to a service, information-processing, and craft-structured economy (Bell, 1973; Piore & Sabel, 1984; Sabel, 1982). The power of the labor unions began to decline with the changes in the role of working-class participation in industry. Managerial capitalism began evolving toward multinational corporate groups, and deregulation of industry by the state became an important theme by the 1980s. The growth of the service industries contributed to further professionalization of social workers, who were moving away from supporting the state in its welfare functions and were beginning to participate in the marketplace as mental health providers. This era also saw substantial growth in the nonprofit sector (Weisbrod, 1988).

The preceding discussion, for the most part, derives from the Anglo-American experience. In other settings, the following items are important: the agents of industrialization (that is, who ushers in industrialization), the role of the state in the process, the involvement of the state in providing welfare functions, and the size of the nonprofit sector (see Esping-Andersen, 1990; Gould, 1993; Rimlinger, 1971). For example, Germany and, later, Sweden did not see much of pre-Fordist industrial society. Instead, their history corresponds with the Fordist model (see Boje, Gephart, Jr., & Thatchenkery, 1996; Peukert, 1992). The pattern in Russia also corresponded to Fordism somewhat, although it was led by revolutionary intellectuals, was planned by the state, and did not have a large voluntary nonprofit sector, as in the Anglo-American setting. The remainder of Western Europe, Canada, Australia, and Japan also followed the Fordist model (Esping-Andersen, 1990; Gould, 1993; Peukert, 1992; Rimlinger, 1971). Thus, only the Anglo-American societies saw a historical progression from pre-Fordist to Fordist to post-Fordist industrial society. Most other industrial societies are Fordist industrial states, although variations within this type can be seen in

- the agents of industrialization (that is, whether they are business elites and their managers or revolutionary elites and their managers)
- the volume of welfare functions provided by the state (high in almost all industrial countries except the United States)
- the volume of the nonprofit sector (high in the Anglo-American setting, low in the Communist countries, and low to medium in other industrial societies)
- the volume of welfare functions carried on by the nonprofit sector (high in the Anglo-American setting, low in the Communist countries, and low to medium in all other industrial states).

Pre-Fordist industrial society relied on market economy, in which the state had a lesser role in the distribution process and in the process of regulation of commerce and industry. The Fordist society had a rudimentary form of collective bargaining by the working class and left social safety nets in the hands of the family and the community, which it called "organized charity" or "scientific charity" (Trattner, 1979). Even though Fordist production style had been around since the early part of the 20th century, a major problem of the Fordist industrial state became obvious with a market failure (the Great Depression) and the possibility that it could happen again. Franklin Roosevelt's social programs, known as the "New Deal" programs, were introduced to thwart a working-class revolt. In contrast, Bismarck's social programs in Germany at the latter part of the 19th century had been introduced without any looming market failure to pre-empt any possibility of a working-class revolt. Both the German and the American efforts led to the formation of different types of welfare policy: anticipatory (or pre-emptive) social policy in Germany and reactive social policy in America (to be discussed again in chapter 4).

The Fordist society grew to a position where the state had a substantial role both in the distribution process and as a regulatory body. Here production moved from the "scientific management" of Taylor (1911) to the principles of group dynamics and intergroup relations (see Anthony, 1977; Bendix, 1956; Forsyth, 1990). This industrial society saw the heyday of the labor movement and of large and politically powerful labor unions. It was referred to as "modern society" (in contrast to the traditional societies of the Third World or to earlier agrarian or feudal eras of the modern societies themselves). After World War II, modern societies were seen as a model of modernization for traditional societies (Frank, 1969; Furtado, 1970; Lenski, Lenski, & Nolan, 1991). In contrast, the post-Fordist industrial society has a reduced role in the regulation of commerce and industry; an increasing trend toward privatization; mounting budget deficits; a service and information-processing economy; a return of craft-based production (Piore & Sabel, 1984); reduction of size and loss of power in the labor unions; reduced job security for the working class; and problems emerging from a new, unskilled or semiskilled labor force, who are either citizens of a foreign country or members of the "underclass" within the country. The new labor force would do jobs that the established labor forces from the working classes would not do. Some French scholars called it a "postmodern society" (Lyotard, 1984; Pardek, Murphy, & Choi, 1994).

Veblen's industrial society existed only in the United States before World War I. In contrast, three variants of the Fordist industrial society emerged after the war: The first was the United States from about 1918 to the early 1970s. The second consisted of most of Western Europe—countries Esping-Andersen (1990) called "statist-corporatist" and "social-democratic"—between World War I and the 1980s. The third variant was the Communist bloc in the period between the Bolshevik Revolution and 1990. Similarly, two variants of the post-Fordist industrial society have emerged: The first is the United States since the early 1970s, and the second is Britain since the middle part of the 1980s. Other capitalist–industrial countries are showing attributes of post-Fordism, but none can be called a post-Fordist economy yet. (Table 1-3 summarizes the six models of industrialization and their related welfare states.)

Sociologists and anthropologists often talk about the capacity for adaptation by a collectivity in given environments (Cohen, 1971; Parsons,

Table 1–3. Six Theoretical Types of Industrial States

PHASES OF INDUSTRIALIZATION	IDEOLOGY OF INDUSTRIALIZATION		NATURE OF WELFARE STATE
	CAPITALIST	SOCIALIST	
Pre-Fordist	Pre-Fordist, capitalist —Britain and USA before World War I	Pre-Fordist, socialist —No empirical entity	No welfare state
Fordist	Fordist, capitalist —Britain and USA between World War I and early 1970s; most Western countries and Japan between WW I and the present	Fordist, socialist —Communist countries between 1917 and 1989	Active-engaged or passive-reluctant welfare states[a]
Post-Fordist	Post-Fordist, capitalist —Britain and USA since the 1970s; some parts of Western Europe approaching it	Post-Fordist, socialist —No empirical entity	Active-engaged or passive-reluctant welfare states[a]

[a]Shown in Figure 2-1, p. 23.

1951). Here, *collectivity* may mean a group, organization, tribe, clan, or nation-state. Seen from this perspective, the welfare state is an adaptation by the nation-state to an industrial environment.

Surplus and Resources

Given the premise that the building and maintenance of a welfare state depends on a surplus, it is important to define what "surplus" really means. In simple terms, *surplus* means that the productivity of a culture (say, a national culture) is higher than what is needed for the mere survival of all of its members. Once a surplus occurs, many ways exist for dealing with what has been produced.

The productivity of a culture is the accumulation of the productivity of different groups within a culture. Groups can be classified according to criteria including the following:

- age (young versus old)
- gender (males versus females)
- social hierarchy (by class, by ethnicity, and so forth)

- knowledge (highly educated to uneducated)
- skills (highly skilled to unskilled)
- ownership (owners versus nonowners of means of production)
- health status (from healthy to not healthy; the concept of *health*, for now, includes mental health and mental retardation).

In examining the productivity of each group, the next question may well be, How does the productivity of this group compare with that of other groups? If a given group's productivity is near zero, then another question follows: Given that the productivity of Group A is near zero, can the consumption requirements of this group be met by the productivity of Group B, which has high productivity? Can some of the items produced by Group B be transferred to Group A, either by a third party or by the state? Is Group B's productivity higher than the national average? How much of the goods and services produced by Group B should the group be able to keep for itself?

What happens if Group A claims that its members were protecting members of Group B from external and internal intruders while the members of the latter group were engaged in the production process, but the job of protecting others was not included in the concept of productivity? Thus, activities that contribute to the production process also need to be included in measuring productivity. Indeed, recently Hechter (1987) and others have seen activities that contribute to productivity as a given group's production of public goods, which may contribute to the production of private and public goods and services by other groups.

What happens if Group C claims that its members were engaged in producing and nurturing future members of Group B? The concept of productivity of a given group and, for that matter, of productivity of the entire culture also can be seen in a time dimension: It is important to produce now, but it is also important to make provisions so that the current production process can continue into the future.

Defining and measuring productivity is a difficult undertaking. The disciplines of economics (as a basic social science) and business management (as an applied social science) have developed measures and guidelines for productivity in international, national, regional, and organizational settings. In these efforts and measures, the market defines productivity. Translated into simple terms, if one's efforts (call them "labor") are marketable, then those efforts can be called productive. The more marketable one's efforts are, the more likely it is that they will be profitable and, consequently, the more likely it is that one can be labeled "productive."

A second way of defining productivity, however, comes from the Frankfurt School in the discipline of sociology (see Berger & Luckman, 1967; Chatterjee, 1996). From this perspective, productivity is socially constructed. In the market orientation, the buyers of a product or service make up the market, and it is their decision to buy or not buy that defines productivity. In the social construction orientation, the sellers contribute to this transaction. In the latter context, behavior of the sellers may take several forms, one of which is "collusion," or avoidance of competition, which leads to price fixing by industries. Collective bargaining by labor, which may contribute to the process of pricing, also affects seller behavior. In capitalist countries, collusion is seen as a form of major deviance and is punishable. Collective bargaining, however, has had a long history of legitimization and is considered right and proper. Another example of the social construction orientation is that of the productivity of those engaged in rearing and nurturing future generations: Their efforts are either devalued or not considered productive at all.

Another example of the market orientation versus the social construction orientation can be illustrated by the following example: "The customer is always right" in the market orientation, and almost any product or service can be defined as productive if it sells. From this perspective, it is proper to commodify anything, including a woman's body, an addictive substance, or child pornography. From the social construction perspective, it is permissible to commodify some but not all marketable goods or services; consequently, they may or may not define certain types of productivity. The market orientation to productivity is more probable when one wants to operate by the norms of efficiency, whereas a social construction orientation is more probable when one wants to operate by the norms of equity (Figure 1-1).

Clearly, the concept of surplus cannot be understood in economic terms (that is, by using procedures from the discipline of economics) alone. It is a concept that requires sociological (the study of division of labor), psychological (the study of motivation to produce or incentives to produce), social work (the study of how certain cultures with a surplus do or do not provide for their children and aged, mentally ill, unskilled, and other populations), and other multidisciplinary input.

Two further points must be made about the concept of surplus:

1. The capacity of a culture to produce and maintain a surplus seems unrelated to its governing body's budgetary provisions. That is, a culture may be able to build a surplus, but its governing body (the state) may have a budget deficit. It is possible (though rare) for a culture not to have a surplus but for its governing body to show a balanced budget or budget surplus.
2. Surplus in a given culture is a dynamic concept and is a result of wealth building through Fordism.

If I expand the first point, it seems that the capacity of a culture to produce and maintain a surplus depends on the following factors:

- *Labor for Meeting Basic Needs.* How much work needs to be done to meet the basic requirements of survival? A list of the require-

Figure 1-1.

Tensions between Equity and Efficiency and Consequent Disciplinary Sympathies in the Study of Social Policy

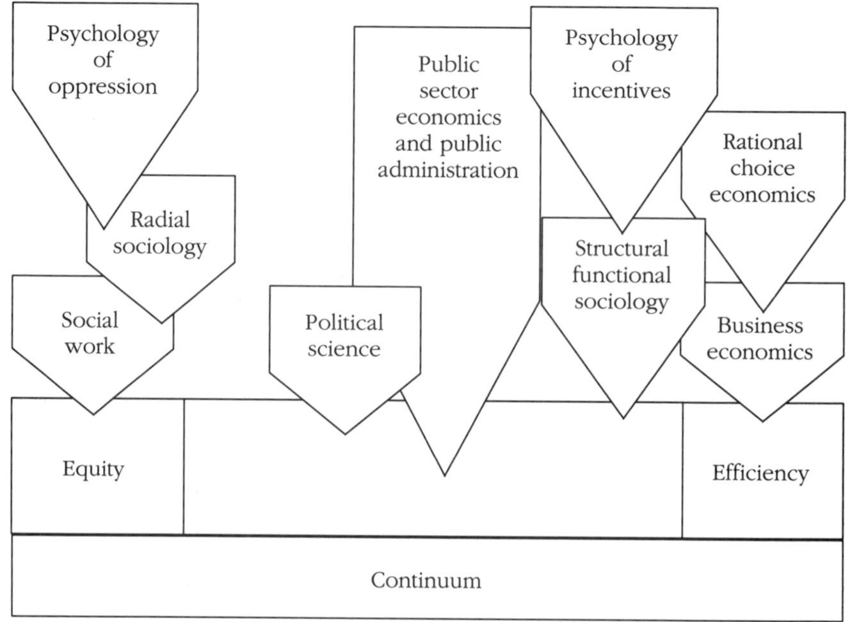

ments for survival includes food, shelter, and medicine. Even those items, however, can be divided into basic items and optional items. Using Maslow's (1962) hierarchy of human needs, what percentage of the day, week, or year is a person's or group's productivity devoted to meeting basic (that is, survival) needs, and what percentage is devoted to meeting what Maslow called "meta-needs" (higher order needs)? For example, in some cultural contexts, members of certain groups may toil for 16 hours a day and almost 365 days a year just to meet basic needs. In contrast, in some other cultural contexts, people in certain groups may work only 7 hours a day and only 300 days a year to meet both basic needs and many meta-needs.

- *Labor for Basic Needs by Working and Lower Classes.* How much work needs to be done by those at the "bottom echelon" of a culture to meet the basic requirements of survival? In industrial societies, this may mean the amount of time spent by members of the working and lower classes in wage-earning endeavors.

Table 1-4. Three Types of Industrial States and Their Relative Surplus

INDUSTRIAL STATE	SURPLUS	EFFORTS TO ENHANCE EQUITY	EFFORTS TO ENHANCE EFFICIENCY
Pre-Fordist	Rising	Low	High
Fordist	High	High	Low
Late-stage Fordist or Post-Fordist	Declining	Reduced	Increased

- *Mass Availability of Consumer Goods.* How available and affordable are certain consumer goods (like automobiles, televisions, vacations, and equipment that heats or cools residences) to members of the middle, working, and lower classes?
- *Movement Away from a Cash Economy.* To what extent has the economy moved away from a cash economy to one in which transactions are handled through financial instruments such as checks, credit cards, promissory notes, and charge accounts? Even though the lower or poverty classes often depend on a cash economy (Lewis, 1959, 1969; Mincey, 1994; Tobin, 1994), the trend of moving away from cash economies in larger society permits the state to monitor a transfer system.
- *Attainability of Basic Comforts.* How attainable is a basic materially comfortable life?
- *The State's Ability to Tax.* Settings may exist in which a society has emerged with a surplus. Has the state in that society thus acquired the wherewithal to levy taxes that can make welfare state possible? Does the state have the ability to tax those in the labor force? How far can the rate of such taxation go? For example, in some societies (such as Western Europe) paying 55 to 60 percent of individual income as tax is not uncommon. In contrast, in some other societies, paying over 31 or 36 percent of one's income would be considered too high and could cause taxpayers' resentments.

The answers to the above questions can only be given from a comparative framework. Thus, viewed from a world-systems perspective, one could rate a national culture as a rising-surplus culture, a high-surplus culture, a declining surplus culture, or a no-surplus culture. Within industrial cultures, three scenarios thus exist: rising surplus, high surplus, and declining surplus (Table 1-4).

Balancing Equity and Efficiency

The preceding discussion highlights how social welfare policy of the Fordist industrial society emerged either to thwart a working-class revolt (as in the United States) or to pre-empt a working-class revolt (as in Bismarck's Germany). The term "social policy," however, came to mean different things to different groups.

The different groups may be divided into two broad subgroups: the academic and the nonacademic communities. Within the academic community, disciplines such as social work, applied sociology, welfare economics, and political science are interested in the study of social policy. Their scholarly efforts, however, do not seem to come together to form a core of accumulated knowledge about social policy. Instead, several independent knowledge structures seem to be evolving. Furthermore, scholars in the various disciplines tend to be caught in tunnel vision, and few efforts bring them together.

In the nonacademic community, the study of social policy is steered by the agendas of various interest groups. The unions politicize and lobby for social policy gains, such as pensions, health care, subsidized day care, and disability coverage. The insurance and other related corporate interest groups work to keep costs down and profits up. Organized social workers and other human service workers are quick to find increased numbers of vulnerable groups who need more and more support from the state, as long as they administer the support programs. Political parties with primary constituencies in the working and middle classes seek the alliance of the unions and other labor groups and work for what may be termed increased social welfare ends. In contrast, political parties expecting support from corporations and from capital-holding groups work to decrease the budget for social welfare ends.

Within the academic community, students and teachers of professional social work are more advocates than they are scholars of social policy. Their position often is that "rich" countries should spend more for their vulnerable populations and that "welfare laggards" (a term originally used by Wilensky, 1975), such as the United States, should emulate the social safety net programs of certain modern Western European countries (Karger & Stoesz, 1998; Van Wormer, 1996). Scholars from the disciplines of economics, economic anthropology, and demography, however, argue that the social safety nets of late 20th-century Europe (and, to a lesser extent, the United States) were based on certain assumptions about a society's demographic structure, capacity to build an economic surplus, and capacity and willingness to pay certain taxes (Elster, Offe, & Preuss, 1998; Offe, 1984; Offe & Heinze, 1992). Scholars from economic history and macrosociology suggest that the development of social policy to facilitate welfare ends is less a function of ideology and more a function of industrialization (Chatterjee,

1996; Gould, 1993; Rimlinger, 1971; Schumpeter, 1950; Wilensky, 1975). Those in the social work field, in contrast, argue that the pursuit of welfare ends is a result of the ideological positions of key interest groups (George & Wilding, 1976; Karger & Stoesz, 1998; Tropman, 1989).

The problem of income maintenance is a good example of the conflicting perspectives. Organized social workers support making income from social insurance programs (for example, social security, disability payments, and unemployment compensation) and general assistance or poverty assistance programs a right for everybody. This approach enhances the dignity of the individual recipients. Most economists and psychologists, however, argue that making income a right for everyone could reduce individual incentive to participate in a market economy, reduce the labor pool for certain low-skilled jobs, contribute to creating a market for legal and illegal immigrant laborers, and create another, somewhat protected, market for members of the working and middle classes who are police officers, social workers, poverty researchers, and welfare administrators (Chatterjee, 1996; Gans, 1972; Rimlinger, 1971; Stiglitz, 1986).

Stiglitz (1986) illustrated the different positions taken by social workers and economists about what social policy is and what it should accomplish. He showed how an inverse relationship exists between equity and efficiency: The more one tries to maximize efficiency in a nation, the less it is possible to foster equity. Conversely, the more one tries to enhance equity, the less efficiency is fostered. The ability to increase the national income can be equated with efficiency, whereas the ability to transfer income and provide services to certain populations through nonmarket distributions can be called equity. It seems that those in the discipline of social work who study social policy are primarily interested in enhancing equity. Consequently, the social work discipline is not interested in efficiency, that is, encouraging work or investment. Most social sciences other than social work and economics, such as macrosociology, social psychology, and psychology, fall at different intervals along the continuum between equity and efficiency. Figure 1-1 on page 14 is a portrayal of this arrangement.

Quite apart from the differences in the study of social policy are the apparent worldwide changes in the nature of welfare states and their social policies. In the wealthy capitalist countries of Western Europe, the trend is toward reducing state spending, and this trend seems to be not just seasonal. The trend in America is toward "welfare reform," which may produce unintended consequences (see Handler, 1995). The newly rich countries from the Third World—Singapore, South Korea, Taiwan, and Malaysia—are proposing to install social safety nets, but they may not follow the European model of many entitlements and built-in dignity for the social welfare recipient. It seems that those Third World countries are opting for a cost-effective model of social policy, since "entitlements afford dignity to the individual recipient but are rarely cost-effective for the collective (that is, the state), whereas gratuities reduce the dignity of the individual but are cost-effective to the collective. Entitlements are directly related to human dignity but are inversely related to cost-effectiveness" (Chatterjee, 1996, p. 260). In the former communist countries, social welfare benefits (in income maintenance and health) are actually decreasing, either because inflation reduces the value of these benefits or because the state is financially unable to continue the benefits.

The purpose of this book is to explore how social welfare policy in the welfare states inherently serves conflicting and contradictory ends; how those ends have been poorly understood by different academic and community groups; and why it is necessary to explore a different paradigm—one from an interdisciplinary perspective—for establishing and maintaining social safety nets into the 21st century.

References

Anthony, P. D. (1977). *The ideology of work.* London: Tavistock.

Arrow, K. (1963). *Social choice and individual values.* New York: John Wiley & Sons.

Ashford, D. (1986). *The emergence of the welfare state.* Oxford, England: Blackwell.

Bell, D. (1973). *The coming of post-industrial society: A venture in social forecasting.* New York: Basic Books.

Bendix, R. (1956). *Work and authority in industry: Ideologies of management in the course of industrialization.* New York: John Wiley & Sons.

Berger, P. (1986). *The capitalist revolution.* New York: Free Press.

Berger, P., & Luckman, T. (1967). *The social construction of reality.* New York: Doubleday.

Boje, D. M., Gephart, R. P. , Jr., & Thatchenkery, T. J. (Eds.). (1996). *Postmodern management and organization theory.* Thousand Oaks, CA: Sage Publications

Burnham, J. (1941). *The managerial revolution.* New York: John Day.

Chatterjee, P. (1996). *Approaches to the welfare state.* Washington, DC: NASW Press.

Clarke, S. (1990). The crisis of Fordism or the crisis of social democracy? *Telos, 83*, 71–98.

Cohen, Y. (1971). *Man in adaptation: The institutional framework.* Chicago: Aldine-Atherton.

Dixon, J. E., & Macarov, D. (1992). *Social welfare in socialist countries.* London: Routledge.

Elster, J., Offe, C., & Preuss, U. K. (1998). *Institutional design in post-communist societies: Rebuilding the ship at sea.* New York: Cambridge University Press.

Esping-Andersen, G. (1990). *The three worlds of welfare capitalism.* Princeton, NJ: Princeton University Press.

Forsyth, D. (1990). *Group dynamics.* Pacific Grove, CA: Brooks/Cole.

Frank, A. G. (1969). *Capitalism and underdevelopment in Latin America.* New York: Monthly Review Press.

Furtado, C. (1970). *Economic development of Latin America.* Cambridge, England: Cambridge University Press.

Galbraith, J. K. (1967). *The new industrial state.* Boston: Houghton-Mifflin.

Gans, H. (1972). The positive functions of poverty. *American Journal of Sociology, 78,* 275–289.

George, V., & Wilding, P. (1976). *Ideology and social welfare.* London: Routledge.

Gould, A. (1993). *Capitalist welfare systems.* London: Longman.

Gould, C. C. (1980). *Marx's social ontology.* Cambridge, MA: MIT Press.

Hall, J. A., & Ikenberry, G. J. (1989). *The state.* Minneapolis: University of Minnesota Press.

Handler, J. (1995). *The poverty of welfare reform.* New Haven, CT: Yale University Press.

Hechter, M. (1987). *Principles of group solidarity.* Berkeley: University of California Press.

Janowitz, M. (1976). *Social control of the welfare state.* New York: Elsevier.

Karger, H. J., & Stoesz, D. (1998). *American social welfare policy: A pluralist approach.* New York: Longman.

Korpi, W. (1987). *Class, power, and state autonomy in welfare state development.* Stockholm: Swedish Institute for Social Research.

Lenski, G., Lenski, J., & Nolan, P. (1991). *Human societies: An introduction to macrosociology.* New York: McGraw-Hill.

Lewis, O. (1959). *Five families: Mexican case studies in the culture of poverty.* New York: Basic Books.

Lewis, O. (1969). Review. *Current Anthropology, 10,* 189–192.

Lyotard, J. F. (1984). *The postmodern condition: A report on knowledge.* Minneapolis: University of Minnesota Press.

Maslow, A. (1962). *Toward a psychology of being.* Princeton, NJ: Van Nostrand.

Mincey, R. B. (1994, Winter). The underclass: Concept, controversy, and evidence. *Focus, 16*(2), 38.

Moynihan, D. P. (1969). *Maximum feasible misunderstanding: Community action in the war on poverty.* New York: Free Press.

Music Today. (1996). *The Bhagvad Gita.* New Delhi: Living Media India, Ltd.

Offe, C. (1984). *Contradictions of the welfare state.* Cambridge, MA: MIT Press.

Offe, C., & Heinze, R. G. (1992). *Beyond employment: Time, work, and the informal economy.* Philadelphia: Temple University Press.

Pardek, J. T., Murphy, J. W., & Choi, J. M. (1994). Some implications of postmodernism for social work practice. *Social Work, 39,* 343–346.

Parsons, T. (1951). *The social system.* Glencoe, IL: Free Press.

Peukert, D. (1992). *The Weimer Republic: The crisis of classical modernity.* New York: Hill & Wang.

Pflanze, O. (1990). *Bismarck and the development of Germany.* Princeton, NJ: Princeton University Press.

Pinker, R. (1979). *The idea of welfare.* London: Heinemann.

Piore, M. J., & Sabel, C. F. (1984). *The second industrial divide: Possibilities for prosperity.* New York: Basic Books.

Quadagno, J. (1988). *The transformation of old age security: Class and politics in the American welfare state.* Chicago: University of Chicago Press.

Reisman, D. A. (1977). *Richard Titmuss: Welfare and society.* London: Heinemann.

Rimlinger, G. (1971). *Welfare policy and industrialization in Europe, America, and Russia.* New York: John Wiley & Sons.

Ritzer, G. (1992). *Contemporary sociological theory.* Boston: Allyn & Bacon.

Sabel, C. F. (1982). *Work and politics.* New York: Cambridge University Press.

Schumpeter, J. (1950). *Capitalism, socialism, and democracy.* New York: Harper & Row.

Skocpol, T. (1992). *Protecting soldiers and mothers.* Cambridge, MA: Harvard University Press.

Snowman, D. (1977). *Britain & America.* New York: Harper & Row.

Stiglitz, J. E. (1986). *Economics for the public sector.* New York: W. W. Norton.

Taylor, F. (1911). *The principles of scientific management.* New York: Harper.

Tobin, J. (1994, Winter). Poverty in relation to macroeconomic trends, cycles, and politics. *Focus, 16*(2), 38–39.

Trattner, W. I. (1997). *From poor law to welfare state.* New York: Free Press.

Tropman, J. E. (1989). *American values and social welfare: Cultural contradictions in the welfare state.* Englewood Cliffs, NJ: Prentice Hall.

United Nations Development Programme. (1994). *Human development report 1994.* New York: Oxford University Press.

United Nations Development Programme. (1996). *Human development report 1996.* New York: Oxford University Press.

Van Wormer, K. S. (1996). *Social welfare: A world view.* Chicago: Nelson-Hall.

Weisbrod, B. A. (1988). *The nonprofit economy.* Cambridge, MA: Harvard University Press.

Wilensky, H. (1975). *The welfare state and equality.* Berkeley: University of California Press.

2

The State as an Agent of Distribution

Surplus seems to be a sufficient condition for welfare state formation. However, given surplus, ongoing productivity and a low dependency ratio are important conditions for its maintenance. Furthermore, industrial capitalism seems to be the best guarantee of a viable state.

Becoming a welfare state essentially means that the state becomes an active agent of distribution, which is a form of nonmarket distribution that can occur either in some form of partnership with the market or in a stand-alone capacity. The Great Depression forced the Anglo-American countries and France to become agents of distribution, and it has been argued that doing so served to preserve the basic structure of the market system (Heilbronner, 1962; Piven & Cloward, 1993). Monarchist Germany and Czarist Russia considered the industrial state an agent of distribution, as seen from the efforts of Bismarck and the rulers of Russia before the Bolshevik Revolution of 1917 (Rimlinger, 1971). These trends continued in the Third Reich and were substantially enhanced in Bolshevik Russia (Peukert, 1992; Rimlinger, 1971).

It took slightly less than 100 years for the Anglo-American industrial states (and France) to become welfare states to some capacity. It took much less time for almost all other capitalist industrial states to become welfare states, and almost no time for communist industrial states to become welfare states. After the break-up of the Communist bloc, the formerly communist countries had problems maintaining the surplus that makes a welfare state possible.

Ideology-driven states are those in which ideology is the reason for welfare state development, whereas *ideology-justified* states are those in which welfare state development happens as a result of wealth building and then is justified by ideology. The role of the state as a distribution agent in the Second World countries thus was ideology driven because the premise of the state was based on socialist ideology. Conversely, the role of the state in nonmarket distribution in the First World countries was ideology-justified (Chatterjee, 1996). A depression and a war forced England and America to make compromises with their ideologies of classic capitalism and family and community caregiving to make the state a distribution agent. In contrast, the central and southern European states, with their culture of the patriarchal family and corporate capitalism, had fewer problems making the state a major agent of distribution, since they were attempting to preserve both the interests of the aristocracy and those of the working class (Esping-Andersen, 1990; Peukert, 1992). In social-democratic Scandinavia, the welfare state was an accommodation between ideology (socialism) and interest (preserving wealth developed from industrialization).

Not all forms of nonmarket distribution are undertaken by the state. The family, the church, and several other agents in society can engage in nonmarket distribution (see Chatterjee, 1996, pp. 3–18). Although not all forms of nonmarket distribution in which the industrial state becomes involved support welfare functions, it is true that welfare functions form a substantial part of redistribution (Chatterjee, 1996).

The sequence shown in Figure 2-1 is helpful in understanding the state as an agent of nonmarket distribution. The outcome at the top right, "not a welfare state," represents pre-Fordist industrial states. The outcome toward the bottom center, "disabled welfare state," represents Fordist industrial states (version 3) from the former communist countries as they struggle to convert to market economy. The outcome at the bottom center, "able and sound welfare state," represents both Fordist industrial states (version 2) from the capitalist First World and post-Fordist industrial states from the First World as they prepare to enter the 21st century. Thus, Fordist industrial states have traveled three paths: two capitalist (the First World countries) and one socialist (the Second World countries). The outcome "troubled welfare state" is arrived at from active-engaged capitalist states (for example, Western Europe) or passive-reluctant capitalist states (for example, the United States and, to some extent, Japan). This outcome is always possible in settings in which the surplus is threatened or diminished for whatever reason (see Table 1-4). In a continuum between equity and efficiency, the pre-Fordist state, which was not a welfare state, was given more to the pursuit of efficiency than of equity. The Fordist states, all of which became welfare states, came to the pursuit of equity in some form or other. Some Fordist states (mostly former planned economy states) became disabled welfare states, whereas other Fordist states (usually market economy states) appeared either "able and sound" or "troubled." As Figure 2-1 illustrates, the able and sound states were often one step away from becoming troubled.

Richard M. Titmuss, a socialist thinker from the London School of Economics, argued that income subsidy and basic health care should be a right in the Fordist industrial states and that this right emanates from the citizenship of persons (Titmuss, 1950, 1959, 1968, 1974). In his work *The Gift Relationship* (1971), he implied that market distribution commercializes and vulgarizes human relationships, whereas human altruism dignifies hu-

Figure 2-1.

The State as a Distribution Agent

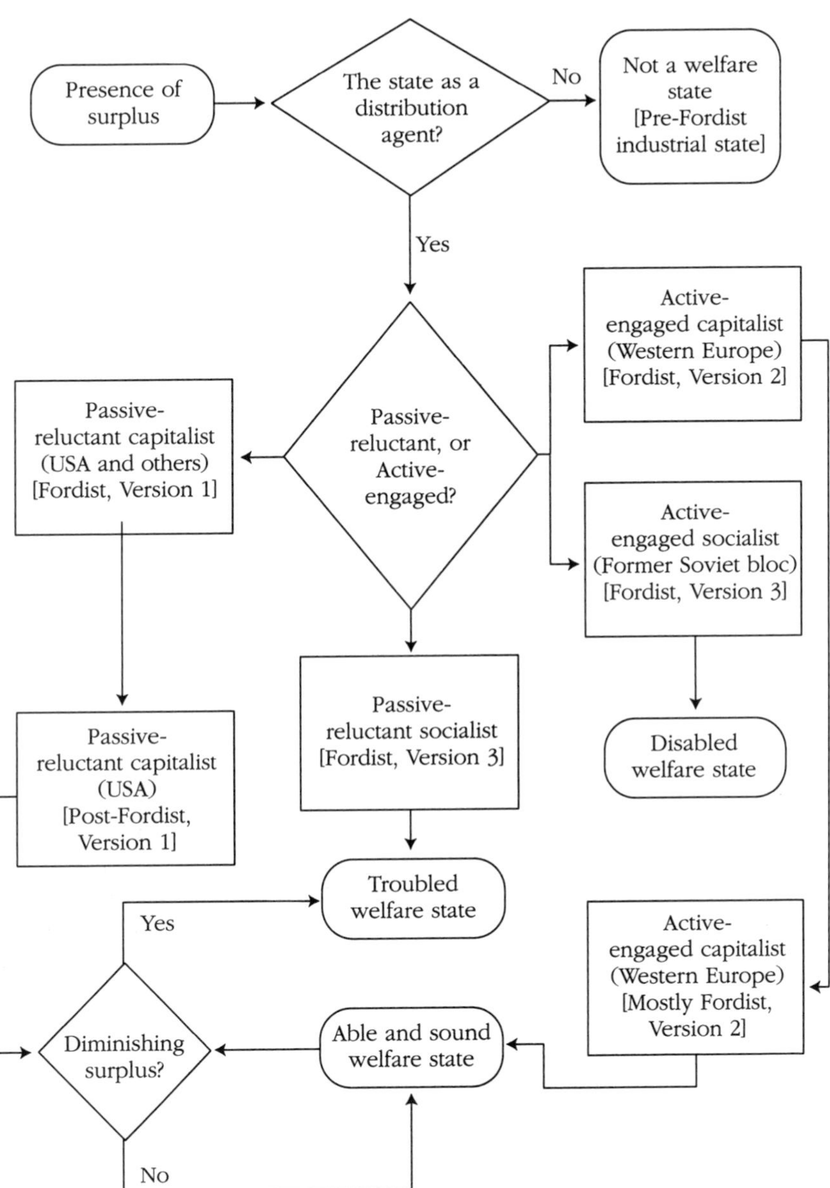

man relationships. Inspired in part by Titmuss, social workers in England, Canada, and the United States called for welfare as a right, although only moderate social security benefits were ever institutionalized in the United States as a right. In contrast, versions 2 and 3 of the Fordist industrial state (Western Europe and the Communist world before 1990, respectively) institutionalized the concept of welfare as a right.

In 1993, less than 20 years after the death of Titmuss, the market principle seemed triumphant all over the world. The planned economies of the Communist world collapsed, and it seemed that the role of the state as a distribution agent had contributed to this collapse. In the active-engaged capitalist part of western Europe, where welfare and health care had come to be viewed as a right, able and sound welfare states (as in Figure 2-1) were facing diminishing surplus and were heading toward becoming troubled welfare states. The passive-reluctant welfare state of the United States instituted cutbacks and underwent further reform in its welfare programs.

The lesson learned by the end of pre-Fordist industrial state or the beginning of the Fordist industrial state was that the state must engage in some form of regulation of commerce and industry and be a serious agent of distribution if it is to deal with many types of human misery. In the United States this approach was called the New Deal. In his classic work, Joseph Schumpeter (1950) predicted that the state's role as a distribution agent was likely to increase many times in the capitalist countries and that this trend reflected a "march toward socialism."

The lessons learned from the New Deal in particular and about the role of the state as a distribution agent in general are being both questioned and refined in post-Fordist industrial states. The questions seem to be centered not on whether the state should be an agent of distribution, but rather on how many types of distribution functions the state can serve without jeopardizing its fiscal health; whether by increasing the distribution functions the state diminishes its capacity for higher productivity; and whether a point exists after which increased state spending does not correspondingly increase human welfare. The focus of this book is on questions such as these.

Measures of Active-Engaged and Passive-Reluctant States

The welfare states are considered to be the countries to which the United Nations assigns a Human Development Index (HDI) rating of 0.875 or above. In 1993, a total of 33 countries were above this threshold, as shown in Table 1-2 (see United Nations Development Programme, 1996).

The term "reluctant welfare state" was coined during a debate between Wilensky (1975) and Barnes and Srivenkataramana (1982). They used "percent of GNP expended on social security in 1966" (p. 237) as an indica-

Table 2-1. Percentage of GDP Expended on Social Security by Reluctant Welfare States in 1966

STATE	% OF GNP EXPENDED ON SOCIAL SECURITY
Canada	10.1
Switzerland	9.5
Australia	9.0
Iceland	8.7
United States	7.9

NOTE: GDP = gross domestic product.

SOURCE: Barnes, J., & Srivenkataramana, T. (1982). Ideology and the welfare state: An examination of Wilensky's conclusions. *Social Service Review, 56,* 237. ©1982 University of Chicago Press. Reprinted with permission of the University of Chicago Press.

tor of active or reluctant welfare states. At that time, there were five reluctant welfare states (Table 2-1). Jansson (1988, 1997) later popularized the term.

The same countries are depicted in Table 2-2, which shows reluctant welfare states in 1993. At that time, only Latvia and Portugal ranked below the United States in percentage of gross domestic product (GDP) expended on social security. Comparing the figures in Tables 2-1 and 2-2, one can clearly see that Canada left the category of reluctant welfare states by 1993. In addition, among the capitalist or market economy countries, Switzerland, the United States, Japan, Israel, and Portugal all could be called reluctant welfare states that year and have been classified as passive-reluctant

Table 2-2. Percentage of GDP on Social Security Expended by Reluctant Welfare States, 1966 to 1993, and by Others

STATE	% OF GDP EXPENDED ON SOCIAL SECURITY
Canada	21.7
Switzerland	14.0
Australia	—
Iceland	—
United States	10.5
Japan	11.5
Latvia	9.1
Portugal	9.0

NOTE: — = Data not available; GDP = gross domestic product.

SOURCE: United Nations Development Programme. (1996). *Human development report 1996.* New York: Oxford University Press.

Table 2-3. Percentage of GDP Expended on Social Security by Active-Engaged and Passive-Reluctant Welfare States, 1993

CATEGORY	COUNTRY	% OF GDP EXPENDED ON SOCIAL SECURITY
Active-engaged capitalist (More than 15.0 percent of GDP)	Sweden	38.3
	Finland	30.5
	Denmark	29.5
	Germany	24.7
	Austria	24.5
	Canada	21.7
	New Zealand	20.2
	Norway	19.6
	Ireland	19.4
Active-engaged socialist (More than 15.0 percent of GDP)	Bulgaria	19.8
	Hungary	17.3
	Poland	17.0
Passive-reluctant capitalist (14.9 percent or less of GDP)	Switzerland	14.0
	Israel	11.8
	Japan	11.5
	United States	10.5
	Portugal	9.0
Passive-reluctant socialist (14.9 percent or less of GDP)	Slovakia	13.3
	Belarus	12.0
	Czech Republic	11.1
	Latvia	9.1

NOTES: All other countries from Table 1-2 omitted because data were unavailable. GDP = gross domestic product.

SOURCE: United Nations Development Programme. (1996). *Human development report 1996.* New York: Oxford University Press.

welfare states for the purposes of this volume. Comparable figures were not available for several countries. Table 2-3 further refines by market type the active-engaged and passive-reluctant classification of the original 45 states listed in Table 1-2.

In Tables 2-2 and 2-3, the percentage of GDP expended on social security is the measure of the active–passive/engaged–reluctant dimension, because it was the measure originally used by Barnes and Srivenkataramana in 1982 (see Table 2-1). Because this approach is based on data that are not available for many countries, however, Table 2-4 uses the figure called "percentage of government expenditure on social security and welfare."

Table 2-4. Percentage of Government Expenditure on Social Security and Welfare, 1992–1995

CATEGORY	COUNTRY	% OF GOVERNMENT EXPENDITURES ON SOCIAL SECURITY
Active-engaged capitalist (More than 33.3 percent of expenditure)	Luxembourg	50.8
	Sweden	48.2
	Austria	45.8
	Finland	45.6
	France	45.0
	Canada	41.3
	Denmark	39.9
	Norway	39.5
	Spain	39.0
	Netherlands	37.2
	New Zealand	36.9
	Japan	36.8
	Malta	34.0
	Australia	33.8
Active-engaged socialist (More than 33.3 percent of expenditure)	Lithuania	37.5
	Latvia	36.7
	Belarus	36.5
Passive-reluctant capitalist (33.3 percent or less of expenditure)	United Kingdom	29.6
	United States	29.6
	Ireland	28.0
	Israel	24.5
	Greece	13.4
Passive-reluctant socialist (33.3 percent or less of expenditure)	Hungary	28.7
	Russia	28.5
	Czech Republic	28.1
	Bulgaria	28.0

NOTE: All other countries from Table 1-2 omitted because data were unavailable.
SOURCE: United Nations Development Programme. (1997). *Human development report 1997.* New York: Oxford University Press.

In comparing Tables 2-3 and 2-4, we see that the United States and Israel remain classified as passive-reluctant, and Canada, Sweden, Norway, Finland, New Zealand, Austria, and Denmark are classified as active-engaged regardless of the measure used. It is our position that the second measure, the percentage of central government expenditure that is for social security and welfare, should be used for our discussion, since it directly reflects the behavior of welfare states.

In comparing Tables 2-3 and 2-4, it seems that Japan is passive-reluctant by the first measure and is just over the threshold for active-engaged, according to the second. Although no data are available for the United Kingdom on the first measure (that is, for Table 2-3), the country emerges as a passive-reluctant welfare state in the second table. Similarly, Switzerland appears to be a passive-reluctant country based on the first measure, but no information on Switzerland as a welfare state is available for the second measure.

Measures of Disabled, Troubled, and Able and Sound States

A combination of factors creates the three categories of disabled, troubled, and able and sound states. The first factor is the productivity of the country, as measured by real per capita GDP. Table 2-5 lists the real 1993 GDPs for selected countries. In Table 2-5, the states in the extreme left column (over $20,000) are categorized as able and sound welfare states, whereas the ones in the far right column (under $5,000) are disabled welfare states. The middle

Table 2-5. Real GDP per Capita, 1993

OVER $20,000	$15,000–19,999	$10,000–14,999	$5,000–9,999	UNDER $5,000
Canada	Australia	Barbados	Argentina	Belarus
Denmark	Austria	Cyprus	Chile	Bulgaria
Hong Kong	Bahamas	Malta	Costa Rica	Lithuania
Japan	Belgium	Portugal	Czech Rep.	Poland
Luxembourg	Finland	Spain	Greece	Russia
Norway	France		Hungary	Ukraine
Switzerland	Germany		Latvia	
United States	Iceland		South Korea	
	Ireland		Slovakia	
	Israel		Uruguay	
	Italy			
	Netherlands			
	New Zealand			
	Singapore			
	Sweden			
	United Kingdom			

SOURCE: United Nations Development Programme. (1996). *Human development report 1996*. New York: Oxford University Press.

NOTES: All countries listed in Table 1-2 are represented in this table. GDP = gross domestic product.

Table 2-6. Dependency Ratio of Welfare States, 1993

CAPITALIST MARKET ECONOMY COUNTRIES				
54.0+	52.0–53.9	50.0–51.9	48.0–49.9	47.9–
Iceland	France	Australia	Austria	Denmark
Ireland	New Zealand	Belgium	Canada	Germany
Israel	United Kingdom	Portugal	Finland	Italy
Norway	United States		Greece	Japan
Sweden			Malta	Luxembourg
				Netherlands
				Spain
				Switzerland

FORMER SOCIALIST COUNTRIES IN PROCESS OF CHANGE				
54.0+	52.0–53.9	50.0–51.9	48.0–49.9	47.9–
	Belarus	Estonia	Bulgaria	
	Latvia		Czech Republic	
	Lithuania		Hungary	
	Poland		Russia	
	Slovakia			
	Ukraine			

SOURCE: United Nations Development Programme. (1996). *Human development report 1996*. New York: Oxford University Press.
NOTE: Not all countries listed in Table 1-2 are represented in this table because corresponding data were not available.

three columns represent degrees of troubled (low, medium, and high) welfare states. As Tables 1-1 and 1-2 indicate, all 45 countries are high-HDI countries, meaning that they rate high in human development efforts. Being high in human development efforts (that is, being included in Tables 1-1 or 1-2) but low in productivity (falling in the far right-hand column of Table 2-5) thus leads to categorization as a disabled welfare state.

Human development and productivity are only one part of the story that determines the ability status of a welfare state. The second factor is the society's *dependency ratio,* which is the "ratio of the population defined as dependent—those under 15 and those over 64—to the working age population, aged 15 to 64" (United Nations Development Programme, 1994, p. 219). The dependency ratio can be used as another measure of a state's ability to continue welfare benefits. After all, the dependency ratio contributes to the state's ability to tax, and this ability is a major foundation of the welfare state.

According to Tables 2-5 and 2-6, states that conservatively can be called able and sound states are those rating high in real GDP and low in dependency ratio (Japan, Switzerland, Denmark, and Luxembourg). Disabled states are those rating low in real GDP and high in dependency ratio: Poland, Belarus, Ukraine, and Lithuania. Russia shows low GDP but a relatively low dependency ratio as well. States falling in the middle thus can be conservatively called troubled states.

Looking at the same tables from a somewhat less conservative orientation, one can observe that the states ranking high to moderately high in per capita GDP (that is, over $ 15,000) and low to moderately low in dependency ratio are Canada, Finland, Austria, Japan, the Netherlands, Switzerland, Denmark, Germany, Italy, and Luxembourg. These 10 First World capitalist countries can be somewhat less conservatively rated as able and sound states. Note that wealthy countries such as France, the United States, and the United Kingdom do not fall in this list, because they meet the high GDP requirement ($15,000 or higher) but not the low dependency ratio requirement (48.0 or lower).

At the other end, again from a less conservative perspective, states that are low to moderately low in GDP (that is, under $10,000) and high to moderately high in dependency ratio (that is, 52.0 or above) are Belarus, Latvia, Lithuania, Slovakia, Poland, and Ukraine. No First World capitalist countries are in this category.

Table 2-7 presents cross-tabulated information from Tables 2-5 and 2-6. In this table, high per capita GDP means more than $20,000; high-medium GDP means $15,000–19,999; medium GDP means $10,000–14,999; low-medium GDP means $5,000–9,999; and low GDP means less than $5,000 (see Table 2-5). High dependency ratio means 54.0 or greater; high-medium dependency ratio means 52.0–53.9; medium dependency ratio means 50.0–51.9; low-medium dependency ratio means 48.0–49.9; and low dependency ratio means less than 48.0 (see Table 2-6).

The large box in the lower left area of Table 2-7 lists able and sound welfare states, whereas the large box to the upper right lists the disabled welfare states. All other states in Table 2-7 are considered troubled welfare states. There are 15 capitalist troubled states—Australia, Belgium, France, Greece, Iceland, Ireland, Israel, Malta, New Zealand, Norway, Portugal, Spain, Sweden, the United Kingdom, and the United States—and four socialist troubled states—Bulgaria, Czech Republic, Hungary, and Russia.

Trade-off: Productivity and Dependency Ratio

Table 2-7 presents two types of data: Real GDP per capita and dependency ratio. It gives equal weight to the two variables toward the assessment of a welfare state. Some problems exist with this assumption, however. According to this format, when two societies have equal productivity but unequal dependency ratio, the latter would determine where in Table 2-7 that society should be placed. Conversely, when two societies have equal dependency

Table 2-7. Disabled, Troubled, and Able and Sound Welfare States

Dependency Ratio	GDP: HIGH	HIGH-MEDIUM	MEDIUM	LOW-MEDIUM	LOW
				Disabled	
High	Norway	Iceland Ireland Israel Sweden		Belarus Latvia Lithuania	Poland Slovakia Ukraine
High-medium	United States	France New Zealand United Kingdom		No capitalist First World countries fall into this category.	
Medium		Australia Belgium	Portugal		
Low-medium	**Able and Sound**		Malta	Czech Republic Greece Hungary	Bulgaria Russia
Low	Austria Canada Denmark Finland Germany	Italy Japan Luxembourg Netherlands Switzerland	Spain		

NOTES: GDP = gross domestic product. Real GDP per capita (from Table 2-5) ranging from high to low. Dependency ratios not available from United Nations data for Hong Kong, Bahamas, Singapore, Cyprus, Barbados, South Korea, Argentina, Costa Rica, Uruguay, and Chile.

Table 2-8. HDI Scores of Welfare States

CATEGORY	COUNTRY	HDI SCORE
Active-engaged capitalist	Canada	0.951
	Japan	0.938
	Netherlands	0.938
	Norway	0.937
	France	0.935
	Finland	0.935
	Spain	0.933
	Sweden	0.933
	Australia	0.929
	Austria	0.928
	New Zealand	0.927
	Denmark	0.924
	Luxembourg	0.895
	Malta	0.886
Mean		**0.928**
Active-engaged socialist	Latvia	0.820
	Belarus	0.787
	Lithuania	0.719
Mean		**0.775**
Passive-reluctant capitalist	United States	0.940
	United Kingdom	0.924
	Ireland	0.919
	Greece	0.909
	Israel	0.908
Mean		**0.920**
Passive-reluctant socialist	Russia	0.874
	Czech Republic	0.872
	Hungary	0.855
	Bulgaria	0.773
Mean		**0.826**

NOTE: HDI = human development index.
SOURCE: United Nations Development Programme. (1996). *Human development report 1996.* New York: Oxford University Press.

ratios but unequal productivity, the former would determine where that society should be placed in Table 2-7.

Increasing productivity can offset a growing dependency ratio. A case in point is the United States, whose increasing dependency ratio (see Table 2-6) does not significantly damage its capacity to be a welfare state because its high productivity compensates (see Table 2-7).

Over the years, this problem has been examined in two disciplines: economics and anthropology. In economics it is known as an old Malthusian problem, where the population of a society increases at a faster rate than the capacity of a society to feed or care for it (see Thomlinson, 1965, pp. 53–59). In anthropology it is called a "cannibals and kings dilemma," in which a given society's increasing population either can or cannot be supported by its prevailing technology (Harris, 1977).

Marx and later Marxians opposed the view that for each level of technology, an optimum population level exists that can be supported by the technology. Furthermore, the Marxian position was that changes in social relations—especially by recruiting the state as a distribution agent—can substantially change the well-being of a population (see Cox, 1970, p. 300). The trends examined in this chapter, it would seem, do not support the Marxian position. In fact, the trends support the reverse position: Without increases in production and decreases in dependency ratio, the well-being of a society is reduced. Thus, the capacity of a welfare state to provide welfare functions to its population appears to be analogous to the Malthusian or the "cannibals and kings" propositions.

HDI Scores of Societies by Groups

In this section, I look at the HDI scores of passive-reluctant welfare societies and compare them with that of active-engaged societies. Table 2-8 shows the mean HDI scores of all societies in descending order. Table 2-8 also shows that capitalist societies, regardless of their reluctance toward or active participation in welfare, seem to come out nearly even on HDI scores. In contrast, socialist passive-reluctant societies fare somewhat better in welfare. Table 2-9 presents further analysis of the data presented in Table 2-7.

It seems, then, that productivity (based on per capita GDP) may influence the HDI levels of industrial states. Coupled with dependency ratio, HDI is a good measure of the caregiving of a welfare society.

Table 2-9. Mean HDI of Welfare States by Ability Status

ABILITY	*N*	MEAN HDI SCORE
Able and sound capitalist	10	0.927
Able and sound socialist	0	NA
Trouble capitalist	15	0.920
Troubled socialist	4	0.824
Disabled capitalist	0	NA
Disabled socialist	6	0.821

Source: Data calculated by the author.

Notes HDI = human development index. NA = not applicable.

Returning to Figure 2-1, the available data seem to indicate that passive-reluctant states, regardless of whether they are capitalist or socialist seem to be troubled. Among the 14 active-engaged capitalist states, seven are able and sound, and seven are troubled. Among the active-engaged socialist states, all are disabled.

Viability of Welfare States

We have seen how two factors (such as productivity and dependency ratio) contribute to the viability of a welfare society. At this point, we return to the concept of the viability of a welfare society and introduce a formula that attempts to quantify it.

If V = the viability of a welfare society, then

$V = {}^{1}/_{k}\ (P_n)(D_r)^{-1}$, where

k = a constant (in this case, k = 1,000),

P_n = a measure of productivity in a state (in this case, per capita GDP), and

D_r = dependency ratio of that state.

Table 2-10 reflects the viability (V) scores of the passive-reluctant, and active-engaged societies. Note that the higher the V score, the greater the viability of the welfare society in question. Table 2-11 lists the same states by their ability status. Figure 2-2 represents a graphic statement about the trends on redistribution discussed so far.

Summary

The social experiment called the welfare state, in which the state becomes a distribution agent and care-provider for selected populations, has begun to show the following trends:

- Socialist states, or the former Soviet-bloc countries, which had promised a welfare system to their populations, were in a poor position to deliver it.
- First World countries with a capitalist market economy in which the promise of a welfare system is either lukewarm or nonexistent are in a better position to provide a social welfare system.
- In capitalist societies, the presence of an active-engaged or a passive-reluctant welfare state seems to make little difference in a society's HDI level.

Table 2-10. Viability Scores of Welfare States by Engagement

CATEGORY	COUNTRY	VIABILITY SCORES
Active-engaged capitalist	Canada	0.448
	Japan	0.497
	Netherlands	0.420
	Norway	0.392
	France	0.388
	Finland	0.353
	Spain	0.307
	Sweden	0.329
	Australia	0.387
	Austria	0.490
	New Zealand	0.319
	Denmark	0.444
	Luxembourg	0.757
	Malta	0.261
Mean		**0.414**
Active-engaged socialist	Latvia	0.065
	Belarus	0.090
	Lithuania	0.078
Mean		**0.078**
Passive-reluctant capitalist	United States	0.496
	United Kingdom	0.344
	Ireland	0.283
	Greece	0.232
	Israel	0.250
Mean		**0.321**
Passive-reluctant socialist	Russia	0.085
	Czech Republic	0.195
	Hungary	0.135
	Bulgaria	0.092
Mean		**0.126**

SOURCE: Numbers were calculated by the author.

- The United States is seen as a passive-reluctant and troubled society. However, its high productivity keeps it from becoming a disabled society.
- Changing demographic structure, as measured with the dependency ratio of countries, threatens the capacity of any country attempting to install and maintain a social welfare system.

Table 2-11. Viability Scores of Welfare States by Ability

ABILITY	COUNTRY	VIABILITY SCORE
Able and sound capitalist	Austria	0.490
	Canada	0.448
	Denmark	0.444
	Finland	0.353
	Japan	0.497
	Luxembourg	0.757
	Netherlands	0.420
	Germany	—
	Italy	—
	Switzerland	—
Mean		**0.487**
Able and sound socialist	There are no countries in this category.	NA
Troubled capitalist	Australia	0.387
	France	0.388
	Greece	0.232
	Ireland	0.283
	Israel	0.250
	Malta	0.261
	New Zealand	0.319
	Norway	0.392
	Spain	0.307
	Sweden	0.329
	United Kingdom	0.344
	United States	0.496
	Belgium	—
	Iceland	—
	Portugal	—
Mean		**0.365**
Troubled socialist	Bulgaria	0.092
	Czech Republic	0.195
	Hungary	0.135
	Russia	0.085
Mean		**0.148**
Disabled socialist	Belarus	0.090
	Latvia	0.065
	Lithuania	0.078
	Poland	—
	Slovakia	—
	Ukraine	—
Mean		**0.077**

SOURCE: Figures were developed and calculated by the author.
NOTES: NA = not applicable; — = not available.

Figure 2-2.

Elaborations on the State as a Distribution Agent

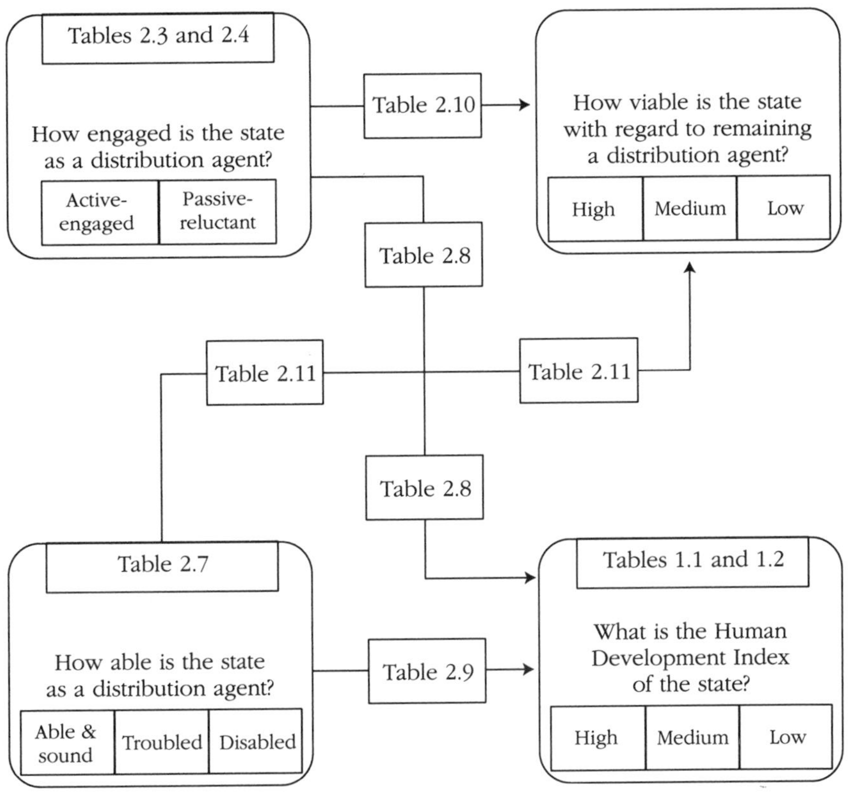

Given productivity, the vulnerability of the welfare state can be seen as a function of its dependency ratio and its styles of redistribution. Later in this book, I show that the ideology of production—that is, industrial capitalism or industrial socialism—as a contributory factor in welfare state development has received more attention from scholars of the welfare state than has the productivity of a society or its demographic structure (which can change the state's ability to tax and engage in transfer). Styles of redistribution also are factors in the development of a welfare state. Chapter 3 presents arguments for and against the state as an agent of redistribution, and chapters 4 and 5 discuss how styles of redistribution affect the welfare state.

References

Barnes, J., & Srivenkataramana, T. (1982). Ideology and the welfare state: An examination of Wilensky's conclusions. *Social Service Review, 56,* 230–245.

Chatterjee, P. (1996). *Approaches to the welfare state.* Washington, DC: NASW Press.

Cox, P. R. (1970). *Demography.* Cambridge, England: Cambridge University Press.

Esping-Andersen, G. (1990). *The three worlds of welfare capitalism.* Princeton, NJ: Princeton University Press.

Harris, M. (1977). *Cannibals and kings: The origins of cultures.* New York: Random House.

Heilbronner, R. (1962). *The worldly philosophers.* New York: Simon & Schuster.

Jansson, B. S. (1988). *The reluctant welfare state: A history of American social welfare policies.* Belmont, CA: Wadsworth.

Jansson, B. S. (1997). *The reluctant welfare state: American social welfare policies—Past, present, and future.* Pacific Grove, CA: Brooks/Cole.

Peukert, D. (1992). *The Weimer Republic: The crisis in classical modernity.* New York: Hill & Wang.

Piven, F. F., & Cloward, R. (1993). *Regulating the poor.* New York: Basic Books.

Rimlinger, G. V. (1971). *Welfare policy and industrialization in Europe, America, and Russia.* New York: John Wiley & Sons.

Schumpeter, J. (1950). *Capitalism, socialism, and democracy.* New York: Harper.

Thomlinson, R. (1965). *Population dynamics.* New York: Random House.

Titmuss, R. M. (1950). *Problems of social policy.* London: Her Majesty's Stationery Office.

Titmuss, R. M. (1959). *Essays on the welfare state.* New Haven, CT: Yale University Press.

Titmuss, R. M. (1968). *Commitment to welfare.* New York: Pantheon.

Titmuss, R. M. (1971). *The gift relationship.* New York: Pantheon.

Titmuss, R. M. (1974). *Social policy: An introduction.* New York: Pantheon.

United Nations Development Programme. (1994). *Human development report 1994.* New York: Oxford University Press.

United Nations Development Programme. (1996). *Human development report 1996.* New York: Oxford University Press.

United Nations Development Programme. (1997). *Human development report 1997.* New York: Oxford University Press.

Wilensky, H. (1975). *The welfare state and equality.* Berkeley, CA: University of California Press.

3

Functions of the State

Analysis of welfare states can never be complete without some form of a theory of the state. What are the functions of the state? Do these functions change over time? How do they change from the preindustrial state to the various types of industrial states? How is the welfare function embedded in all the functions that the state serves? Should the state be involved in redistribution, and if so, what are the consequences?

Whether by design or by default, industrial societies seem to produce a welfare state; that is, the state becomes an agent of redistribution. Thus in practice, providing redistribution seems to have become an important function of those states. According to the vocabulary of functionalist sociologists (see Bailey, 1990; Gans, 1972; Granovetter, 1985; Merton, 1957; Parsons, 1951), the welfare state is a form of adaptation by a culture to a changing technological environment.

What are the consequences of this form of adaptation? The fact that the formerly socialist (or planned-economy societies) are universally low in their capacity for production (see chapter 2) would not surprise most economists, sociologists, and moral philosophers. As shown below, their argument would be that (1) producers of wealth in socialist societies have less incentive to produce it because it is not in their interest to do so, and (2) it is human nature to pursue ends that are more in one's own interest than in the collective interest.

In the arguments for and against the state as a distribution agent, the second point often has been discussed more explicitly than the first (Barry, 1990; de Jouvenel, 1952/1990; George & Wilding, 1977). Consequently, it makes sense to first discuss the state as a distribution agent in the context of a self-interest–collective interest continuum. George and Wilding first introduced a widely discussed continuum called a "continuum of collectivism," which consist of linear categories of anticollectivism, reluctant collectivism,

Fabianism, and Marxism. After describing that continuum, this chapter will update it and then discuss scholars' positions on the state as an agent of redistribution.

Continuum of Collectivism

George and Wilding's (1977) scheme, presented in Table 3-1, has certain built-in biases. First, it is constructed with an emphasis on collectivism (it has three different collectivist categories, compared with one anticollectivism category, giving the appearance of a fundamental ideological schism in the Western world: Christ, and anti-Christ). Second, even in its collectivist orientation, it shows an English bias because it leaves out the entire school of thought of the communal Marxists and anarchist Marxists of the European continent (for example, Petr Kropotkin, 1902/1955, and Pierre Proudhon, 1927/1969, and their ideas about welfare universalism). Third, their scheme does not incorporate well the works of thinkers like John Rawls or Robert Nozick, because their writings first appeared in the 1970s, which is when George and Wilding also published their work. Fourth, it lumps together thinkers such as Adam Smith, Friedrich von Hayek, and Milton Friedman in a single category called "anticollectivists." Indeed, Pinker (1979) and Barry (1990) have already summarized some of these criticisms.

To remedy the problems inherent in the continuum George and Wilding (1977) offered, we suggest a six-interval continuum (Table 3-2): Marxist–state socialist, Marxist–communal socialist, Fabian socialist, reluctant collectivist, individualist–libertarian, and individualist–social Darwinian. In Table 3-2, George and Wilding's anticollectivists category becomes two categories: individualist–social Darwinian, and individualist–libertarian. Similarly, we break George and Wilding's Marxist category into two: Marxist–state socialist, and Marxist–communal socialist.

George and Wilding Revised

George and Wilding (1977) either omitted or ignored the ideas of certain classical scholars. For example, the work of Adam Smith, who suggested the paradox of "private gain yielding social good" (see Atherton, 1990; Barry, 1990; "The Modern Adam Smith," 1990), should be categorized as individualist–libertarian. The work of Friedrich von Hayek (1944, 1948), who predicted the loss of liberty to impersonal bureaucracies, should be placed in that category as well. Milton Friedman's (1962) work also should be seen as that of an individualist libertarian: Friedman was insistent that the unfortunate members of a society be aided by direct transfer payments, which would retain the liberty of both the payers and the recipients of transfer. The wel-

Table 3-1. Four Orientations to the State as a Redistribution Agent

	MARXIST	FABIAN SOCIALIST	RELUCTANT COLLECTIVIST	ANTI-COLLECTIVIST
Values	Liberty Collectivism Equality	Liberty Fellowship Pursuit of equality	Liberty Individualism Reform inequality	Liberty Individualism Rights of individuals
Incentive	Is suspect in individuals	Negates fellowship	To be encouraged	Is the basis of society
Assumption	Planned economy by the state	Planned and incremental state role	Regulated market economy	Market economy
Vision	Remove class conflict	Promote equality	Remove blatant inequality	Inequality is the price for liberty
Market	To be controlled by the state	To be tamed by the state	To be regulated by the state	To be left alone
Tax	For total redistribution	Progressively for redistribution	Progressively for welfare programs	Not for redistribution
State	Expansive	Incrementally expansive	Some expansion necessary	Minimal
Is the welfare state	Incremental	Reluctant welfare state	Welfare state	Often not a welfare state

SOURCE: Adapted from text of George, V., & Wilding, P. (1977). *Ideology and social welfare.* London: Routledge.

Table 3-2. Revisions to the State as a Redistribution Agent

MARXIST–STATE SOCIALIST	MARXIST–COMMUNAL SOCIALIST	FABIAN SOCIALIST	RELUCTANT COLLECTIVIST	INDIVIDUALIST–LIBERTARIAN	INDIVIDUALIST–SOCIAL DARWINIAN
Liberty as defined by the state	Liberty as defined by the community	Liberty as defined by the fellowship	Liberty as defined by an aristocratic tradition	Liberty as defined by the individual	Liberty as defined by those who are successful at the marketplace
Equality enforced by the state	Equality enforced by the community	Pursuit of equality by a fellowship	Change inequality through social reform	Equality is desirable but unattainable	Equality is unattainable
Reward loyalty	Reward loyalty and merit	Reward merit and loyalty	Reward merit and placate the unmerited	Reward merit and patronize the unmerited	Reward merit
Individual rights are less than survival of the state	Individual rights are less than survival of the community	Individual rights are less than the norms of fellowship	Defend the rights of the individual	Promote the rights of the individual	Promote the rights of the individual
Justice by above criteria	Justice by above criteria	Justice by above criteria	Justice by above criteria	Justice by above criteria	Justice by above criteria
Individual incentive is suspect	Individual incentive is a problem	Individual incentive is contrary to norms of fellowship	Individual incentive should be supported	Individual incentive should be rewarded	Individual incentive is the basis of society
Planning by the state	Planning by the community	Planning by the fellowship	Planning by the state and the individual	Planning by the individual	Planning by the individual

continued

Class hierarchy is class conflict	Class hierarchy is overcome by communal solidarity	Class hierarchy is avoided by the fellowship	Class hierarchy is managed by the state	Class hierarchy is managed by the state	Class hierarchy is left alone
State-party partnership to remove class conflict	Communal solidarity removes class conflict	Fellowship undoes class conflict	Reform some class-related issues	Appearance of concern for some class-related issues	The lower classes are unfit for survival
Market to be controlled by the state	Collective bargaining by the state	To be tamed by the state	Market to be regulated by the state	Market to be deferred to by the state	Market to be left alone
Taxation for total redistribution	Taxation progressive for equality of outcome	Taxation progressive for equality of outcome	Taxation progressive for equality of opportunity	Taxation to help the state secure individual's rights	Taxation to help the state secure individual's rights
Expansive state and a welfare state	State is an ally or an enemy of interests of the community	State incrementally a welfare state	Increasing but reluctant welfare state	Minimal state but a partial welfare state only for "the deserving"	Minimal state and not a welfare state
Ideas influenced the socialist welfare states	Ideas influenced the socialist and many European welfare states	Ideas influenced the socialist and British welfare states	Ideas influenced the British, American, and Japanese welfare states	Ideas influenced the British and American welfare states	Ideas opposed the welfare state
Authors/architects: Marx Lenin Trotsky	Authors/architects: Marx Rousseau Proudhon Kropotkin	Authors/architects: Booth Webbs Tawney T. H. Marshall Titmuss	Authors/architects: Bismarck Beveridge Hopkins Galbraith Moynihan	Authors/architects: Smith A. Marshall von Hayek Schumpeter Friedman de Jouvenel	Authors/architects: Spencer Sumner Ward Jensen

fare state is cumbersome; by its very operation, it creates large, impersonal bureaucracies (as von Hayek observed) as well as certain new professions from the middle class, who consume a great deal of the state's expenses for the unfortunate. (See the section below on third-party involvement in welfare transactions). In addition, the work of Bertrand de Jouvenel (1952/1990) (summarized below) should be seen as a major position paper for the category individualist–libertarian. Another famous scholar, who would rate somewhere between reluctant collectivist and individualist–libertarian, is Joseph A. Schumpeter (1950), based on his concept of the workfare state (discussed in chapter 4).

In addition, George and Wilding's (1977) scheme says almost nothing about classical scholars who should be classified as individualist–social Darwinist. Classical scholars, such as Herbert Spencer in England and William G. Sumner, Lester Ward, and Arthur Jensen in America, could be classified in this category (see Hofstadter, 1955; Jensen, 1970). Jensen (1970), for example, clearly stated that it is not worthwhile for the state to engage in redistribution efforts aiming at the reduction of unequal status of biologically inferior persons.

In the category called "Fabian," George and Wilding (1977) omitted the work of T. H. Marshall (1964, 1981), who introduced the ideas of "social rights" (rights to certain goods and services stemming from one's membership in a collectivity), "civil rights" (rights to certain behavioral styles, like free speech, freedom of movement, or freedom of assembly), and "political rights" (rights to participate in the governance of the state) (see also Grønbjerg, 1977). In fact, T. H. Marshall's (1964) idea about a citizen's entitlement to a basic income or a certain level of health care places him as an important partner of Titmuss in the Fabian fellowship.

At the extreme left, George and Wilding (1977) ignored the classical works of communal socialists such as Kropotkin (1902/1955) and Proudhon (1927/1969), who are also called anarchist socialists because of their commitment to the concept of community at the expense of the concept of the state. Both were socialists and believed that a collective—be it a clan, a tribe, a community, or a nation—is obligated almost universally to provide welfare services ("aid-giving," or "mutuality," as they called it) to the needy. Their ideology resembled that of the Fabians. Among their work, Kropotkin's *Mutual Aid* (1955) is perhaps the best-known position paper on the necessity of the welfare state. And even further to the left, missing in George and Wilding's work are the works of Lenin (1943) and Trotsky (1933) and their ideas about the necessity of the welfare state.

In the reluctant collectivist category, Bismarck in Germany and Harry Hopkins and Franklin D. Roosevelt in the United States are key people who supported the welfare state, but George and Wilding (1977) did not discuss them. They discussed in detail, however, the other reluctant collectivist, Lord Beveridge of England. Hopkins, Roosevelt, and Beveridge saw the pursuit of full employment as one key function of the state and were clear in their thinking that when the market cannot attain it, the state should (see Beveridge, 1942; Graham, 1976).

Key Authors since George and Wilding

I deliberately omitted from Table 3-2 certain key authors, because their works appeared either at about the same time as or after George and Wilding. Here we summarize their work and its relevance to the idea of the state as an agent of distribution.

Two works that were noticed and discussed widely are those of John Rawls (1971) and Robert Nozick (1974). Rawls's ideas, which are highly sympathetic to disadvantaged populations, called for egalitarianism and state intervention to aid marginalized populations, ideas that put him near the Fabians. However, the Fabians are considered to be exclusively a British fellowship that originated around 1883 or 1884 and were incorporated into what is now called the British Labour Party; the name is now used as an umbrella term for the party's research arm. It is therefore not appropriate to classify Rawls as a Fabian. His ideas, however, certainly would place him somewhere slightly to the left of the reluctant collectivist category in Table 3-2.

Rawls advances two principles: (1) One should be entitled to a maximum amount of liberty as long as it does not jeopardize the liberty of anyone else; and (2) the welfare of the most disadvantaged members of society should be maximized through applying a redistributive principle, which would make the most-disadvantaged people as well off as possible. The second principle, however, does not call for equal distribution of wealth, because the talented members of society produce enough wealth so that their share of wealth is always higher than that provided by the nontalented and the disadvantaged. Rawls based his positions on what he called the "maximin" principle, also known as the "Rawlsian theory of justice." Commenting on Rawls's work, Coleman (1974, p.741) summarized a basic concern of moral philosophers: "This book constitutes the culmination of a long preoccupation of Rawls with the question of how one can characterize, in principle, a just society, one in which the dual problems of preserving individual autonomy and rights and obtaining the benefits that arise from a social order are solved." It would seem that Rawls is caught in a tug-of-war between liberty, as understood by the individualist–libertarian thinkers, and redistribution, which is an idea we place, albeit reluctantly, near those of the Fabians.

Whereas Rawls's work represents a struggle between the positions of Fabians and individualist–libertarians, Nozick's work is absolutely in the far corner of the latter camp. Nozick (1974) argued that as long as people have acquired wealth (or income, although Nozick did not differentiate between the two) in a lawful and legitimate way, they have a right to keep it, and the state does not have the right to take it from them for purposes of redistribution. The right to hold on to private property is a just and absolute right and is inviolable. Elaborating on the idea of rights, Dworkin (1977, 1986) added that the state indeed cannot take wealth away from one group and transfer it to others for the purposes of welfare, because it violates—in addition to the right suggested by Nozick—the right to equal consideration and respect. At times, however, this right also can mean that respect for others may mean respect for disadvantaged people and that under those circumstances, the state may intervene on their behalf.

These debates occurred, it seems, mostly in the context of income-maintenance policy. It is easy to see how Rawls or other reluctant collectivists would want the state to redistribute income so that the poor also would have some income and, consequently, some minimum buying power. What if the disadvantaged, however, are not the poor per se but children in an abusive environment within their own family or community? Should the state take money from those who have justly acquired income or property and pay a group of social workers with that money to protect those children? Is the principle of taking money from those who have it and using it for child welfare policy a just principle? It is possible to argue that a conflict may exist here between the implications for justice and implications for protection. The issue may be that, given a conflict between the protection and the justice functions of the state, which one has supremacy? This point is covered in greater detail later in this chapter.

Further updating the concepts of justice, rights, and equality in theories of distributive justice are Kolm (1996), Roemer (1996), and Sen (1992). Kolm, attempting to update Rawls, suggested that four approaches to justice exist: (1) the utilitarian model, (2) the full process freedom model, (3) the Marxist-socialist model, and (4) the fairness model. Comparing Kolm's approaches with the categories described in Table 3-2, we see that the utilitarian model resembles that of the reluctant collectivists; the full process freedom model, essentially a French model, is similar to the communal socialist model; the Marxist-socialist model is close to the Marxist–state socialist model; and the fairness model is that of Rawls, which we have rated somewhere between the reluctant collectivist and Fabian models. Kolm also suggested that the utilitarian model views society as just when it is devoted to maximizing utility, which allegedly can be accomplished by providing maximal happiness for the maximal number. According to the full process freedom model, society is just when a social contract exists among the members of society to decommodify and redistribute certain basic goods and services to all. In the Marxist-socialist model, a just society exists when all production and distribution is carried out by the state, with an eye to benefiting the interests of the collectivity. Finally, in the fairness model, a just society occurs when a fair distribution of goods and services exists, regardless of how the production occurs. The fairness model resembles the Scandinavian model of the welfare state.

Kolm (1996) suggested that Rawls, who opposed utilitarianism, laid out the most important point: Redistribution must benefit the least advantaged. To this principle Kolm added that the norms of fairness and equality demand that redistribution be left neither to a random selection nor to an "invisible hand" (Adam Smith's metaphor for the market), but to a clearly understandable social contract as exists in the full process freedom model (the communal socialist model in Table 3-2). Sen (1992), an economist and moral philosopher, stated that equality of capability must not necessarily be a factor in redistribution: What appears to be individual capability or merit is really a function of many generations of cumulative inequality manifested through the accident of birth.

Roemer (1996), on reviewing those theories of distributive justice, suggested that the understanding and possible rebuilding of the welfare state, at the least, has to depend on both the "tools of economists" and the "tools of philosophers." (We believe that such a task also should include the "tools of social workers," the "tools of sociologists," the "tools of anthropologists," and the "tools of historians.") Roemer goes on to say that because economists can view a problem with more precision than other scholars can, they should be consulted about the structure of the welfare state; in the final analysis, however, developing knowledge and position papers about the welfare state is the domain of moral philosophers.

Other key authors since George and Wilding (1977) include Berger (1986); Castro (1983); Esping-Andersen (1990); Gould (1993); Murray (1984); and Murray and Herrnstein (1994). Murray's (1984) work essentially advances the thesis that income redistribution to the poor by the state essentially does not alleviate poverty and, in some ways, contributes to its continuity. Using the case of the inner-city underclass (a euphemism for the inner-city black low-income class, which causes debates about its usage), Murray demonstrated that in the United States prolonged transfer payments to the poor did not alleviate the poverty and culture of poverty (see Lewis, 1959, 1969) of the inner cities. At about the same time, Castro's (1983) position paper, delivered in New Delhi, argued for strengthened welfare states in the Second World (at the time, the Communist bloc Second World still existed) and the formation of a Welfare World that would provide help to the Third World. Castro's treatise is an argument for redistribution at not only the state but also the global level. Conversely, Berger (1986) confirmed that at a worldwide level, there seemed to be no better agent than industrial capitalism for alleviating poverty, a position originally taken by Adam Smith (see Atherton, 1990; "The Modern Adam Smith," 1990) and later strongly supported by Joseph Schumpeter (1950).

Esping-Andersen's (1990) work is both sociological and empirical. However, his criterion (and bias) for a just society is clear: Total commodification (a metaphor known as "fetishism of commodities," borrowed from Marx) in any society moves it further from being a just society, whereas partial decommodification moves it toward being a just society. In

1980 Esping-Andersen's data showed that the states under the Anglo-American umbrella (Australia, Canada, Ireland, New Zealand, the United Kingdom, and the United States) are the least decommodified and that the northern European states (Denmark, Norway, and Sweden) are the most decommodified. Given that his data represent trends before the reforms of Thatcher in the United Kingdom and Reagan in the United States, it is likely that reforms pushed those countries even further away from decommodification.

Esping-Andersen (1990, p. 149) pointed out another trend: "Modern welfare states are no longer systems of social provision only. They have, in many nations, become virtual employment-machines, often being the only source of job growth. Today, the Danish and Swedish welfare states employ about 30 percent of the labor force." By implication, it would seem that another sign of a just society is the conversion of its state into an employment machine.

Gould (1993) presented a comparative case study of three capitalist nations: the United Kingdom, a reluctant welfare state (defined in this book as passive-reluctant); Sweden, an exemplar of a welfare state (defined as active-engaged); and Japan, which rates between the two. He argued that public-sector employment in Sweden constituted 33 percent of all employment and that public-sector expenditures made up 60 percent of its GDP. Those expenditures have reduced Sweden's economic productivity. Gould's conclusion was that "the *only way* out of Sweden's economic difficulties [is] to reduce the size of the public sector and the burden of high taxation" (Gould, 1993, p. 230). Recalling the idea of commodification, he suggested that "labour, even in Sweden, is in the process of recommodification" (Gould, 1993, p. 233) and that the trend was "the Japanisation of welfare," in which a middle road of reluctant collectivism is pursued as the basis for social policy.

Murray and Herrnstein (1994) added a psychological and biological view to these considerations. They reminded us that sexual selection, as both Darwin and Freud pointed out, is an important part of human behavior: Human females choose mates who are powerful, who can provide protection and support to the family, and with whom their reproductive destiny can be optimized. Given this biological tendency of humans, the information age is fostering sexual selection that is causing the formation of two groups: those who inherit high IQs and those who do not. (IQ scores are usually passed on biologically from one generation to another.) In this light, the entire question of who can participate in the market (and consequently be taxed to support welfare) becomes an open one. The end is likely to be the emergence of a society in which the elites are those with high IQs and the masses are those with low IQs. The implication of this discussion is that the state, even if it wanted to, would become incapable of the pursuit of justice and equality. In many ways, this work resembles that of Jensen (1970), discussed earlier.

ARGUMENTS FOR REDISTRIBUTION: A SUMMARY

The first and perhaps one of the most important reasons why the state needs to engage in redistribution is family failure. It has been documented (Bell, 1973; Blumer, 1990; Kottak, 1979) that industrialization as a technocultural mode changes family structure from an extended to a nuclear one, and then changes even the nuclear structure to a blended structure. The main functions of the family in industrial societies are primary socialization of children and stabilization of adult personalities (Blumer 1990; Parsons & Bales, 1955). Furthermore, for some members of industrial societies, even minimally functioning families are not available. Consequently, the state takes over many social-control, socialization, and role-management functions ordinarily performed by the family. For example, child, adolescent, and elder role-management functions of the family become state child protection, juvenile justice, and elder-abuse prevention efforts.

A second important reason for the state to be engaged in redistribution is to deal with market failure. The market crash of 1929 and the Great Depression that followed clearly taught that the consequence of state inaction (as a redistribution agent) is an immense magnitude of human suffering. Any prolonged human suffering may spur violent change in society. Thus, state redistribution to deal with actual or potential market failure is an effort to alleviate human suffering and to maintain stability in society.

A third important reason for the state to redistribute is "nature failure." Natural disasters, such as typhoons, tornadoes, hurricanes, famines (which can be caused by humans as well as nature), and earthquakes, may devastate market-led distribution systems. In such cases, the state has to take on short-term or long-term redistribution functions. The problem of failure to thrive or being born biologically disabled, in which nature does not allow certain people to develop appropriately, is another type of nature failure. A state may be required to step in when nature failure occurs either in isolation or in combination with family or market failure.

In the absence of market failure, the market for labor should work well, and consequently, successful labor force attachment—also called continuous employment—should solve needs for housing, health care, education, child care, and elder care. The assumption here is that successful labor force attachment is a sufficient condition for the ability to purchase goods and services from the marketplace. This assumption, however, is not always correct; such cases are examples of the problem of distribution failure (Sen, 1981).

Distribution failure may occur under several circumstances. It can occur in cases in which a wage-earner's wages are adequate by market standards for the wage-earner's position and qualifications, but his or her purchasing power is insufficient to procure certain goods and services (that is, health care or housing) for the family. The term "market standards" refers to what the marketplace will actually pay for labor of a certain type. It can also occur in cases in which the wage-earner's wages are inadequate by market standards and thus housing, health care, education, child care, and elder care are not affordable for the family. Distribution failure can occur in settings in which there is one wage earner and the family size is large (literally, too many mouths to feed) or in situations in which there is no wage earner at all. Foremost, distribution failure happens when the person with poor labor force attachment, who cannot buy most goods and services, buys into a set of rising expectations that somehow he or she (and their families) is owed better housing, better health care, better education, and so forth. In those cases, the economic efficiency of market distribution is fine and fully operational, but the normative expectation of what a human must minimally have is not in parity with the market distribution. In many poor countries with no welfare state, no such normative expectation exists. In wealthy countries with welfare states, the state steps in with a subsidy, which can be in the form of an income supplement or an in-kind payment, such as state-operated housing or health care. Such state subsidies, in turn, may create a normative expectation that certain goods and services are owed to certain consumers.

Arguments against Redistribution: A Summary

Two kinds of arguments against redistribution seem to exist. The first opposes all forms of redistribution and corresponds with the individualist–social Darwinian position in Table 3-2; the second supports a limited amount of redistribution and corresponds with either the individualist–libertarian or the reluctant collectivist categories in the table.

The classic arguments of de Jouvenel (1952/1990) against redistribution are mostly of the second type and occasionally of the first type. He argued that the efforts of the welfare state resemble those of a socialist state. Small communities may be able to sustain socialism, but not the state, a point understood by Rousseau but not by Marx. (Note that our six-category typology differentiates state socialism from communal socialism.) de Jouvenel's chief arguments are as follows:

- The state has several functions, but they do not include redistribution.
- Economic inequality, by itself, is not an evil and is a fact of life.
- It is not the state's function to arbitrarily assign a floor or a ceiling of income standards.
- The standards of redistribution are set by a marginalist principle, that is, those in the margins (as in a bell curve) have to be brought into the middle, either by giving to them or by taking away from

them. This principle violates the norms of liberty, an argument Nozick (1974) later repeated when he suggested that the state has no right to take away income or property earned in a just and lawful way.

- The resources needed to provide a subsistence minimum for the poor cannot be obtained by taxing only the rich, and redistribution often must include taxing those who are in the middle class.
- Any policy of redistribution will discriminate against minorities, because standards of redistribution will be set by majority norms (a point also made by von Hayek, 1976, 1978).
- Redistribution can confer tax immunities or tax advantages to businesses, benefits ordinarily denied to families; the redistributionist state thus also becomes an antifamily state.
- The state's redistributionist efforts create serious disincentives for individual and family saving.
- By giving a subsidy, the state gains control over the recipients of that subsidy and thereby transforms the recipient population into a hostage population who must surrender their liberty to receive the subsidy.
- Redistribution curtails private initiatives and leads to a process of centralization and massive bureaucratization, a point also developed by both von Hayek (1976, 1978) and Friedman (1962).
- Redistribution does not alleviate poverty but institutionalizes it and creates disincentives for the poor to leave that condition.

de Jouvenel (1952/1990) forcefully made the last point, and he has since been strongly supported by Murray (1984). Nozick, in *Anarchy, State and Utopia* (1974), and von Hayek, in *The Constitution of Liberty* (1978), added the following points to those above:

- Redistribution benefits the middle class because it creates new markets for them, such as occupations and professions that recruit from the middle class to manage the poor.
- The redistributionist state is also an ever-increasing, or expansionist, state with large bureaucracies (which employ the middle class) and requires continued interference with individual liberties.
- The large bureaucracies of the redistributionist state often develop immense discretionary powers, as seen in the powers exercised by welfare officers, immigration officers, and so forth.
- The large bureaucracies of the redistributionist state cannot be a surrogate family but often are antifamily.
- Redistribution efforts legitimize the interests of state bureaucracies and members of the middle class who develop territories in the poverty market.

Paradigm Lost in the Welfare States

Arguments for and against the state as a distribution agent have branched out, leading to George and Wilding's (1977) four paradigms (see Table 3-1) and then to the six paradigms described in this chapter (see Table 3-2). Some of those paradigms, however, stand totally untested, discredited, or absorbed into other paradigms. Table 3-3 illustrates this point.

For example, in the days preceding the New Deal efforts, the individualist–social Darwinist model (see Table 3-2) was an influence in the United States. It did not dominate the country, however, because many state-supported programs benefiting the interests of organized labor had been enacted in the United States before the New Deal. The individualist–libertarian and reluctant collectivist models influenced both Britain and the United States, and the Fabian socialist model influenced Britain as well. Japan emerged as a unique type of reluctant collectivist state. Ultimately, Fabian socialism was absorbed into a British political party, but the Marxist–communal socialist model, its roots tracing back to Rousseau (1915), Kropotkin (1902/1955), and Proudhon (1927/1969), maintains credibility in all of Europe. The model should be renamed "communal socialist," however, because the term "Marxist" is now discredited. Thus, we are essentially left with three models of the welfare state as the 21st century approaches: individualist–libertarian, reluctant collectivist, and communal socialist.

Returning to the three capitalist welfare systems that Esping-Andersen (1990) discussed earlier, it seems that his so-called liberal states are one type of reluctant collectivists, his "statist" welfare systems rest somewhere between reluctant collectivists and communal socialists, and his "social-democrat" systems resemble "communal socialists."

Table 3-3. Late 20th-Century Paradigms of the State as a Redistribution Agent

MARXIST— STATE SOCIALIST	MARXIST— COMMUNAL SOCIALIST	FABIAN SOCIALIST	RELUC-TANT COLLECT-IVIST	INDIVID-UALIST LIBER-TARIAN	INDIVID-UALIST– SOCIAL DARWINIAN
Discredited since the collapse of the Soviet Union	Remains a key idea in most of Western Europe	Absorbed in the British Labour Party; still an influence in Britain	Remains a key idea in America, Britain, and Japan	Remains a key idea in America and Britain	Was an influence in America before the New Deal; no state approximates this today

Third-Party Transactions: Consequences

In elementary economics, third-party systems are inefficient mechanisms whereby the presence of the proverbial middlemen contributes to price increases of a product. That is, when a product goes directly from the maker of the product to the buyer, its cost is lower than when it goes from the maker to the buyer through several middlemen.

At least, that was the wisdom in agricultural economies. In many ways, however, the process is more complex in industrial economies, and certain transactions are not possible without the presence of middlemen. The problem of cost-escalation in the welfare states may, in part, originate here, with what is called "third-party payments and activities." Many transactions in industrial societies, both within and outside the area of social welfare, are supported by third-party activities. Literature on the use of third-party systems is almost nonexistent, however, in the arguments for and against the state as a distribution agent.

The State as the First Third Party

As it stands, the state is the first third party between the recipient and the taxpayer. In this status, the state frequently keeps a part of the money paid by the taxpayer to offset the costs of transfer. Often, the state can balance its budget (as was accomplished in the United States during the late 1990s) with money collected for social security or social welfare purposes or spend money collected for social welfare for other items.

Professions as the Second Third Party

When the state provides an in-kind service to a recipient group, it has at least two choices. It can establish a bureaucracy, employ qualified people in the bureaucracy, and then have those state employees deliver those services (for example, health or social services); or it can establish a bidding procedure and award a contract to a qualified professional group to deliver the same services. In the first setting, the service provider is the employee of the state, whereas in the second setting, the service provider is an independent contractor. The first path leads to increased bureaucratization, and both the first and second paths lead to pressure for increased professionalization (see Mintzberg, 1993). Professionalization is, among other things, a form of collective bargaining (Friedson, 1994; Larson, 1977; Macdonald, 1995). Organized groups of professionals promote their own interests first in their quest for professionalization (Larson, 1977; Trattner, 1979). When they become a third party in the transactions between the taxpayer and the welfare beneficiary, their role also becomes a factor in cost escalation.

Role of the Social Work Profession

The social work profession is the most developed in the most passive-reluctant states. By *most developed,* we mean the number of years of postsecondary education it takes to qualify as a social worker as well as the degree of professionalization achieved by the occupational groups who call themselves social workers. Social work as a profession not only is the most developed in the passive-reluctant states but also originated, for the most part, in those states. For all practical purposes, the profession is American in origin, and the model of professional social work has since been exported to other Fordist industrial settings.

In simple terms, the social work profession originated as managers of the poor and other marginal members of society. As we approach the 21st century, however, the profession has become an important provider of mental health services and has shifted away from serving the poor (see Specht & Courtney, 1994). The profession has at least two important functions for society: (1) managing the poor and marginal members of society and (2) providing mental health services to both the poor and the nonpoor (perhaps with an emphasis on services to the nonpoor). To perform the first function, social workers relied on combining socialization services (through the settlements and community centers) with demands for universal (rather than means-tested) income maintenance by the state. To perform the second function, those in the profession adopted a medicalized vocabulary (for example, the *Diagnostic and Statistical Manual of Mental Disorders* [American Psychiatric Association, 1987, 1994]) and awarded elaborate titles to clinical social workers (LCSW, MSWAC, BCD, and so forth) that often exceeded the number of letters in the titles awarded by the British monarchies to their outstanding citizens.

It is easy to claim that social work professionals failed to develop methods that would change the status of those they served, except to unite in the position that the state spend more money to raise the floor of poverty. In this regard, the profession became an advocate for the state taking on an increasingly greater redistribution function. The alleviation of poverty, or the alleviation of absolute poverty in capitalist countries, was accomplished mostly by capitalism and not by social workers. (All countries have some form of poverty, but in capitalist countries poor people have been given a floor—and often a roof over their heads.) Joseph Schumpeter (1950) first made this point, and he has been supported since by Esping-Andersen (1990), Friedman (1962), Furniss and Tilton (1977), and Sen (1982, 1997).

The formula for alleviating poverty through increased redistribution by the state, coupled with the right to welfare (see Marshall, 1981; Piven & Cloward, 1971) and universal distribution, is quite similar to the ideology of communal socialism (see Tables 3-2 and 3-3). Even as we approach the 21st century, the cry for redistribution remains the social work profession's only methodology. Socialization services for teaching the poor how to get out of poverty are less popular and waning and are almost no longer carried out by professional social workers. The other role that was popular with the profession was that of welfare administrators (called "welfare bureaucrats" by Stoesz, 1989), a role that helped legitimize their third-party status.

Organized Labor as the Third Third Party

A major function of unions or organized labor is collective bargaining with firms (see Dickman, 1986; Rayback, 1966). In the process of collective bargaining, unions demand not only higher wage levels but also in-kind benefits.

The activities of organized labor have implications for social welfare that fall into two main categories. First, they affect union members, on whose behalf unions claim to participate in the bargaining process. Second, they affect the prices of a firm's products (see Hogler, 1995). With regard to the first implication, the higher wages obtained through collective bargaining seem to come with a high price: high membership dues, undemocratic governance of unions, corruption, low tolerance for dissent, and high demand for centralized loyalty. In this context, one interpretation of collective bargaining is that it constitutes the trade of liberty (of individual members) for temporary protection from the market. A second interpretation is that organized labor as the third third party creates another set of intermediaries, who extract a price for their advocacy.

With regard to the second implication, unions add to the cost of doing business, lead to increased labor costs, and reduce a firm's ability to compete, thereby creating a dilemma for state regulatory agencies over how to formulate labor policy (see Freeman & Medoff, 1984; Hirsch, 1991). If regulatory agencies formulate policies that are overly prolabor, then firms will become inefficient in their competitiveness, which in turn may lead to a shift of capital from a prounion to an antiunion geographical area. If agencies formulate policies that are overly probusiness, then the sponsoring government is likely to lose the political support of organized labor.

In a recent work, Freeman (1992; see also Hogler, 1995) outlined the following five attributes of labor unions:

1. They contribute to prolonged careers of the workforce, which in turn leads to stability at the workplace.
2. They obtain fringe benefits, such as health insurance and pensions; the benefits contribute to capital development, which can be used for investment.
3. They restrict managerial discretion.
4. They do not have a negative impact on productivity.

5. They have a negative impact on the profit margins of firms and their ability to compete.

In summary, the activities of organized labor are far from free organizing by disenfranchised workers. Their activities lead to a set of third-party activities, which are paid for by those whom the activities are supposed to protect. I revisit this item again when we discuss the issue of protection and the idea of who should provide protection in any given society.

Organized Interest Groups as the Fourth Third Party

In addition to organized labor, other interest groups may emerge who claim to be for or against the interests of candidates for welfare benefits. Many of them appear to be privately organized groups for or against given causes; however, most of them ask the state for nonprofit status, which makes them exempt from certain taxes. These groups are thus beneficiaries of state activities without paying their share of taxes. Essentially, their activities are to some extent subsidized by the state, meaning that the state has fewer resources to support—as Rawls would call them—the most disadvantaged members of society.

Problem of Rationing

The matter of rationing is another issue comparable to third-party transactions that is relatively absent in the literature on the state as a redistribution agent. Lipsky (1980) documented how street-level bureaucracies set up almost invisible barriers between the state and the recipients of certain types of welfare beneficiaries. Those barriers are rationing devices; because the services provided by the state are not subject to market forces, the bureaucracy needs rationing devices such as making a recipient wait for a long time, humiliating recipients, or sending them away without any information about the availability of certain goods and services.

Edwin Chadwick foresaw this problem (see Barry, 1990, p. 26): "A good or a service provided at zero price will attract an infinite demand." Modern managed care and the health care provided by the state in many societies are examples of this principle. What is still unsettled is the following question: If the market rationing principle is removed, then what should take its place? Furthermore, if the state engages in redistribution, then according to which principles should it do so? Should it redistribute according to need? According to the recipient's ability to contribute to society, life station, or demographic life expectancy? These issues, although hotly debated, remain unresolved.

FUNCTIONS OF THE STATE

The human institutions of the family and the community (or its equivalents, such as the clan and the tribe) evolved naturally. In each technocultural environment, the two institutions had important functions. For example, we have already pointed out that the family has two important functions in the industrial environment: stabilization of adult personalities and primary socialization of children (Parsons & Bales, 1955). The community also has two important functions: identity maintenance and reference-group creation (Merton, 1957).

In contrast, the human institution called the state was created somewhat artificially (see Locke, 1698/1987). Its origins go back to the institutions of monarchy, empire, kingdom, and other large entities forged together by military or economic forces. Marshall Sahlins, an anthropologist, showed that neither people with hunter-gatherer technology nor nomads in a pastoral society need a state (Sahlins, 1972, 1985, 1995).

Hall and Ikenberry (1989) suggested that a state usually involves three elements. First, the state consists of a set of institutions that are staffed by the state's own personnel. The state's most important institution (because it ensures the state's survival) is its apparatus of control over the means of violence and coercion. Second, the institutions are at the political center of a geographically bounded territory, usually referred to as a society. Third, the state monopolizes rule-making within its territory. This monopoly tends to create a common political culture shared by all citizens.

The evolution of the modern state, as shown by Oppenheimer (1975) and Eberhard (1965), began with the forced settlement of agricultural communities by nomads (over other nomads or over people already committed to agriculture). The major functions of the state in this first rung on the evolutionary ladder were to maintain sovereignty and protect subjects from outside predators and inside criminals. The state's ability to tax, or procure the resources to perform its key functions, was also established at this time, as were its boundary-maintenance functions. Those functions were fortified by the establishment of the military (which protects against outside predators), the police (which protects against inside criminals), behavior prescriptions regarding foreigners (which may be called foreign policy), and behavior prescriptions regarding the subjects of the state (which may be called domestic policy).

The second evolutionary rung consisted of the military conquest of existing kingdoms or monarchies that could be supported by a religious infrastructure, such as Christianity or Islam (Hall & Ikenberry, 1989). The state at this point usually had an aristocratic class and a clerical class, and often an alliance existed between the two as they governed the masses. In medieval Europe, the emergence of a mercantile class created a third type of power group (Hall & Ikenberry, 1989). An important goal of many states was to attain ideological unanimity; one approach to this goal was to convert the masses to the "King's religion."

The third rung on the evolutionary ladder of the state consisted of the efforts to secure certain basic rights, justice, and equality for all; some examples of those efforts are the Magna Carta in England and the separation of the clerical and the aristocratic classes, known as the "separation of church and state" (Tilly, 1975). This separation also reconfirmed the sovereignty of the state.

The fourth rung emerged when the ideas of French (and perhaps British) intellectuals led to two revolutions within 13 years (one in 1776, and the other in 1789), leading to the emergence of the modern state. It is on this rung that the state took on an identity separate from the clerical infrastructure, mercantile infrastructure, and aristocracy (although in many cases the aristocracy became the governing elite) and moved from a monarch–subject to a state–citizen orientation (see Crone, 1989; Maier, 1987; Poggi, 1978). One key function of the state at this point was to manage the sovereignty of the state through an alliance with the representatives of key power groups within the state.

The fifth and uppermost rung on the evolutionary ladder is the "confrontation" between industrial capitalism and the state, where each had to make accommodations to the other (Mann, 1988). Furthermore, the states that fall in the fifth rung are the industrial states (as referred to by Galbraith (1967) and discussed in chapter 1), which seem to fall into three subcategories: pre-Fordist, Fordist, and post-Fordist. The welfare state, whatever its form (see Tables 3-1 and 3-2), appears in Fordist industrial societies; before the welfare state appeared, the family, the community, the church, and private charity managed human vulnerability.

This evolutionary view is supported only by certain schools of anthropologists and political scientists (Eberhard, 1965; Sahlins, 1972, 1985). In the field of political science, another position explaining the functions of the state is roughly as follows: States' functions vary, depending on who is making a list of the functions (see Tables 3-2 and 3-3). The liberals (called "libertarians" in both tables) at one end and the Marxists (including the communalists and the Fabians) at the other end agree that the state should eventually become disposable. In the middle of Table 3-3 are the realists (the reluctant collectivists), who suggest that the state performs certain necessary functions, such as protecting against internal and external predators, maintaining peace, and struggling to provide justice and equality (see Hall & Ikenberry, 1989). Added to those three schools of thought (that is, liberal, Marxist, and realist) is the theory of Michael Mann (1988), which seems to be a further development of the realist school. He asserts that two dimensions to state power exist: despotic and infrastructural. The infrastructural power in modern states is very important, because it can penetrate and organize society; this power creates new commitments, obligations, pressure groups, and so forth, which bind the state in subsequent decisions (see Evans, Rueschemeyer, & Skocpol, 1985). Despotic power, however, emerges when any one group committed to one coherent ideology infiltrates the avenues of infrastructural power.

Scholars in the field of cultural anthropology, who usually provide evidence from technologically less developed cultures, tend to take the position that any linear and neatly sequential theory of social "evolution" of a human institution (like the state) should be suspect (see Steward, 1958). Some agreement, however, seems to exist that the fifth rung (that is, the "confrontation" and subsequent accommodation), which lies between the somewhat secular state and industrial capitalism, is a landmark from which an understanding of the modern state can be pursued (Kottak, 1979; Rimlinger, 1971).

On the fifth rung—called the "industrial state" in industrial societies—which consists of an accommodation between industrial capitalism and the state, it seems that the ability to perform three specific functions becomes extremely important. These three functions are "regulation" (of industry and other things), "redistribution" (of income and other things), and "attainment of full employment." In the pre-Fordist state the performance of the first two functions by the state were sometimes hotly debated (Bendix, 1964), but in the Fordist states they were a fact of life. In post-Fordist states, efforts were made to remove the first two functions from the list of state functions (as in the Reagan and Thatcher administrations in the United States and England), but those efforts were not very successful.

Table 3-4 lists the major state functions described in this section: sovereignty, resource procurement, protection, securing rights, protecting

Table 3-4. Functions of the State

STATE	FUNCTIONS
The preindustrial state	Maintaining sovereignty
	Resource procurement
	Protecting loyal subjects from outside predators
	Protecting loyal subjects from inside predators
	Protecting rights
	Securing liberty
	Administering justice
	Managing demands for equity
	Managing representation of diverse groups
The Fordist industrial state	All of the above, plus
	• Regulation
	• Redistribution
	• Attaining full employment
	• Pursuit of equality

liberty, administering justice, promoting equality, representation, regulation, redistribution, attaining full employment, and pursuit of equality.

Sovereignty

Maintaining sovereignty is an important function of the state. Loss of sovereignty may mean balkanization of the state, colonization by some other state, or the according of client status by another body. Loss of sovereignty may also mean wealth transfer, both within the state and from the vanquished state to a dominant state. Maintaining sovereignty is the prime function of the state. Without it, performing all other functions becomes difficult.

Resource Procurement

Without resources, the state cannot perform any functions. Resources, however, are procured from different sources and by different means. For example, if a society has abundant natural resources of a given kind (for example, fossil fuel), then the state may seek revenue only from the sale of that fuel and use the resources procured as it sees fit without imposing any form of taxation on its citizens. Most states, however, need to obtain resources by imposing one or more types of taxation.

First, the state must develop policy about whom it is going to tax. For example, should it levy taxes on certain goods produced by foreigners and exempt the same goods from taxation if they are of domestic origin? If it does, then the objective of such taxation is to protect certain domestic business interests. Should the state tax citizens, giving the appearance that they are paying for certain services provided by the state; and if it does, should it then make the citizens pay those taxes based on a flat rate or according to their ability? Should it exempt certain groups from taxation altogether because the groups are not involved in profit-seeking activity?

Second, the state must clarify the activities it is going to tax. Should it tax production, so that the more one produces, the more taxes he or she should pay? This type of taxation is often easy to implement, but it may create disincentives for production. Should the state tax certain kinds of consumption, such as liquor or chocolates? This type of tax is often used to discourage or reduce the consumption of certain items. Should it tax exchange, such as the sale of certain items? If this form of taxation is used, then should the tax cover all forms of exchange, or only certain kinds of exchange? Income, wealth, property, inheritance, sales, and value-added taxes are examples of different forms of taxation.

Third, taxation can be multifunctional. On the one hand, taxation can bring in resources needed by the state. On the other hand, it can create incentives or disincentives for engaging in certain behaviors. For example, taxing tobacco or liquor serves two ends: producing revenue and discouraging the heavy use of the item. Certain forms of welfare or income-maintenance policy, in which the policy requires discontinuance of income support if the recipient has an intact family, is another example of this form. In such cases, the state's income maintenance policy may have very serious negative effects on the family as a basic institution. Some groups may not be able to form or maintain a family at all when such antifamily policies are in effect.

Fourth, taxation often is accompanied by the right of taxpayer representation in the formulation of state policy (see Curran, 1974; Groves, 1973; Stiglitz, 1986). A state needs to maintain its ability to tax (see chapters 1 and 2) to support its activities, but it also needs to manage the threshold of tolerance its taxpayers may have for paying certain taxes.

Protection

Providing protection from external and internal predators is one of the most primitive functions of the state (Alford & Friedland, 1985; Simmie & King, 1990). This function is related to both maintaining sovereignty and procuring resources for military and police forces to ensure sovereignty.

The idea of a two-tiered system originates in the matter of providing protection. For example, if and when given citizens become successful in amassing wealth, they may tell the state that they need ever-increasing police protection because they are now vulnerable and open to criminal encroachments by internal predators. The state may make them pay higher taxes and provide increased police protection, or it may allow this group to purchase the services of private groups of protectors. The central point is that all citizens receive a basic minimum of police protection, but groups needing extra protection may purchase it at the marketplace.

In the modern states, this protection function has become rather elaborate and, as a result, is subject to a two-tiered system. For example, protection from ignorance is another form of protection, because a lack of education, skills, or information may mean the inability to earn a livelihood. To counter ignorance, many modern states set up educational programs, and some have set up elaborate educational systems that begin at the grade school level and end at the university level. When the state sets up such an elaborate system, it must also establish some form of rationing of education, because it cannot provide education to everyone at every level on demand. Thus, some states have a testing system for people that begins at age 12, and others set up screening procedures (as has been done in many European countries) by which only "the best and the brightest" are channeled to higher education. The response to protection from ignorance became universal education, then rationed education. Given this situation, some citizens may still want to pursue higher education, but being unable to do so under their existing system, may have to "purchase" education in the marketplace, which may be available from the second tier.

Protection from ill health is another example. Nowhere in the existing literature is there evidence that protection from ill health is a state function in the preindustrial state. It became a state function in the Fordist industrial state, however, in at least two ways: through a public health movement, which required the state to take certain steps to prevent the spread of epidemics or other poor health conditions and through the emergence of new health technologies that prolong human life (Trattner, 1979).

Yet another example is protection from poverty. Again, this function appears only in the industrial states, because nowhere is there evidence that this was a state function in preindustrial states.

In most industrial states, protection from ignorance and ill health have become a two-tiered system, in which one tier (usually the bottom tier) is provided by the state, whereas the other tier (usually the top tier) is provided by the market. This often means the existence of two tiers in industrial societies, where the state becomes the first-tier provider of education or health services, and the market remains second-tier provider of the same. In some cases, the first-tier provision of education or health is done either on a means-tested basis or on a universal basis. In contrast, the services in the second tier, provided by the market, are for selective buyers who want specific types of services. In many settings, the first-tier services are available either on a rationed basis (because of high demand and limited supply) or on some other basis under which the provider determines the amount of services available to the consumer. Again in contrast, the services in the second tier are usually available on demand, because the buyer (the client) influences the amount of services he or she should have. In some cases, it may appear that the services provided by the state are inferior to those provided by the market.

Protection from poverty is found only in some industrial states, usually in capitalist societies with a "communal socialist" orientation (see Tables 3-2 and 3-3) and in socialist societies. According to the categories in chapters 1 and 2, it seems that active-engaged states are more frequently given to providing protection from poverty than passive-reluctant ones. The extent to which, as well as the quantity in which, these protections will remain state functions seems to be a crucial question.

Securing Rights

In human history, the signing of the Magna Carta in 1215 was an important step that established certain rights of humanity. These rights included protection from undue taxation, the right to worship, rights against illegal search and seizure, and certain civil rights. Although it is possible to argue that the concept of natural rights dates back to Greek stoicism, the events around the Magna Carta clearly place it in the realm of modern political philosophy.

A key event between the time of the Magna Carta and the English Bill of Rights (1689) was the shift in Europe in the concept of natural law. As a result of the teachings of Thomas Aquinas and Hugo Grotius, natural law during this time came to be seen less as a set of duties and obligations and more as a set of rights (Freeden, 1991).

Key writings in England and France during the 17th and 18th centuries further shaped the concept of rights. In England, Thomas Hobbes and John Locke defined rights within the realm of a social contract. Locke believed that natural rights derived from natural law, meaning that humans always retain "the right to life, liberty, and property"; that in the emergence of the state and the social contract the enforcement of those rights came under the jurisdiction of the state; and that the state's inability to secure those rights justifies a revolution (Harmon, 1964). In France, the works of Montesquieu, Voltaire, and Rousseau established the idea of inalienable "rights of Man." In England, Adam Smith, who was to become the foremost scholar on the marvel that is the market, published *The Wealth of Nations* in 1776. He argued for a right to education, which he believed was necessary for the exercise of citizenship (Atherton, 1990; Smith, 1891).

The foregoing ideas gave legitimization to the English Revolution of 1688, which resulted in the English Bill of Rights. They also influenced the Declaration of Independence in the United States and the American Revolution of 1776, affirming that certain human rights were inalienable, and these were the rights to life, liberty, and the pursuit of happiness. In 1791 this was further affirmed as the rights to life, liberty, and property in the Fifth Amendment to the Constitution contained in what became the Bill of Rights. From the French Revolution of 1789 came the Declaration of the Rights of Man and of the Citizen, which defined rights as liberty, property, safety, and resistance to oppression. *Liberty* is further defined as the right to free speech, association, religion, and freedom from unlawful confinement.

A debate between two famous scholars of that time, Edmund Burke and Thomas Paine, enhanced the concept of rights. To Burke, the possession of property was the best insurance against arbitrary encroachment on liberty, and society was a partnership consisting of those who are living, those who are dead, and those who are yet to be born (Durant & Durant, 1967). No absolute rights exist, only convention or tradition, which has bridled human nature. The institutions of religion, aristocracy, and property arose as a response to human nature, which is basically self-serving.

Paine, an American by birth, responded to Burke in the two volumes of *Rights of Man*, published in 1791 and 1792 (Foner, 1945). Historically, the two volumes not only affirmed the earlier notion of human rights—that people have a right to protection from the state and from each other—but also introduced a new notion, that people have a right to certain basic goods and services that are requirements for life. This second notion of rights included the right to education, poverty relief, pensions for elderly people, and public works to create employment, all of which the state should provide from the taxes it collects. The first notion of rights would come to be known as "civil rights," as Marshall (1964) called them, whereas the second notion came to be known as "social rights."

Inherent in the debate between Burke and Paine is the dichotomy between minimalist versus expansive states, or the continuum between the libertarian–individualist and communal–socialist models (as suggested in Table 3-3). State-socialist and social Darwinist models were added to the continuum later in the 19th century and carried over to the 20th century.

Thomas H. Green, writing in the mid-19th century, argued against natural rights and maintained instead that rights emanate from society and are guaranteed by the state. He asserted that rights are "a power of which the exercise by the individual or by some body of men is recognised by a society, either as itself directly essential to a common good, or as conferred by an authority of which the maintenance is recognised as so essential" (Freeden, 1991, p. 20). Furthermore, for Green, no rights existed in the abstract sense except for those "embedded in the community" (Barry, 1990, p. 37).

Against the positions of Paine and Green, Herbert Spencer (in *The Man versus the State,* 1884) claimed that the right to welfare (that is, to certain goods and services) could not be a guaranteed right without curtailing the right to liberty. He argued that such a right would mean unfair taxation to those who produce wealth and that it would create vested interests in certain parts of the middle class, who would form occupations enforcing such rights (see Spencer, 1884/1892). In other words, guaranteeing those rights would create a special market for the middle class.

L.T. Hobhouse (1911, 1922) made the idea of the right to welfare more specific. He argued in favor of a right to a minimum income for everyone, which would ensure the right to existence. The state has to enforce the right to existence, and in doing so, must require the more-successful citizens to pay somewhat higher taxes (a point to which Spencer objected). The idea of people receiving welfare, however, inevitably leads to the concept of "reciprocity." That is, the recipient must perform some duties for the state in return.

Later in the 20th century, Richard Morris Titmuss, in *Essays on the Welfare State* (1959), *The Irresponsible Society* (1960), *Commitment to Welfare* (1968), and *Social Policy* (1974), argued that the right to welfare is indeed a basic human right and that it emanates from the idea of citizenship. That is, citizenship secures one's right to belong; and in the securing of the right to belong, the right to existence follows. The only way to secure the right to welfare is to tax the more successful members of society, who also have the right to belong to a given collectivity. The right to welfare thus comes from the right to existence and the right to belong.

Although Titmuss argued forcefully for citizenship and the rights emanating from it, he did not foresee the efforts that were to follow in several wealthy capitalist states during the last quarter of the 20th century.

Those efforts included restricting citizenship to certain groups; such restrictions seemingly were developed to pursue goals that included restricting welfare benefits to particular ethnic or racial groups and maintaining ethnic homogeneity. For example, Soysal (1994) pointed out how different countries in Europe were dealing with various immigrant groups, mostly by creating laws and provisions that make citizenship difficult to obtain. On the same subject, Dauenhauer (1996) suggested that in a complex society, citizenship should not be a unitary role entitling the role-occupant to a set of privileges (such as being able to vote or having the right to welfare assistance), but instead should be placed in a set of obligations that correspond with a set of rights.

Two models of citizenship seem to be emerging. The first one, which Titmuss (1960, 1968) used in his arguments for rights, is called the "family model," and the second, which Dauenhauer (1996) used, is known as the "club model." In the family model, one is a citizen of a state because one is born within its boundaries, marries a citizen from its boundaries, or is otherwise "adopted" into the membership of the state (a process called "naturalization"). In the club model, one has to be "initiated" into the membership of the state. Such initiation depends on how the candidate is "introduced" to the country. One can be introduced by the appropriate ethnic group or by some other special status, but not automatically by birth within the state's borders. Although Titmuss assumed that the family model was the basis of citizenship, his own country (England) later followed the club model for granting or withholding citizenship to many immigrants (see Soysal, 1994). Switzerland, Austria, and Germany followed the club model even more rigorously (Soysal, 1994).

Barry (1990) pointed out that Hobhouse and Titmuss offered two different sources of legitimization for the idea of welfare rights. For Hobhouse, the idea is embedded in reciprocity, whereas for Titmuss, the idea emanated from citizenship. Even for those who agree with the concept of the right to welfare, the fundamental differences between Hobhouse and Titmuss lead to two very different types of welfare policy, as is shown later in this book.

T. H. Marshall, in *Class, Citizenship, and Social Development* (1964), added that there are basically two types of rights: civil rights and social rights. *Civil rights* can be defined as the right to certain behaviors, whereas *social rights* can be defined as the right to certain basic goods and services (Chatterjee, 1970). In a study of welfare in the 50 states in the United States, Grønberg (1977) concluded that attainment of a third type of right, which Marshall had called "political rights," makes the other two possible.

In the United States Piven and Cloward, in *Regulating the Poor* (1971), *Poor People's Movements* (1977), and *The New Class War* (1982), supported the idea of right to welfare. Their ideas were closer to those of Titmuss and Marshall in the United Kingdom.

Henry Shue (1996) proposed that three rights are fundamental: the right to security, the right to subsistence, and the right to liberty. He argued that a powerful country like the United States should work toward having those rights guaranteed by every nation in this world.

Securing Liberty

The term "liberty" must be differentiated from what has been called "sovereignty." The first term is better applied to individuals' rights as citizens, whereas the latter describes collectivities' powers as states. The assurance of liberty is another description for civil rights, wherein a person's right to protection from harassment, incarceration, restriction of movement, and illegal search and seizure—all translated into the word "freedom"—is secured by the state and recognized by law. It has been clearly established that liberty equates with civil rights. However, whether liberty also entails the provision of social rights is still in dispute. The libertarians, supporters of minimalist government in the tradition of Edmund Burke, argued against the concept of social rights, whereas the socialists and the communitarians argued in favor of such rights.

Liberty has been justified for basically three reasons: morality, efficiency, and community. The first reason, morality, was used in the solemn words of the Magna Carta, in the passions of the American and the French Revolutions, in the introduction of civil rights, in the American civil war of the 19th century, and in the civil disobedience movements (for example, in India and in the United States) of the 20th century. This interpretation of liberty means freedom from bondage of any kind. The second reason, efficiency, was used by Bernard Mandeville in *The Fable of the Bees* (1723/1924) and by Adam Smith in *The Wealth of Nations* (1776 /1891). In this second approach to liberty, "public good is an accidental outcome of self-interest rather than the product of a rational plan" (Barry, 1990, p. 16). Green (1886/1941) offered the third reason, community, when he suggested that liberty does not mean just avoidance of bondage or facilitation of public good but the power to act as a member of a community toward a common goal (see Barry, 1990). This approach is known as the "community-sanction" orientation to liberty.

The three major 20th-century scholars of liberty are F. A. von Hayek (*The Constitution of Liberty,* 1960), Milton Friedman (*Capitalism and Freedom,* 1962), and Robert Nozick (*Anarchy, State, and Utopia,* 1974). All three scholars see liberty from a morality and efficiency orientation. Etzioni (1995) and Wuthnow (1989, 1994), on the other hand, follow the community-sanction orientation to liberty, in which liberty is defined by a local community.

Administering Justice

Administering justice is one of the ancient functions of the state, which administers justice when its sovereignty-maintaining functions are threatened. The state also administers justice when its protective functions are threatened. Most of the time, administering justice means making individual citizens and groups comply with a developed legal system.

The concept of justice encompasses at least five different elements:

1. justice stemming from the state's protective functions
2. justice arising from the state's resource-procurement functions
3. justice emanating from the different forms of representation within the state
4. justice needed to recompense victims of human aggression or nature's calamities
5. justice resulting from the vulnerability of given groups.

All five elements are interrelated and are referred to here as "protective" justice, "correctional" justice, "distributive" justice, "restorative" justice, and "representational" justice.

Protective justice starts with the state's efforts to protect the citizens from external and internal predators (Table 3-4). Usually those efforts lead to building military and police infrastructures and subjecting offenders to the state's correctional justice system. Protective justice at times may also include protecting certain domestic industries (the loss of which may lead to the loss of many jobs and domestic economic problems); in this case, it is called "protectionist trade policy." However, other elements of protective justice exist as well, such as protecting mentally ill, mentally disabled, and developmentally disabled people; children; and other vulnerable groups from opportunism, exploitation, abuse and neglect. Some states may even consider the unemployed a vulnerable group and may set up policies to protect them.

In administering protective justice, a state may also administer distributive justice. For example, distributive justice occurs when the state begins to provide income or services to vulnerable groups to protect them from predictable catastrophes. In this example, redistribution activities, which occur through taxing people in the labor force to benefit the vulnerable, help support the state's protection function.

Restorative justice reflects the state's efforts to compensate individual citizens or groups who have been victimized by individual predators or through past injustices. Criminal acts are examples of victimization by individual predators; people who commit crimes are, when caught, subjected to the correctional justice system, and the state compensates the victim either from the resources of the offender or from its own sources. An example of a past injustice for which the state compensated its victims occurred when the United States paid Japanese Americans lump-sum amounts as restitution for having incarcerated them during World War II.

Included in the concept of distributive justice is the idea of fair taxation. Regressive taxes, such as sales tax on food, which is unfair to the poor, are not within the norms of distributive justice, nor are they within the norms of representational justice. The concept of representational justice refers to the state's ability to develop a climate in which various cultural (including ethnoreligious and ethnolingual) groups are properly represented and whose interests are taken into account in making various policy decisions.

Another normative element in representational justice is equality, which is manifested as equality before law. That is, parties subjected to the state's justice system are supposed to be equal and are not supposed get any preferential treatment because of their social position. In most settings, however, the realities are different from the normative position: People who can afford well-trained lawyers and people who are well placed in society often are treated better by the justice system than are people who are marginal. To counter this trend, most modern states have instituted procedures whereby the poor, the vulnerable, the indigent, and otherwise marginal groups are represented by public defenders or court-appointed defenders. Consequently, the equivalent of a two-tiered system is also emerging in the state's ability to administer justice. Like the two-tiered system for providing protection described earlier, the tiers for the justice system comprise a bottom tier for basic justice (provided by the state) and a top tier for better justice-related services, such as attorneys (provided by the market).

Without specifically calling it a two-tiered system, John Stuart Mill (Barry, 1990) argued that justice entails protection of and, at times, redistribution to marginal and powerless groups. In *The Subjection of Women* (1869/1970), he argued that justice requires equal opportunity for and equal redistribution to women. This idea recently resurfaced in the writings of several feminist scholars (Korpi, 1989; Orloff, 1993), who claimed that the social insurance and social security systems of most modern states are biased in favor of men. Hobhouse (1922) introduced the term "social justice," by which he meant some form of redistribution in favor of the marginal and less privileged populations. Hart (1967) further developed this argument and suggested that the less privileged are entitled to a portion of the redistribution because justice demands it. Rawls (1971) supported Hart's contention and adds that the state's distribution of goods or services in favor of the less privileged is a form of administering justice (that is, distributive justice). Plant (1988), countering von Hayek's (1976) notion that justice is a mere response to market processes, suggested that although the effects of market processes are unintended, they can be anticipated, and rules of justice require that they be anticipated.

Managing Demands for Equality

The concept of equality, like that of liberty and rights, is an ancient idea that strongly surfaces in the Magna Carta and in the American and French revolutions. It is again John Stuart Mill, however, who reformulated this idea into two related concepts: equality of opportunity and equality of results (Barry, 1990). *Equality of opportunity* means that the state creates conditions in which applicants for educational seats, jobs, or other positions have equal ability to qualify for them, and the selection is made based on merit. Equality of results, also called "equality of outcome," occurs when the state sets a quota for jobs or other positions, and a certain number of people are then put into the slots because of their group membership. The people may or may not be well qualified to fill those slots, but they represent a given group. Such policies thus fulfill representational justice functions.

Among the welfare states defined in chapters 1 and 2, the United States has experimented with both equality of opportunity and equality of results during the latter half of the 20th century. India, a vast and diverse country that is emerging into the industrial world, has also experimented with both approaches, which are often programmatically called "affirmative action." On the one hand, affirmative action has helped create a new middle class that is upwardly mobile from the less-privileged classes in India. On the other hand, it has fostered resentment in that country among some members of the privileged middle class who have been denied key positions to make room for people from the less-privileged groups. The situation in the United States is comparable to that of India in this regard.

Many authors further discussed the opportunity versus outcome approaches to equality. Le Grand (1982) saw it from a different perspective: He argued that equality is better achieved not by redistributing from the rich to the poor but by subjecting all members of society to a common standard of care without any means test. That is, when all members of society receive a minimum income or health care on a universal basis and without a means test, a type of equality will occur that is not otherwise attainable by merely allowing people successful in the marketplace to buy those commodities. Esping-Andersen (1990) later named this concept "decommodification."

Every state has to make some form of either tacit or explicit decision about how to manage inequality at birth. Every child born in a society is born as either a male or a female and is subsequently subjected to a society's norms about gender. Furthermore, every child born is also a member of a social class, an ethnoracial group, an ethnolingual group, an ethnoreligious group, and a family, all of which may be privileged to various degrees. A fundamental problem for every state is how to reduce this form of inequality without reducing the role of the family, which is the bearer and transmitter of culture.

Sooner or later, most industrial states return to the question of equality. Although the pursuit of equality may take place through taxation policy, protection policy, justice policy, and many other policies, a special form of pursuit of equality occurs through affirmative action policy. This policy is one of the most controversial pursuits undertaken by the industrial state, because it trades rewarding merit for rewarding representation or group membership. However, it is one of the few policies the state has to counter the inequality status many children inherit at birth.

Manage Representation

In any society, the state has to manage, respond to, or develop positions about various small and large groups within or around its territories. Often these groups are ethnoracial, ethnolingual, or ethnoreligious groups. Superimposed on these groups may be social class groups, majority and minority groups, and privileged and less privileged groups. Jeremy Bentham (see Stark, 1952) resolved the problem emanating from managing these diversities by saying that the state's most important function is to create "happiness" and, in fact, to create "maximal happiness of the maximal number" (Barry, 1990, pp. 28–29). This view of the function of the state, known as "utilitarianism," has been the underlying principle in most recent political democracies. Consequently, the state has to administer representational justice, as discussed above.

Although the Benthamite "maximal happiness of the maximal number" is an important guiding principle, the following outcomes are possible in the execution of this principle. Let the maximal number (that is, those who are being made happy) be n, and let the total population in that society be N. It follows that $[N-n]$ are not happy. The policy of the state to this $[N-n]$ population may be one or a combination of the following:

- adversarial policy (attempt expulsion or extinction of $[N-n]$)
- colonial policy (allow n to patronize or exploit $[N-n]$)
- assimilationist policy (force $[N-n]$ to merge into n)
- pluralistic policy (allow both n and $[N-n]$ to coexist with equal rights of citizenship).

By the scheme above, $[N-n]$ is by definition an oppressed group, and n is the dominant group. We have observed above that the dream of Titmuss was to have the fourth option to reduce oppression (as outlined earlier), but this option is not necessarily followed by all nation-states (for an extensive discussion of such majority–minority, or dominant–oppressed, relations, see Farley, 1988).

Regulation

Regulation is a relatively new function of the industrial state. Barry (1990) and Hall and Ikenberry (1989) have traced how various forms of state regulation can be traced to medieval times; these forms can be called "standardization functions." Examples are the state's efforts to set up maritime procedures, regulations governing the use of public facilities and roads, decisions to use a certain language, and the like. Standardization functions maintain order and in many ways reduce ambiguity.

A second type of regulation is the use of regulation as protection. Examples of such regulations include the state's efforts to set standards in the food industry to reduce food-related health hazards; to control which drugs are sold over the counter, by prescription only, or not at all; to license certain occupational groups, so that they operate in the marketplace with a certain standard of knowledge; and to set certain wage and price controls to control inflation or protect certain vulnerable groups. Requiring feuding parties (for example, labor and management groups or key professional groups engaged in collective bargaining efforts) to come to closure is another example of regulation as protection.

The regulation-as-protection function has increased substantially in the industrial state (Galbraith, 1967; Hall & Ikenberry, 1989). During the past two decades, environmental protection regulations have been added to this function as well.

A relatively new function of the general area of regulation is monopoly prevention. During the early part of the 20th century, some groups (for example, certain oil companies) in the market became very successful and were about to operate without much competition in the United States. Regulation in the form of monopoly prevention or monopoly reduction was used then, and since then this form of regulation has become another important form of state regulation.

A recent statement ("Lessons from the Brink," 1998) summarized the importance of the regulation function as follows:

> **Conventional Wisdom:** Free markets always lead to prosperity. The spread of laissez-faire capitalism around the world is inevitable, now that the cold war is over and the United States has won.
>
> **Reality:** Freedom can also lead to anarchy. Asia and Russia are good reminders that the rule of law, *regulation* of banks, bankruptcy courts, accounting transparency, and a whole web of legal do's and don't's are necessary to channel high octane, short-term capital flows to efficient investments. Without government playing a major role, international capital flows can lead to corruption, overcapacity, currency devaluation, recessions, and even a backlash against capitalism itself. Capital and foreign exchange controls are returning with a vengeance in Asia and Russia. Free markets need government action to work best. (p. 148) (emphasis added)

Hall and Ikenberry (1989), quoting Michael Mann, argued that regulatory efforts form an infrastructural dimension in the state's power. They pointed out that "the infrastructural dimension of state power—the ability to penetrate society and to organize social relations—is quite important. . . . [I]nitially indicative of capacity to shape internal political and economic practices, [it] may eventually lead to commitments and obligations" (Hall & Ikenberry, 1989, p. 13).

Redistribution

Redistribution existed in the preindustrial state, most frequently in the form of nature failure (see "The Arguments for Redistribution: A Summary," above). During natural calamities, the state's engagement in some form of redistribution has been recorded in history (see Claessen & Skalnik, 1978; Eberhard, 1965; Oppenheimer, 1975). The industrial state, however, saw a multifold increase in the redistribution functions of the state (Galbraith, 1967; Hall & Ikenberry, 1989, pp. 70–71). Most agricultural societies seem to engage close to 90 percent of their work force in agricultural production, but in contrast, most advanced industrial societies engage about 10 percent of its work force in industrial production (Hall & Ikenberry, 1989). In addition, work forces in agricultural societies are more capable of absorbing people whose labor is valued near zero than are industrial societies. This situation forces the industrial state to develop substantially larger redistribution functions.

Redistribution is possible only when the technology base of the society generates a surplus. Whether this surplus should be redistributed on a means-tested basis or on a universal basis, whether it should be in cash or in-kind, and how it should be legitimized are matters for collective decision making after a surplus has been secured. The next chapter will elaborate on these ideas.

Attaining Full Employment

The Beveridge report acknowledged attainment of full employment as a state function (see Atkinson, 1993; Beveridge, 1942). The modern industrial state, as discussed in the foregoing paragraphs, often finds that much of its population is without significant family or workforce attachment. In addition, many types of vulnerabilities, such as age and disability, contribute to human vulnerability. The state, by promoting a universal full-employment policy, provides a special form of protection from poverty (see "Protection," p. 61).

Summary

In this chapter, we have reviewed the many functions of the state over time as it became the industrial state. Table 3-5 summarizes those functions and

Table 3-5. Functions of the State and Embedded Welfare Functions

FUNCTIONS OF THE STATE	EMBEDDED WELFARE FUNCTIONS
Sovereignty maintenance	Welfare is usually not provided by a foreign state. It is sometimes provided by a sovereign state, provided there is a surplus. Sovereignty and surplus are prerequisites for the welfare state
Resource procurement by taxation	Almost all taxation questions lead to: Is it a progressive or regressive taxation? • from whom • by taxing which activities • creating what form of incentives or disincentives • with what threshold of tolerance
Protection	
• from external predators	This is two-tiered, with the state providing basic protection, while additional protection can be purchased at the marketplace
• from internal predators	Yes (as in protective services for vulnerable people, which is in addition to police services)
• from ignorance	Yes
• from ill health	Yes
• from poverty	Yes
Securing rights	
• civil rights	
• social rights (right to welfare)	Yes
* based on citizenship either in the family model or the club model	Yes
* based on reciprocity	Yes
* based on community	Yes
Protecting liberty • as morality • as efficiency • as community	Debated. Argument for: Liberty cannot be attained unless basic human needs are met Argument against: Liberty is surrendered to the state by having welfare
Administering justice	This is (unfortunately) also two-tiered, with the state providing "basic" justice, while "additional" justice can be purchased at the marketplace
• protective	Yes
• correctional	Yes
• distributive	Yes

(Table continues)

Table 3-5 (continued)

FUNCTIONS OF THE STATE	EMBEDDED WELFARE FUNCTIONS
• restorative	Yes
• representational	Yes
Promoting equality • of opportunity • of outcome	Debated. Argument for: Some equality of outcome is needed for restorative justice Argument against: The principle of equality of opportunity is sacrificed thereby
Representation	
• adversarial	No
• colonial	Mostly no
• assimilational	Conditionally
• pluralistic	Yes
Regulation	
• as standardization	Yes
• as protection	Yes
• as monopoly-prevention	Maybe
Redistribution	Yes—it is the basis for the modern welfare state. The basic issue here is which form of redistribution should be means-tested and which should be made available on a universalistic basis
Attainment of full employment	Yes—it is the basis for the modern welfare state The basic issues here are (1) whether the state should become "the employer of last resort" and (2) whether and how much productivity should be expected from such programs
Pursuit of equality • affirmative action	Debated. Same arguments as in "Promoting equality" above

lists the ways in which most of them have key welfare functions embedded in them.

The functions of the state begin with the idea of protection as security, which requires maintaining sovereignty, providing military and police services, and the like. Over time, and especially after attaining a surplus, protection as basic survival becomes important; welfare functions are added not only to the concept of protection but also to the concepts of rights, liberty, justice, and equality. In modern welfare states (which exist only in the capitalist West), welfare functions are always a part of the expanded functions of redistribution, pursuit of full employment, and equality.

A Conflict in the Modern State: Liberty or Equality?

A fundamental conflict exists within the modern industrial state: a conflict between the pull to optimize liberty and the pull to optimize equality. In a market economy, those who are relatively successful in the marketplace want the state to pursue policies that enhance liberty so they can enjoy their success. Those who are not successful (or those who have clients who are not) want the state to do everything possible to pursue policies that foster equality, so they have second or subsequent chances to re-enter the game. Every industrial state has to manage this conflict in one way or another.

References

Alford, R. R., & Friedland, R. (1985). *Powers of theory: Capitalism, the state, and democracy.* New York: Cambridge University Press.

American Psychiatric Association. (1987). *Diagnostic and statistical manual of mental disorders* (3rd ed., rev.). Washington, DC: Author.

American Psychiatric Association. (1994). *Diagnostic and statistical manual of mental disorders* (4th ed.). Washington, DC: Author.

Atherton, C. R. (1990). Adam Smith and the welfare state. *Arete, 15,* 24–31.

Atkinson, A. B. (1993). *Beveridge, the national minimum, and its future in a European context.* London: London School of Economics, Welfare State Programme and Suntory-Toyota International Center for Economics and Related Disciplines.

Bailey, K. D. (1990). *Social entropy theory.* Albany: State University of New York Press.

Barry, N. (1990). *Welfare.* Minneapolis: University of Minnesota Press.

Bell, D. (1973). *The coming of post-industrial society: A venture in social forecasting.* New York: Basic Books.

Bendix, R. (1964). *Nation-building and citizenship.* New York: John Wiley & Sons.

Berger, P. (1986). *The capitalist revolution.* New York: Basic Books.

Beveridge, W. (1942). Social insurance and allied services. New York: Macmillan.

Blumer, H. (1990). *Industrialization as an agent of social change.* New York: Aldine de Gruyter.

Castro, F. (1983). *The world economic and social crisis.* Havana: Publication Office of the Council on State.

Chatterjee, P. (1970). "Community" in social science and social work. *Indian Journal of Social Work, 31*, 125–134.

Claessen, H. J., & Skalnik, P. (1978). *The early state.* The Hague, Netherlands: Mouton.

Coleman, J. (1974). Inequality, sociology, and moral philosophy. *American Journal of Sociology, 80,* 739–764.

Crone, P. (1989). *Pre-industrial societies.* Oxford, England: Blackwell.

Curran, D. J. (Ed.). (1974). *Tax philosophers: Two hundred years of thought in Great Britain and the United States.* Madison: University of Wisconsin Press.

Dauenhauer, B. (1996). *Citizenship in a fragile world.* Lanham, MD: Rowman & Littlefield.

de Jouvenel, B. (1990). *The ethics of redistribution.* Indianapolis: Liberty Fund. (Original work published 1952)

Dickman, H. (1986). *Industrial democracy in America.* LaSalle, IL: Open Court.

Durant, W., & Durant, A. (1967). *The story of civilization* (Vol. 7). New York: Simon & Schuster.

Dworkin, R. M. (1977). *The philosophy of law.* New York: Oxford University Press.

Dworkin, R. M. (1986). *Law's empire.* Cambridge, MA: Belknap Press of Harvard University.

Eberhard, W. (1965). *Conquerors and rulers.* Leiden, Netherlands: Brill.

Esping-Andersen, G. (1990). *The three worlds of welfare capitalism.* Princeton, NJ: Princeton University Press.

Etzioni, A. (1995). *New communitarian thinking.* Charlottesville: University of Virginia.

Evans, P. B., Rueschemeyer, D., & Skocpol, T. (1985). *Bringing the state back in.* New York: Cambridge University Press.

Farley, R. (1988). *Majority–minority relations.* Englewood-Cliffs, NJ: Prentice Hall.

Foner, P. H. (1945). *The complete writings of Thomas Paine.* New York: Citadel Press.

Freeden, M. (1991). *Rights.* Minneapolis: University of Minnesota Press.

Freeman, R. (1992). Is declining unionization of the U.S. good, bad, or irrelevant? In L. Mishel & P. Voos (Eds.), *Unions and economic competitiveness* (pp. 143–169). Armonk, NY: M. E. Sharpe.

Freeman, R., & Medoff, J. (1984). *What do unions do?* New York: Basic Books.

Friedman, M. (1962). *Capitalism and freedom.* Chicago: University of Chicago Press.

Friedson, E. (1994). *Professionalism reborn.* Chicago: University of Chicago Press.

Furniss, N., & Tilton, T. A. (1977). *The case for the welfare state: From social security to social equality.* Bloomington: Indiana University Press.

Galbraith, J. K. (1967). *The new industrial state.* Boston: Houghton-Mifflin.

Gans, H. (1972). The positive functions of poverty. *American Journal of Sociology, 78,* 275–289.

George, V., & Wilding, P. (1977). *Ideology and social welfare.* London: Routledge.

Gould, A. (1993). *Capitalist welfare systems.* London: Longman.

Graham, O. L., Jr. (1976). *Toward a planned society: From Roosevelt to Nixon.* New York: Oxford University Press.

Granovetter, M. (1985). Economic action and social structure: The problem of embeddedness. *American Journal of Sociology, 91,* 481–510.

Green, T. H. (1941). *Lectures on the principles of political obligation.* London: Longman. (Original work published 1886)

Grønbjerg, K. (1977). *Mass society and the extension of welfare, 1960–70.* Chicago: University of Chicago Press.

Groves, H. M. (1973). *Financing government.* New York: Holt, Rinehart, & Winston.

Hall, J. A., & Ikenberry, G. J. (1989). *The state.* Minneapolis: University of Minnesota Press.

Harmon, M. J. (1964). *Political thought: From Plato to the present.* New York: McGraw-Hill.

Hart, H. L. (1967). Are there any natural rights? In A. Quintom (Ed.), *Political philosophy* (pp. 55–56). Oxford, England: Oxford University Press.

Hirsch, B. (1991). *Labor unions and the economic performance of firms.* Kalamazoo, MI: W. E. Upjohn Institute.

Hobhouse, L. T. (1911). *Liberalism.* London: Williams & Norgate.

Hobhouse, L. T. (1922). *The elements of social justice.* London: Allen & Unwin.

Hofstadter, R. (1955). *Social Darwinism in American thought.* Boston: Beacon Press.

Hogler, R. L. (1995). *Labor and employment relations.* Minneapolis: West.

Jensen, A. R. (1970). How much can we boost IQ and scholastic achievement? *Harvard Educational Review, 39,* 1–123.

Kolm, S. C. (1996). *Modern theories of justice.* Cambridge, MA: MIT Press.

Korpi, W. (1989), Power, politics as state autonomy in the development of social citizenship. *American Sociological Review, 54,* 309–328.

Kottak, C. P. (1979). *Cultural anthropology.* New York: Random House.

Kropotkin, P. (1955). *Mutual aid.* Boston: Porter Sargent. (Original work published 1902)

Larson, M. (1977). *The rise of professionalism.* Berkeley: University of California Press.

Le Grand, J. (1982). *The strategy of equality.* London: Allen & Unwin.

Lenin, V. I. (1943). *Selected works.* New York: International Publishers.

Lewis, O. (1959). *Five families: Mexican case studies in the culture of poverty.* New York: Basic Books.

Lewis, O. (1969). Review. *Current Anthropology, 10,* 189–192.

Lipsky, M. (1980). *Street-level bureaucracy.* New York: Russell Sage Foundation.

Locke, J. (1987). *Two treatises on government.* (P. Laslett, Ed.). Cambridge, England: Cambridge University Press. (Original work published 1698)

Macdonald, K. M. (1995). *The sociology of the professions.* Thousand Oaks, CA: Sage Publications.

Maier, C. (1987). *In search of stability.* Cambridge, England: Cambridge University Press.

Mandeville, B. (1924). *The fable of the bees; or private vices, publick benefits.* Oxford, England: Clarendon Press. (Original work published 1723)

Mann, M. (1988). *States, war, and capitalism.* Oxford, England: Blackwell.

Marshall, T. H. (1964). *Class, citizenship, and social development.* Garden City, NY: Doubleday.

Marshall, T. H. (1981). *The right to welfare and other essays.* New York: Free Press.

Merton, R. (1957). *Social theory and social structure.* Glencoe, IL: Free Press.

Mill, J. S. (1970). The subjection of women. In A. S. Rossi (Ed.), *Essays in sex equality* (pp. 125–242). Chicago: University of Chicago Press. (Original work published 1869)

Mintzberg, H. (1993). *Structure in fives.* Englewood Cliffs, NJ: Prentice Hall.

Murray, C. (1984). *Losing ground: American social policy, 1950–80.* New York: Basic Books.

Murray, C., & Herrnstein, R. J. (1994). *The bell curve: Intelligence and class structure in American life.* New York: Free Press.

Nozick, R. (1974). *Anarchy, state, and utopia.* New York: Basic Books.

Oppenheimer, F. (1975). *The state.* New York: Free Life Editions.

Orloff, A. S. (1993). Gender and the social rights of citizenship. *American Sociological Review, 58,* 303–328.

Parsons, T. (1951). *The social system.* Glencoe, IL: Free Press.

Parsons, T., & Bales, R. F. (1955). *Family, socialization and interaction process.* Glencoe, IL: Free Press.

Pinker, R. (1979). *The idea of welfare.* London: Heinemann.

Piven, F. F., & Cloward, R. (1971). *Regulating the poor.* New York: Pantheon.

Piven, F. F., & Cloward, R. (1977). *Poor people's movements: Why they succeed, how they fail.* New York: Pantheon.

Piven, F. F., & Cloward, R. (1982). *The new class war.* New York: Pantheon.

Plant, R. (1988). Needs, agency, and welfare. In J. D. Moon (Ed.), *Responsibility, rights, and welfare* (pp. 60–76). Boulder, CO: Westview Press.

Poggi, G. (1978). *The development of the modern state.* London: Hutchinson.

Proudhon, P. (1969). Mutualism. In *Selected writings of Pierre Proudhon* (pp. 57–70). Garden City, NY: Anchor Books. (Original work published 1927)

Rawls, J. (1971). *A theory of justice.* Cambridge, MA: Harvard University Press.

Rayback, J. G. (1966). *A history of American labor.* New York: Free Press.

Rimlinger, G. (1971). *Welfare policy and industrialization in Europe, America, and Russia.* New York: John Wiley & Sons.

Roemer, J. E. (1996). *Theories of distributive justice.* Cambridge, MA: Harvard University Press.

Rousseau, J. J. (1915). *The political writings of Jean Jacques Rousseau* (Vol. 1). (C. E. Vaugh, Ed.). Cambridge, England: Cambridge University Press.

Sahlins, M. (1972). *Stone-age economics.* Chicago: Aldine.

Sahlins, M. (1985). *Islands of history.* Chicago: University of Chicago Press.

Sahlins, M. (1995). *How "natives" think.* Chicago: University of Chicago Press.

Schumpeter, J. (1950). *Capitalism, socialism, and democracy.* New York: Harper & Row.

Sen, A. K. (1981). *Poverty and famines.* Oxford, England: Clarendon Press.

Sen, A. K. (1982). *Choice, welfare, and measurement.* Cambridge, MA: MIT Press.

Sen, A. K. (1992). *Inequality reexamined.* Cambridge, MA: Harvard University Press.

Sen, A. K. (1997). *On economic inequality.* New York: Oxford University Press.

Shue, H. (1996). *Basic rights.* Princeton, NJ: Princeton University Press.

Simmie, J., & King, R. (Eds.). (1990). *The state in action: Public policy and politics.* London: Macmillan.

Smith, A. (1891). *An inquiry into the nature and causes of the wealth of nations.* London: Nelson & Sons. (Original work published 1776)

Soysal, Y. (1994). *Limits of citizenship.* Chicago: University of Chicago Press.

Specht, H., & Courtney, M. (1994). *Unfaithful angels: How social work has abandoned its mission.* New York: Free Press.

Spencer, H. (1892). *Social statics* (Abridged and revised). New York: D. Appleton. (Original work published 1884)

Stark, W. (Ed.). (1952). *Bentham's economic writings.* London: Allen & Unwin.

Steward, J. H. (1958). Evolution and process. In A. L. Kroeber (Ed.), *Anthropology today* (pp. 313–326). Chicago: University of Chicago Press.

Stiglitz, J. E. (1986). *Economics for the public sector.* New York: W. W. Norton.

Stoesz, D. (1989). A theory of social welfare. *Social Work, 34,* 101–107.

The modern Adam Smith. (1990, July 14). *Economist,* pp. 11–12.

Tilly, C. (Ed.). (1975). *The formation of national states in Western Europe.* Princeton, NJ: Princeton University Press.

Titmuss, R. M. (1959). *Essays on the welfare state.* New Haven, CT: Yale University Press.

Titmuss, R. M. (1960). *The irresponsible society.* London: Fabian Society.

Titmuss, R. M. (1968). *Commitment to welfare.* New York: Pantheon.

Titmuss, R. M. (1974). *Social policy: An introduction.* New York: Pantheon.

Trattner, W. I. (1979). *From poor law to welfare state.* New York: Free Press.

Trotsky, L. (1933). *The history of the Russian revolution.* New York: Simon & Schuster.

von Hayek, F. A. (1944). *The road to serfdom.* Chicago: University of Chicago Press.

von Hayek, F. A. (1948). *Individualism and economic order.* Chicago: University of Chicago Press.

von Hayek, F. A. (1976). *The mirage of social justice.* Chicago: University of Chicago Press.

von Hayek, F. A. (1978). *The constitution of liberty.* Chicago: University of Chicago Press.

Wuthnow, R. (1989). *Communities of discourse.* Cambridge, MA: Harvard University Press.

Wuthnow, R. (1994). *Sharing the journey: Support groups and America's new quest for community.* New York: Free Press.

4

STYLES OF REDISTRIBUTION 1

The welfare states, to date, have developed identifiable forms of redistribution. There has been speculation about desirable forms of redistribution. This chapter discusses 10 such patterns of redistribution. Each type of redistribution policy has its advantages and disadvantages. Each fosters a different end in a continuum between equity and efficiency.

Undertaking redistribution requires social policy, the creation of which is a form of human behavior. First, it is a form of collective human behavior; formulating social policy includes all types of group, organizational, community, administrative, crowd, and boundary-defining behavior. It is more often a special form of organizational and administrative behavior (that is, administering the state), although it includes, at one time or another, all other forms of collective human behavior. As a result, social policy making suffers from all the drawbacks of collective behavior.

Second, formulating social policy is a form situational human behavior. All human behavior takes place in a cultural, technological, political, or historical context. Long ago, sociologist W. I. Thomas (1923) suggested that "if men define situations to be real, then they are real in their consequences" (p. xx). Later, sociologist Talcott Parsons (1951) updated this axiom, suggesting that about five dichotomous situations, called the "pattern variables" existed, from which a person, a group, a community, or an organization may define any given situation. These variables are affectivity or affect neutrality; particularism or universalism; self or collectivity orientation; ascription, or achievement; and diffuseness or specificity.

Third, social policy formulation is a form of adaptive human behavior. For example, an automobile manufacturer has to adapt its behavior when it realizes that it has been producing rear-wheel driven vehicles, which are big and fun to drive, but are neither very fuel efficient nor good on slippery roads. The market is now changing, and the demand for smaller, fuel-efficient vehicles with better traction on slippery roads is rising. In addition, fuel prices are going up rapidly, making big and fun-to-drive vehicles more expensive to operate. In such a situation, a manufacturer who insists on building these vehicles will not be engaging in adaptive behavior and may risk the possibility of going out of business. Making big and fun-to-drive automobiles was adaptive when gasoline was cheap, and there was also high demand for big cars. The basic point is that behavior that is adaptive in one cultural, political, or technological situation may not be so in another situation.

Fourth, most collective behavior is either anticipatory or reactive. Anticipatory behavior takes place when a given person, group, community, or other collectivity behaves in relation to another party with a given assumption about the future. On the other hand, reactive behavior takes place when one party behaves in relation to another from one or more experiences of the past, and where these past experiences prescribe the behavior in the present. For example, anticipatory behavior occurs when a dental student introduces herself to a clinic patient as "Doctor so-and-so," when in reality she has not yet earned the title "doctor." Reactive behavior occurs, for example, when a street gang spots certain strangers in their "territory," defines them as intruders, and "reacts" with hostility.

Fifth, formulation of social policy is a form of goal-directed behavior. At times such goals may include plans to benefit a clearly defined target group, such as poor people, or at other times, they benefit other groups, such as certain service providers to poor people or a constituency of policy makers.

Over the years, the disciplines of political science and public administration have specialized in developing models of policy analysis. Dye (1995) lists nine such models. The discipline of social work, specializing only in welfare policy, uses some of them, but it does so with a different vocabulary. The following section lists the models that Dye described and shows their linkages to the four types of behavior that are part of social policy formulation as well as to welfare policy as social workers know it.

Public Policy Models as Proposed by Dye

Public policies can be analyzed from one or more of the following models (as proposed by Dye, 1995):

- The institutional model looks at how a government is positioned to respond to a given situation. Given that government structures in nation-states vary, this model also asks which level of government is positioned (or not positioned at all) to respond to a given situation (for example, crime, unemployment, industry disputes leading to a strike or a lock-out, and natural disasters).

- The process model focuses on the process by which a problem is identified, government action plans in relation to the problem are proposed, action plans are legitimized and then implemented, and efforts are made to evaluate the impact of that policy. In this model, public opinion, elite opinion, media coverage, and other influential interest groups or "think tanks" all can identify a problem.
- The group interaction model examines how decisions that may lead to some form of redistribution are contested between groups. At times dyads form within a group as a coalition against an individual (see Simmel, 1902). Similarly, two or more groups may form coalitions or alliances against a third group so that the third group cannot monopolize decisions about redistribution.
- The elite preference model begins with the premise that the governing elite makes policy. This model focuses on the elites' definition of the situation (that is, an explanation for the problem and how the nation should respond to it). It studies how that elite influences the masses and government officials to accept their definition of the situation and formulate policies accordingly.
- The maximal social gain model focuses on how a government body (as in the institutional model above) responds to a situation; in this model, however, the government's response is shaped by a focus on achieving the maximum possible social gain. The policy's benefits must far exceed the costs, and the policy chosen (from several alternatives) must lead to the greatest possible benefit. Often this model is called the "rationalism model."
- The incrementalism model is one in which existing commitments are taken for granted, and new efforts are added on slowly and incrementally. This model also tacitly acknowledges that interest groups defend the continuity of existing commitments and hence, that new policies requiring additional resources that may compete with the existing allocations are not seriously encouraged. New policies thus are formulated only on an incremental basis.
- Game theory assumes that groups and individuals are "players," who engage in a "game," that complete information about the game is rarely "available. Given the circumstances of uncertainty, policy decisions must be made. Game theory assumes that there is a "payoff matrix": Some outcomes make one party win while another loses, whereas some other outcomes call for both parties winning or both parties losing.
- The public choice model (Buchanan, 1968, 1969) sees groups

with their own interests coming together and developing policy in their self-interest. However, just as individuals behaving in their own interest in the marketplace enhances the welfare of all (see ideas of Adam Smith in chapter 3), people making policy in their own interest also enhance collective welfare. James Buchanan, Nobel-Prize winner and famous economist, developed this theory of public choice.

- Systems theory views policy as the output of the political system. In both the general systems theory of Ludwig von Bertalanffy (1968) and the social systems theory of Talcott Parsons (1951), systems require input (nourishment from the environment), process throughput (that is, processing of the nourishment), and produce output (the transformed input). Over time and cumulatively, outputs affect in some way the environment from which the inputs came. Thus, the environment creates a demand on the political system that requires some form of input; after processing by the political system, the input is output as policy.

Models Developed for Analyzing Social Welfare Policy

The models listed more or less constitute the universe of policy models. In contrast, the models in the following section have been developed only for the analysis of social welfare policy. All the models have elements of some, if not most, of the policy models Dye (1995) enumerated.

Pre-emptive Welfare Policy and Situational Welfare Policy

I discuss pre-emptive and situational welfare policy in this book, because I feel that most welfare policies emanate from one or the other. They form dichotomous approaches. In one approach, the state anticipates a situation and develops social policy to prevent that situation, and in the other, it is suddenly faced with a situation as a crisis and must respond to it.

A classic example of the pre-emptive model is Otto von Bismarck's decision to institute social insurance programs in Germany during the latter part of the 19th century (for a discussion of Bismarck's efforts, see Rimlinger, 1971). In contrast, a classic example of the situational model is Franklin D. Roosevelt's efforts to implement several social welfare policies and programs (that is, the New Deal) in the United States during the early 1930s in response to the national crisis created by the resounding market failure.

The pre-emptive/situational model is useful for describing social welfare policy and can be used to explain historical events. It also can be

Table 4-1. Pre-emptive versus Situational Social Policy

PRE-EMPTIVE	SITUATIONAL
The state	The state
develops policy to prevent certain behaviors or situations	develops policy to deal with a problem already in hand
develops policy to build alliances and loyalties on a planned basis, so key groups will not be hostile to the state	attempts alliances and loyalties, but these are 11th hour efforts; loyalties of key groups are no longer guaranteed
precommits the state's resources, which may lead to a culture of entitlement	commits the state's resources only for crisis alleviation
may end up pursuing equity functions heavily (see Figure 1-1)	tries to pursue equity without a culture of entitlement
is often an active-engaged state	is often a passive-reluctant state

SOURCE: Model developed by the author.

used to speculate about the timing of collective efforts to change or solve social problems. Table 4-1 compares pre-emptive with situational policy.

KEYNESIAN WELFARE POLICY AND SCHUMPETERIAN WELFARE POLICY

Keynesian and Schumpeterian (1950) welfare policies are those in which the approach to government spending differentiates welfare policy. In short, the Keynesian version calls for increased state spending and the creation of a "decommodified" arena to support poor and marginalized people, whereas the Schumpeterian version calls for the integration of poor and marginal people into the labor force and the market structure as much as possible.

John Maynard Keynes, famous economist known for his studies of state spending, advised Franklin D. Roosevelt to institute the New Deal, even if it had to be done with deficit financing (Heilbronner, 1961). Mishra (1984) referred to this type of welfare policy as "differentiated" welfare policy, which emerges as a response to the demand side of the economy. Mishra also suggested an "integrated" form of welfare policy, which emerges as a response to both demand and supply. In the latter case welfare expenditures

Table 4-2. Keynesian Welfare State versus Schumpeterian Workfare State

KEYNESIAN WELFARE STATE	SCHUMPETERIAN WORKFARE STATE
supports responsible trade unionism and collective bargaining	promotes innovation and competitiveness in the marketplace
consolidates big business and social partnership	promotes the retrenchment of social welfare and its subordination to market forces
works to link the interests of both capital and labor to attain full employment	promotes a market-guided full employment plan as much as possible
generates tax revenue to finance welfare programs	reduces taxes that finance welfare programs, creates incentives for market participation
creates income maintenance with or without market participation	encourages income maintenance with market participation
uses arbitrary criteria	uses commercial criteria, encourages privatization and deregulation
holds that poor people should receive transfer payments from the state (but this is not clearly expressed)	holds that poor people should maintain reciprocity with the state (which is clearly expressed)
enhances equity function (see Figure 1-1)	tries to balance both equity and efficiency (see Figure 1-1)
surfaces in both active-engaged and passive-reluctant states	surfaces in mostly passive-reluctant states

SOURCE: Adapted from the text of Jessop, B. (1994). Post-Fordism and the state. In A. Amin (Ed.), *Post Fordism: A reader* (pp. 251–279). Oxford, England: Blackwell.

are indexed to the spending capacity of the state and the purchasing capacity of the national currency. Taking Mishra's observations into account, it may be possible to view differentiated policies as early Keynesian and the integrated policies as modified Keynesian.

Janowitz (1977) pointed out that integrated welfare policy was intended to accomplish the dual goals of rationing welfare payments and services while retaining their value (also see Chatterjee, 1996). The objective of rationing was related to Chadwick's (as cited in Barry, 1990) notion that "a good or service provided at zero price will attract an infinite demand" (p. 26) (see chapter 3). According to Janowitz, the objective of retaining value was never accomplished, because politically motivated interest groups kept increasing the number of welfare recipients and the amount they should be paid. Note that the politically motivated interest groups included labor unions and social workers (see Edwards, 1993; W. Gould, 1993).

The Keynesian model does not say much about whether poor people should do anything in return for receiving welfare; but the Schumpeterian model, in contrast, supports reciprocity between poor people and the state, an idea Hobhouse (1911, 1922) introduced. The Schumpeterian workfare state discourages providing income to poor people without some form of reciprocity between them and the state (see Jessop, 1994). Schumpeterian policy calls for systematic state efforts so that the poor people are engaged in workfare. Furthermore, in the Schumpeterian model, state efforts are subject to market forces and privatization of programs is encouraged, as are deregulation and passive support of problems based on market solutions. The key ideas of the two models are reproduced in Table 4-2.

As policy recommendations, Schumpeter's (1950) and Keynes's templates are well-outlined theoretical positions that lead to clearly different types of policies. The policies can be examined in historical terms, and some educated observations can be made about their abilities to foster certain social welfare ends (see Table 3-5). The Keynesian policies are generally situational and are engineered to handle crisis situations (such as the market failure during the Great Depression) and to promote equity (see Figure 1-1). In contrast, Schumpeterian policies, also situational and meant for crisis alleviation (as well as future growth of both the economy and human well-being), are meant to promote both equity and efficiency (see Figure 1-1). Social workers and labor unions are usually not supportive of the Schumpeterian workfare state (see Edwards, 1993; W. Gould, 1993).

Residual Welfare Policy and Institutional Welfare Policy

In residual welfare policy and institutional welfare policy, the nature and conditions of coverage are seen as the policy foundation. Wilensky and Lebeaux (1958) originally introduced the typology, which Titmuss (1960) than adopted. Ever since its introduction, the typology has been very popular in social work. Recently, Segal and Brzuzy (1998) defined the two policy types in the following manner: *Residual policy* responds to situations when the family or the community is unable to respond to human problems, and the state or the larger society provides help as a crisis intervention. *Institutional policy,* however, responds as though the problem emerges from predictable and normal situation of industrial settings; the help is given as if the problem were routine.

Table 4-3. Residual and Institutional Welfare Policies

RESIDUAL POLICIES	INSTITUTIONAL POLICIES
are crisis oriented	are prevention oriented
require recipients to prove a need	require recipients to enter a role (such as child, aged person, sick, and so forth, as shown in Table 5-4)
require officials to be familiar with recipients' lives	do not require officials to know everything about recipients' lives
hold that only "deserving" poor people should receive assistance	provide assistance by categories and roles of recipients
measure program success by how much the number of assistance recipients is reduced	measure program success by how well all categories and roles are served
promote stigmatization of recipients	do not stigmatize recipients
view recipients as inadequate	do not use clinical definitions
lean toward fostering efficiency (see Figure 1-1)	lean toward fostering equity (see Figure 1-1)
are common in passive-reluctant states	are found in passive-reluctant and active-engaged states

Source: Adapted from the text of Wilensky, H, & Lebeaux, C. (1958). *Industrial society and social welfare.* New York: Free Press; and van Wormer, K. (1996). *Social welfare: A world view.* Chicago: Nelson-Hall.

Wilensky and Lebeaux (1958) themselves suggested that the United States followed more of a residual welfare policy before the Great Depression and that the introduction of the New Deal showed a shift from residual policies to a position somewhere between residual and institutional. Pre-Fordist industrial society (see chapter 1) seems to have had primarily a residual policy—that is, it did not have much of a welfare state. The crisis that developed from the market failure in 1929 moved the United States somewhat away from residual policy, but it remained a somewhat passive-reluctant welfare state compared with some of the other western European capitalist welfare states.

It is often (incorrectly) assumed that institutional policies by nature are universal, whereas residual policies are selective or means-tested. The dimensions of residual policy versus institutional policy and universalism versus selectivism are independent of each other. Segal and Brzuzy (1998) showed that the United States has both institutional and means-tested policies (for example, Medicare, which provides health care for all elderly people) and residual and universal policies (for example, the Federal Emergency Management Agency, which provides disaster relief).

The typology of residual versus institutional policy is an ideal-type construction, similar to Weber's (1946) ideal-type construction of bureaucracy. In this type of construction, an abstract model is built with attributes of a given phenomenon. The residual versus situational model has been the dominant paradigm for both social workers and sociologists (who are given to a structural–functional orientation). Table 4-3 represents a summarized presentation of this model as developed initially by Wilensky and Lebeaux (1958) and van Wormer (1996).

The Wilensky and Lebeaux (1958) typology has been popular for reviewing social welfare policy and is one of several important tools for policy analysis. However, given its popularity and given its tilt in favor of institutional social welfare, it is difficult to use it for answering important empirical or historical questions. The very application of it biases any assessment questions concerning social welfare assessment or impact evaluation.

Individualist–Libertarian and Communal–Socialist Welfare State

Milton Friedman (1962) and Richard M. Titmuss (1959; 1968) proposed the individualist–libertarian versus communal socialist welfare states. Their key question was, Which function should the state enhance? (see chapter 3) Should it be liberty or equality? (see Table 3-5) Moroney and Krysik (1998) provided a comprehensive review of these two ideal types. Although they summarized both positions as being value driven, and as having a normative-ideological nature, I strongly disagree. Rather, the two positions lead to two mutually exclusive theories of the state.

The libertarian position is as follows: The primary function of the state is to ensure and enhance liberty; industrial capitalism is the only way to enhance liberty and increase choice. The state is not capable of egalitarian redistribution, and when it attempts to do so, it creates huge bureaucracies and third parties and eventually contributes to diminishing returns (Feldstein, 1994). It also makes the state a paternalistic state, in which what poor people should consume or what their lifestyles should be like are dictated by the state. If choices increase, which occurs when productivity increases, then poverty reduction happens simultaneously.

In contrast, the socialist (whether communal or Fabian) position views the primary function of the state as ensuring and enhancing equality within the confines of a humane community; only various forms of socialism can achieve this function. Industrial capitalism, with its market forces, is incapable of fostering either equity or equality (see Figure 1.1), and the only institution capable of egalitarian redistribution is the modern state. Furthermore, industrial capitalism contributes to an "alienating state"—where even citizens feel as if they are aliens—and the communally oriented redistributive state, with a fervent commitment to universal citizenship, can counter such alienation.

Moroney (1991) pointed out that the libertarian position influenced many members of the Republican Party in the United States, whereas the communal or Fabian socialist ideas have had a serious impact on the members of the British Labour Party. His observations of historical events are indeed correct. However, I dispute his claim that the positions of both Friedman (1962) and Titmuss (1959, 1968) are simply normative. I argue that the Friedman position has led to a macro-level hypothesis, to which certain natural experiments have provided a great deal of empirical support. In contrast, the position of Titmuss, which can also be translated into a macro-level hypothesis, has not been supported by the same set of natural experiments.

At its core, both hypotheses have two components. The first one is epistemological and centers on the individual's decision making and choice within a state. The second one is about group behavior, and centers on collective decision making by key groups on behalf of a nation. The Friedman (1962) hypothesis assumes that individuals are incentive driven and that the state should create policies that give individuals incentives to participate in the wealth-building process and to give away a part of their wealth as taxes. This approach enhances productivity, which makes possible certain forms of welfare for selected groups (discussed in chapter 5). Given this epistemological foundation, groups compete to produce, which eventually leads to better products. The function of the state is to see that the groups compete during the production process; this function is called the regulatory function. The greater the competition between groups in the production process, the more the welfare of the nation is enhanced.

The Titmuss (1958, 1962) hypothesis assumes that not all individuals see the options available to them, especially individuals at the lower end of the stratification matrix. In addition, individual choice in a capitalist society is not a constant but varies according to one's position in the social strata. Thus, the higher the position on the socioeconomic ladder, the more choices available. Given this situation, those at the bottom of the stratification matrix have less incentive to participate in the production process than to engage in behavior that is immediately gratifying. An emphasis on egalitarian redistribution creates communal solidarity within and between groups and also leads to a better integration of the poor and other marginal groups in society.

A natural experiment tested the two macro-level hypotheses during the latter half of the 20th century. The economic behavior of the Soviet Union represented that of the socialist states, whereas that of the First World countries represented the capitalist states' economic behavior. By the end of the century, all the First World countries had welfare states and very high HDI levels, whereas the Soviet Union and all Second World countries showed poor productivity and consequently, their welfare states were performing the welfare functions in a very poor manner (see chapters 1 and 2). Within the First World countries, passive-reluctant welfare states were in far better shape than the heavily entitlement-oriented active-engaged welfare states (see chapters 1 and 2 for a discussion of this experiment). Berger (1986) succinctly stated a lesson from this experiment: Socialism appears to be morally dignified because of its apparent altruism, but it is not capable of the kind of productivity that will enhance the state's welfare functions. Capitalism, on the other hand, which appears to be morally suspect because of its emphasis on individual incentives, does build wealth sufficient to cover certain basic welfare functions. At midcentury, Joseph A. Schumpeter (1950) observed that capitalism is capable of and has eradicated absolute poverty in the countries where it is in practice. The poverty that exists in rich countries like the United State is relative poverty, which cannot be alleviated but has to be managed. (The bottom of the stratification ladder will always be relatively poorer than the top.)

Berger (1986) applied Schumpeter's (1950) observation to the Third World. During the middle of this century, many Third World countries were emerging from colonial rule. A large number of them (led by Nehru of India and Sukarno of Indonesia) followed a socialist path and remained poor. A small number of Third World countries in the Pacific Rim opted to follow capitalist policies and, by the end of the century and are substantially wealthy. Furthermore, Indonesia discarded its socialist policies and adopted capitalistic policies (although under somewhat authoritarian rule) during the 1970s and was showing substantial more wealth development than India by the 1990s.

Perhaps the most profound issue illustrated by the differences between Friedman (1962) and Titmuss (1959, 1971) is the matter of exchange versus gift relationships. Friedman suggested that people engage in self-centered acts and that their transactions with others are motivated from self-interest. Such transactions, by nature, are "exchange" relationships, in which there is a quid pro quo between exchanging parties. Mauss (1990) commented on this idea, suggesting that essentially all gifts given in human relationships are attempts to create an incentive to reciprocate the gift. Blau (1964) and Emerson (1987), developers of modern exchange theory in sociology and social psychology, have taken the same position, as did Malinowski (1926) from anthropology. The implication of this debate is that gift relationships, in which something is given with no reciprocity, are rare; using terminology from behaviorism, gift giving behavior is likely to become extinguished if it continues without any reciprocity.

Titmuss (1959, 1971) began his "moral entrepreneurship" from these ideas. In *The Gift Relationship* (1971), he suggested that donors should give

Table 4-4. Social Policy from Friedman and Titmuss

FRIEDMAN'S VIEW OF SOCIAL POLICY	TITMUSS'S VIEW OF SOCIAL POLICY
aims to enhance liberty	aims to enhance equality
aims to enhance choice	aims to enhance egalitarian redistribution
holds that enhancing liberty and choice will reduce absolute poverty	holds that setting a floor and promoting a universalist policy of income subsidy will reduce poverty
calls for enhancing and increasing productivity	calls for enhancing and equalizing redistribution
should closely follow Adam Smith and Joseph Schumpeter	should follow closely Fabian socialism or communal socialism (see Table 3-2)
views the state described by Titmuss as paternalistic	views the state described by Friedman as the alienating state
views the state described by Titmuss as caught in bureaucracies that absorb resources	holds that only the state can be an agent of redistribution
attempts to enhance both equity and efficiency (see Figure 1-1)	attempts to enhance equity (see Figure 1-1)
has more following in passive-reluctant states	has greater following in active-engaged states

SOURCE: Adapted from text of Friedman, M. (1962). *Capitalism and freedom*. Chicago: University of Chicago Press; Titmuss, R. M. (1968). *Commitment to welfare*. New York: Pantheon; and Moroney, R. M. (1991). *Social policy and social work*. New York: Aldine de Gruyter.

blood as a gift to patients who need blood transfusions. When a human being needs something so precious as blood, he or she should receive it from another human being or from a community of humans as a gift. Blood should never be subjected to a commodification process, where a patient needing blood purchases it from the market using an exchange relationship (that is, blood received for money paid). States that allow the commodification of blood, like the United States, suffer from waste, mismanagement, and human degradation. States where all blood is voluntarily given, such as the United Kingdom, almost never see waste, mismanagement, and human degradation. (One may elect to read between the lines: states supporting the principle of gift relationships are morally superior to those supporting exchange relationships.)

In a sharp dissent, Sapolsky and Finkelstein (1977) suggested that Titmuss (1971) was guilty of gross errors in his study's methodology. Titmuss based his claims on poor sampling procedure. Sapolsky and Finkelstein concluded that Titmuss's specific thesis about blood donorship and his broader one about the superiority of one-way gift relationships were not based on adequate methodology, and were not empirically supportable.

An earlier debate put forth this very proposition of gift versus exchange relationship (the question whether one-way gift relationships could build efficient welfare states). Recall from chapter 3 the position of Hobhouse (1911. 1922) that human relationships, including those of welfare recipients receiving benefits from the taxpayer through the state, are more stable when they are based on a system of reciprocity rather than on one-way transactions of gifts or entitlements.

Returning to Berger's (1986) metaphor, Titmuss seems to have an immense normative dignity but poor empirical support for his positions. In contrast, Friedman's (1962) and Schumpeter's (1950) positions from a generation earlier, which seem very mercantile and prosaic, are empirically supported (see chapter 2). This, indeed, creates a problem for an entire generation of professional social workers at the end of the 20th century, because most of them are believers of Titmuss and his ideas and are suspicious of those of Friedman or Schumpeter. Returning to Figure 1.1, most social workers seem to prefer enhancing equity rather than both equity and efficiency. Table 4-4 summarizes the two forms of redistribution.

Manifest Function– and Latent Function–Oriented Social Policy

Manifest function–oriented and latent function–oriented social policies are redistribution efforts in which policies developed benefit both an intended group or target population and one or more unintended groups or target populations. At times, it is quite possible that the unintended benefits for interest group X almost equal or exceed the intended benefits of targeted group Y. This form of policy analysis may be called "manifest and latent benefits." Robert Merton (1957), a sociologist, introduced this conceptualization, suggesting that most actions by individuals or groups may have intended as well as unintended functions. Merton's ideas have never been formally applied to social policy analysis, except that Gans (1972) used it to show how certain social problems such as poverty benefit members of the middle class. In such cases, policies are intended to benefit the poor, but those providing services to the poor become unintended beneficiaries.

This mode of welfare policy analysis may be appropriate in some settings, however. One such setting may be the Great Society programs of

Table 4-5. Social Policies with Two Different Groups of Beneficiaries

CLEARLY TARGETED BENEFICIARIES	MANIFEST AND LATENT BENEFICIARIES
Social policy	Social policy
clearly designates beneficiaries	does not clearly designate beneficiaries, and the social arrangements call for too many intermediaries, even when the beneficiaries are clearly designated
allows low overhead and administrative costs	creates high overhead administrative costs
allows lesser number of third parties	creates higher numbers of third parties
increases choices of recipients	reduces choices of recipients and increases choices of service providers
makes impact analysis and cost-benefit analysis relatively easy	makes impact analysis and cost-benefit analysis relatively difficult because it is hard to isolate the effects of policy and programs on the beneficiaries
makes policy assessment in relation to equity or efficiency relatively easy	policy assessment in relation to equity or efficiency is relatively difficult
may found in active-engaged states	may be found in passive-reluctant states

Source: Model adapted from ideas of Merton, R. (1957). *Social theory and social structure.* Glencoe, IL: Free Press.

the United States, which began in 1965. The objectives of Great Society social policy was eradication of poverty with maximal feasible participation of poor people. Moynihan (1969), an architect of these policies, has suggested that the programs were not politically adequate to make the given ends possible. Murray (1984) has charged that the Great Society programs were more supportive of the political interests of the Democratic Party than the socioeconomic interests of poor people. Moroney and Krysik (1998) documented that the housing policies of the Great Society programs, which had contradictory, multiple goals, ended up benefiting the middle class more than poor people. It is possible to argue that the manifest function of the Great Society policies was to benefit poor people but that the latent function was to benefit members of the middle class, who could claim to be custodians of the poor or who could support the interests of the Democratic Party.

Other examples of manifest and latent benefits can be shown to exist in health policy, especially in health policy for elderly people. Medicare, a health care program for people over age 65, was introduced in the United States during the Great Society days is still in operation. Feldstein (1994) claimed that U.S. health policy in general and Medicare in particular was producing what economists call "diminishing returns," that is, increased state spending was not producing increased benefits. A number of third parties in the United States (see chapter 3), were absorbing resources intended to benefit elderly people. Japan has similar problems, in which many third parties are as much beneficiaries of health expenditures as the elderly population (see A. Gould, 1993). Key ideas from this form of social policy analysis are summarized in Table 4-5.

The Positive State, the Social Security State, and the Social Welfare State

Furniss and Tilton (1977) suggested three types of state responses to the problem of human vulnerability: the positive state, the social security state, and the social welfare state. These three reflect three different visions of the state and consequently, call for three different types of social policy.

The positive state is committed to the owners of property, and the state's efforts are directed toward providing protection to them first. To that end, state policy is formulated to accomplish the following goals:

1. to promote good relationships between the market and the state (Furniss and Tilton, 1977, called it government–business collaboration for economic growth)
2. to promote full employment as much as possible so that levels of public consumption and business production are kept relatively high
3. to please organized labor, because it influences key political blocs, by working in or accommodating its demand as much as possible.

The positive state, as a result, turns to social insurance programs to accomplish those ends. Social insurance programs are based on actuarial assumptions (that is, life expectancy and years of participation in the labor force) and forge the destiny of wage earners to the economic and political health of the state. That connection builds social control of the workforce and prevents organized working-class revolt. Bismarck's efforts in late 19th century Germany resembled a positive state, and Furniss and Tilton (1977) acknowledged that this kind of social policy is also similar to Titmuss's (1958) residual approach (although Wilensky and Lebeaux, 1958, not Titmuss, coined the terms "residual" and "institutional").

The social security state is, in many ways similar to the positive state, except that it guarantees a national minimum to all of its citizens (Furniss & Tilton, 1977). The minimum may be income or surrogate property, but often it is income. This concept of guaranteed minimum avoids the problems inherent in welfare coverage permissible in the positive state, which extends coverage only to those who are in the workforce and selected others, such as blind and disabled people and veterans. Industrial societies have other vulnerable populations, such as unskilled people; single-parent families, in which the only parent present is not employable; has a chronic illness, or is disabled, and people designated as mentally ill. Furthermore, a guaranteed minimum means that a form of entitlement exists to which every citizen has a right. The state or any other groups in a political alliance cannot selectively grant or withhold this right from a citizen. Thus, this type of policy reduces social control by the state or its agents.

The social welfare state also resembles the social security state. In addition to providing a guaranteed minimum income, the social welfare state promotes cooperation between business and unions and seeks cooperation between the government and the unions. In addition, the social welfare state seeks policies to promote what is known as "solidaristic wages" and "environmental planning." (The term *solidaristic wages* refers to the situation in which the wage gap between the workers and the managers is relatively low. For example, the United States is very far from having solidaristic wages, because the wage gap between workers and managers is very high. In contrast, Japan and Sweden are close to having such wages, because the wage gap in those two countries is much narrower than that of the United States. *Environmental planning* refers to state intervention (at times in alliance with selected communities) to conserve the environment. Without such state interventions, many industries would not be likely to do what they could to conserve the environment in which they engage in their production.) The latter two objectives are designed to foster equality and solidarity, with consideration for conservation for the future generations. Furthermore, a social welfare state struggles for the social integration of marginalized groups.

An example of the positive state is the United States. In comparison, Great Britain is a social security state, and Sweden is a social welfare state. It should be noted that the examples given by Furniss and Tilton (1977) are from the latter part of the 1970s. During and after the Thatcher administration (1980s), Great Britain moved somewhat away from being a social security state and somewhat closer to a positive state (see A. Gould, 1993). However, by the end of the 1990s, the United States remained the best example of the positive state.

Furniss and Tilton (1977), in their efforts to form a scale to assess the welfare state, seemed biased in favor of communal socialism (as shown in Table 3-2). They acknowledged a debt to Gunnar Myrdal (as quoted in Furniss & Tilton, 1977, pp. 24–25) when they suggested that "socialistically inclined liberalism" and "liberalized socialism" are the concepts by which a state should be assessed.

Recall from chapter 3 that in Europe in general, and in England in particular, the word "liberal" means one who is firmly committed to the idea of liberty. In classical economics, such a commitment also meant a position close to anticollectivism in Table 3-1 or a position somewhere toward the right in Table 3-2. (In contrast, in the United States, "liberal" means one who subscribes to the adequacy of New Deal or Great Society programs and who believes that social programs supported by state spending will solve social problems.) Myrdal's (as cited in Furniss & Tilton, 1977) notion of socialistically inclined liberalism falls somewhere between reluctant collectivism and individualist–libertarian in Table 3-2, and his notion of liberalized socialism falls somewhere between Marxist–communal socialism and Fabian socialism (see Tables 3-2 and Table 3-3).

Furniss and Tilton (1977) further pointed out that (elaborating from Gunnar Myrdal, John Stuart Mill, and Adolf Wagner) that improvements in birth control technology is another factor that must be considered in analyzing the state's role in redistribution. This technology has made it possible to limit population growth and labor market oversupply, which, in turn, offsets the Malthusian prophesy. The matter of redistribution by the state, then, becomes a matter that should be seen in relation to the demand for basic resources for survival that are not excessive in proportion to supply. When high birth rates are coupled with low death rates and longer life expectancies, the Malthusian nightmare is likely to return. Table 4-6 presents Furniss and Tilton's models, which seem to form a linear scale.

Furniss and Tilton's (1977) assumption that the "Malthusian nightmare" is relatively absent in the welfare states is only partly true. Blake (1989) demonstrated, as have many others before her, that poor people all over the world have more children, that is, have higher birth rates than nonpoor people. In poor countries, it is the poor and the peasant populations who have high birth rates, and these populations are in the majority. Their high birth rates counteract any economic development. Thus, poor countries need to achieve a level of economic development that far exceeds the birth rate of their majority population to achieve a viable level of economic growth or reduce their birth rate. Rich countries, where poor people constitute a minority of the population, have high productivity and economic growth, so they can ignore the higher birth rates of their poor population (Hernandez, 1993; Tanner, 1996; U.S. Bureau of the Census, 1995). However, this situation can further contribute to the problems generated by a country's dependency ratio, as discussed in chapters 1 and 2.

Arthur Gould (1993) offered other criticisms: He commented that "Furniss and Tilton were writing too early to be able to consider the implications of some of the more radical reforms introduced by the Social Democrats in the mid-1970s" (p. 223). Quoting from Wilson's (1979) work, Gould suggested that "high social benefits, taxes and social security contributions were becoming a *disincentive for employees to work and for employers to*

Table 4-6. Three Types of Redistributive Responses by the State

THE POSITIVE STATE	THE SOCIAL SECURITY STATE	THE SOCIAL WELFARE STATE
protects owners of property	protects owners of property	protects owners of property
promotes harmony between the market and the state	promotes harmony between the market and the state	promotes harmony between the market and the state
promotes full employment	promotes full employment	promotes full employment
uses social insurance	uses social insurance creates surrogate property guarantees a national minimum to all protects vulnerable groups	uses social insurance creates surrogate property guarantees a national minimum to all protects vulnerable groups
uses high social control	uses decreased social control	uses substantially decreased social control
has limited concern for equity	has increased pursuit of equity	seeks solidaristic wages
has high commitment to efficiency	has high commitment to efficiency	has high commitment to equity risks possible loss of efficiency protects the environment for future generations
is often a passive-reluctant state	is somewhat of an active-engaged state	is an active-engaged state

SOURCE: Adapted from text of Furniss, N., & Tilton, T. A. (1977). *The case for the welfare state: From social security to social equality.* Bloomington: Indiana University Press.

invest [italics added]" (p. 223). Gould's further criticism of the Swedish welfare state was that educational programs in Sweden were heavily influenced by the trade unions who "brainwashed" children and youths to become firm believers in socialism, and even scholars such as Korpi (1978, 1983, 1989) acted like advocates for socialism or socialist welfare state rather than as analysts of the consequences of the welfare state. Quoting Sodersten (1991), Gould claimed that "with the growth of public sector employment from 25 percent to 33 percent of all employment, and the expansion of public sector expenditure from 35 percent to over 60 percent of GDP, *Sweden's economic performance has declined* [italics added]" (Gould, 1993. p. 231).

Having criticized the preferred model of the welfare state of Furniss and Tilton, A. Gould (1993) then suggested that the model for the welfare state should not be Sweden or Germany (also see Petty, 1996; "The politics of unemployment," 1997). It instead should be Japan, which is somewhat of a positive state (see Table 4-6) with certain features of the social welfare state. I called it a passive-reluctant state earlier.

Three Welfare State Regimes

Esping-Andersen (1990) offered a study of redistribution in the First World capitalistic states, examining 14 western European countries, the United States, Canada, Australia and New Zealand. He classified redistribution into three types: conservative, liberal, and social democratic. In his classification, the conservative states are the middle European states, the liberal states are the Anglo-Saxon states (that is, the United Kingdom, the United States, Australia, New Zealand, and Canada), and the social democratic states are the Scandinavian states.

According to Esping-Andersen (1990), a welfare state is a country in which some degree of nondependence on the market exists for day-to-day living. This point alone establishes Esping-Andersen as one who prefers a certain kind of state—one with a high rate of decommodification. His preference is a value-based, not a scientifically based choice: It is perfectly acceptable for an able human being to not participate in the labor force, to sit outside the market structure, and to allow the welfare state to meet his or her day-to-day living needs. Decommodification (the degree to which social rights permit people to live independently of the market structure); social stratification; interrelationships between the state, market structure, and family; the nature of the public–private mixture; and key historical forces all vary to different degrees across the three types of welfare state regimes. (Table 4-7 summarizes the major attributes of the welfare state regimes.)

The term "public–private mix" refers to a set of conventions in each country that have emerged over time and that may be unique in that country. These conventions dictate, for example, whether the functions of the state as identified in Tables 3-4 and 3-5 will be performed by the state; partly by the

Table 4-7. Three Welfare State Regimes

CONSERVATIVE	LIBERAL	SOCIAL–DEMOCRATIC
has moderate decommodifications	is lowest in decommodification	is highest in decommodification
produces stratification	maintains stratification	reduces stratification
is a monarchial welfare state	is market oriented	has parliamentary reform orientation
offers compulsory state social insurance with strong entitlements	offers means-tested and modest social maintenance	offers equal benefits to all regardless of market participation
has state paternalism: dependent on family, morality, and traditional authority	is dependent on contract	is independent of individuals
has dominance of the (Catholic) Church and the aristocracy	has dominance of laissez-faire ideology	has dominance of working class mobilization
is high on equity with some efficiency loss—a culture of entitlements	is high on efficiency and makes only situational accommodation to equity (see Table 4-1)	is high on equity with some efficiency loss—a culture of entitlements
is often an active-engaged state	is often a passive-reluctant state	is often an active-engaged state

Source: Adapted from Esping-Andersen, G. (1990). *The three worlds of welfare capitalism*. Princeton, NJ: Princeton University Press.

state and partly by the community; or partly by the state, partly by the community, and partly by the market.

The work of Esping-Andersen, although empirical, seems biased in favor of partial decommodification of labor (and by extension, health care) and somewhat biased against the idea of free operation of the market. In addition, he can be seen as an ideologue closer to Fabian socialism or communal socialism (see Table 3-3). Furthermore, A. Gould's criticisms (1993), summarized above, are also applicable here.

Liberal and Conservative Orientations to Social Policy

Establishing a dichotomy between liberal and conservative orientations to social policy is a popular American approach to reviewing styles of redistribution. In the United States, "liberal" means a position that resembles Fabian socialism and "conservative" means a position close to reluctant collectivist or one of the "libertarian" categories as shown in Table 3-3. Schlesinger (1949) and Schlesinger, Jr. (1986) have proposed that the United States has seen spiral-like swings in social policy since the Civil War and that the swings have oscillated between liberalism and conservatism. Liberalism is interpreted as concern for alleviating the misery of many people, preoccupation with public issues, and democratic pulls toward equality, freedom, social responsibility, and general welfare. Conservatism is interpreted as concern for the rights of the few (people with property); absorption in private affairs; capitalist pulls toward private property, profit, and free market; and survival of the fittest (Hirschman, 1980; McClosky & Zaller, 1984). Furthermore, liberals believe that increased state spending on social programs enhances social welfare objectives, whereas conservatives believe that substantial reduction in state spending enhances social welfare.

The above description of liberal and conservative beliefs, however, is also a liberal view (Schlesinger, Jr., 1986), which creates an impression that liberals only care about democracy and welfare of many people and that conservatives are agents of capitalism and do not care about democracy or conditions of the masses. This is not quite the case, however, and questioning the state's ability to solve social problems often means that one gets labeled "conservative." However, U.S. social policy scholarship has long been dependent on this typology, which for all practical purposes is better described as a proequity (liberal) or a proefficiency (conservative) orientation. It is entirely possible to find conservatives in the United States who are for democracy, freedom (that is, liberty, as discussed in chapter 3), and social responsibility but who do not think that the state can become a surrogate family.

Using this liberal versus conservative typology, Tanner (1996) has suggested that both the liberals and the conservatives are wrong in their approaches to ending problems of poverty in the United States. He argued

Table 4-8. American Liberalism and Conservatism

AMERICAN LIBERALISM	AMERICAN CONSERVATISM
is concerned for the miseries of many people	is concerned for the privileges and rights of a few people
is preoccupied with public issues	is preoccupied with private concerns of a few people
pulls for equality	pulls for liberty
pulls for greater redistribution	pulls for optimizing private profit
pulls for democratic processes	pulls for elitism
is suspicious of capitalism and the free market	is supportive of capitalism and the free market
believes in state spending and its ability to solve social problems	has disbelief in state spending and its ability to solve social problems
pulls for equity (see Figure 1-1)	pulls for efficiency (see Figure 1-1)
would prefer the state to be active-engaged	would prefer the state to be passive-reluctant

SOURCE: Adapted from Schlesinger, A. M. (1949). *Paths to the present*. New York: Macmillan; Schlesinger, A. M., Jr. (1986). *The cycles of American history*. Boston: Houghton Mifflin; Hirschman, A. O. (1980). *Morality and the social sciences: A durable tension*. Memphis, TN: P. K. Seidman; and McClosky, H., & Zaller, J. (1984). *The American ethos: Public attitudes toward capitalism and democracy*. Cambridge, MA: Harvard University Press.

that liberal solutions create captives of a welfare system and that "solving problems of poverty is beyond the power of government programs" (Tanner, 1996, pp. 109–110). He further argued that conservatives also are wrong in their views, because they

> should realize that government programs are far less capable of changing human behavior than is simple economic reality. A more realistic approach is stated by Mickey Kaus 1989, in *The End of Equality*: Instead of attempting to somehow teach mainstream culture to people who spend most of their day immersed in ghetto culture, we should make ghetto culture economically unsustainable. (Tanner, 1996, p. 128)

Tanner goes on to suggest that government cannot get people out of poverty, and government efforts to do so are flawed. A civil society should not make welfare a better choice than market participation. For those who cannot participate in the market, there should be "a reinvigorated private charitable sector" (p. 181).

An irony inherent in the position of Tanner (1996) is that after taking both liberals and conservatives to task and suggesting that most welfare programs are designed with an inadequate understanding of poor people and of human nature, he suggests that the modern state should return to the days of organized charity (Trattner, 1977). In this position, he is very close to Titmuss's view of the gift relationship, that members of society should give voluntarily to solve problems of marginality. Table 4-8 summarizes the basic ideas of U.S. liberals and conservatives.

Economic Efficiency, Social Conflict, and Collective Welfare Models

Using health care as an example, Melhado (1998) outlined three models of redistribution. He called them the "economic efficiency," the "social conflict," and the "collective welfare" models. Melhado offered his policy analysis as an alternative to the economic efficiency model, which he claimed, stems not from value-free economic analysis but from a "cluster of values that inhibit the expression of social solidarity and the formulation of policies intended to foster distributive justice" (p. 215).

In his outline, the economic efficiency model emerged in the United States in the 1960s as an alternative to the idea of a national health insurance plan. During the 1960s, two models of redistribution were being discussed in the United States: the collective welfare model and the social conflict model. These two models resembled each other somewhat in their epistemological assumptions and in their proposed program structure. The social conflict model assumed that health care is a basic necessity for survival, just like food, shelter, and basic security. The collective welfare model assumed that health care, like food, shelter, and security, is a special item needed for survival and that consequently, its production and distribution are matters of collective concern. Under the economic efficiency model, however, various components of health care are subjected to commodification and private ownership.

The basic variations among Melhado's (1998) models occur around four dimensions: epistemological assumptions, ownership, cost, and program structure.

The basic assumption in the economic efficiency model is that health care is a commodity, and it is produced by private individuals. All these private individuals who produce health care must make a profit. Furthermore, the demand for and supply of health care would have an effect on its cost, just as they would for any product in the marketplace. Demand always seems to be high, and supply, in comparison, is always insufficient. So, health care costs are high. Furthermore, health care requires a program structure under which individual or group practitioners behave like private business entrepreneurs and practice medicine with the support of private or public hospitals or health maintenance organizations.

The basic assumption in the social conflict model is that health care has become a commodity when it should not be a commodity or part of the marketplace at all. Because of its commodity status, health care has been monopolized by the wealthy, because they are the only ones who can afford to pay the high prices associated with care. Physicians and other health care providers have been allowed to acquire sacred knowledge, which belongs to the community; those who acquire this knowledge should not be free agents and profit from it. They should be allowed a decent wage for their labor, but knowledge about health care and the means of production should be publicly owned. When that happens, the distribution of health care will depend, not on who can pay for it, but on who has membership in the community. The program structure for health care in such a decommodified setting can only take place in a health maintenance organization or in something equivalent to national health insurance.

The basic assumption of the collective welfare model is that all members of a community (or nation) are owed a basic level of health care, and thus health care cannot be allowed to become commodified. All forms of health care facilities and knowledge are publicly owned and should be held under some form of public trusteeship. This trusteeship will determine how health care is dispensed, thereby achieving cost control. The program structure of such health care practice can only be through some form of national health insurance or service. Table 4-9 summarizes these three models.

Sharing-Surplus Orientation and Marketing-Surplus Orientation

The sharing-surplus and marketing-surplus orientations make up a paradigm that I introduce to review how the state's tradition in managing surplus develops, given the presence of a surplus. In this regard, surplus seems to be managed according to two principles. The first of them can be called a "sharing-surplus" principle, whereby the state finds ways of merely redistributing the surplus. Given that social welfare is, for the most part, a transfer system in which the state transfers income from those in the labor force to those who are not or passes on the cost of services such as health care to those in the labor force (see Chatterjee, 1996), sharing surplus means direct transfer by the state from the payers to the recipients. This principle involves a smaller number of third parties. The second principle can be

Table 4-9. Melhado's Summary of Three Models of Health Care

ECONOMIC EFFICIENCY MODEL	SOCIAL CONFLICT MODEL	COLLECTIVE WELFARE MODEL
Key authors: J. Buchanan M. V. Pauley M. S. Feldstein	Key author: E. M. Melhado	Key author: V. R. Fuchs
Basic question: What is economically efficient?	Basic question: What is most conflict resolving?	Basic question: What is most beneficial to the collective?
Basic assumption: Supply is always limited	Basic assumption: Wealthy people monopolize what should be more evenly distributed	Basic assumption: All citizens are owed certain basic goods; hence their production and distribution are a collective concern
Health care is a special form of public good selectively consumed; the problem is how to optimize subsidy to consumption	Health care has been commodified; the challenge is how to decommodify it	Health care is a collective utility: The challenge is how to change its ownership from private hands to public trusteeship
Problem can be solved by cost sharing	Problem can be solved by ownership sharing	Problem can be solved by ownership sharing
Program structure: Individual and group practice with private insurance and with health maintenance organizations	Program structure: National health insurance and health maintenance organizations	Program structure: National health insurance

SOURCE: Adapted from Melhado, E. M. (1998). Economists, public provision, and the market: Changing values in policy debate. *Journal of Health Politics, Policy, and the Law, 23,* 215–263.

called "marketing surplus," whereby the state, while attempting to manage surplus, creates a demand structure. New markets and new forms of productivities then emerge, with a supply structure responding to the demand structure created by the state. For example, when the U.S. government allocates block grants to the states and sometimes, to voluntary agencies or for-profit ventures to provide goods or services to those not in the labor force), that use of intermediaries (third or fourth parties) in the transfer process leads to marketing surplus. Like the proverbial middlemen in any marketing situation, the intermediaries consume a part of what is being transferred. A more precise observation here can be stated in the following terms:

Let the amount being transferred in a sharing surplus situation be S_{s1} and the amount reaching the recipient, after administrative and other costs be S_{s2}. It is clear that

$$S_{s1} > S_{s2}.$$

Now, let the amount being transferred in a marketing surplus situation be S_{m1} and the amount reaching the recipient, after administrative costs and other costs, be S_{m2}. It is also clear that

$$S_{m1} > S_{m2}.$$

However, if $S_{s1} = S_{m1}$,

then $S_{s2} > S_{m2}$;

and $S_{m1} - S_{m2} > S_{s1} - S_{s2}$.

On the face of it, it would appear that the tradition of sharing surplus is more desirable than marketing surplus. This objective is probably true if the objective of social policy is to promote equity only (see Figure 1-1). However, if the objective of social policy is to promote both equity and efficiency, then perhaps basing social policy on the marketing surplus model is more desirable. Social policy based on the marketing-surplus model is more often "multifunctional," that is, devoted to promoting more ends or more functions than those based on the sharing-surplus model. Table 4-10 outlines some of the similarities and differences between the sharing-surplus and marketing-surplus models.

The United States and, increasingly the United Kingdom since the Thatcher administration, are closer to marketing-surplus, whereas the other Western European and former socialist countries are closer to a sharing-surplus policy. In different policies within nations, direct cash transfers are more akin to sharing surplus, whereas in-kind benefits provided by third parties (and supported by the state through a transfer process) are closer to a marketing-surplus approach.

The term "relative deprivation" was introduced by several U.S. soci-

Table 4-10. Two Approaches to Social Policy

FACTOR	SHARING SURPLUS	MARKETING SURPLUS
Function(s)	single	multiple (multifunctional)
Objective	to promote equity	to promote equity and efficiency
Surplus shared with	target populations	target populations and other entrepreneurs
Number of third parties	low	high
State's role	transfer agent	transfer agent and customer for new entrepreneurs
Economic functions	supply to target populations	supply to target populations and support demand for the labor of new entrepreneurs
State's ability to tax	high consensus for high taxation for many types of welfare	absence of consensus on taxation for many types of welfare
Structure of the state	centralized	decentralized
Social policy leads to	consumption by target population	consumption by target population and incentive for new production
Means of service delivery	either completely state owned or state supported; efforts to nationalize key services (such as health care)	some state owned or state supported, but trends of purchase of services; partnership between the state and the market; efforts to privatize services (such as health care)
Policies may lead to	relative deprivation	diminishing returns
Nature of industrial state	active-engaged (capitalist or socialist)	passive-reluctant (capitalist)

SOURCE: Model developed by author.

ologists (see Stouffer, 1949) during their study of black soldiers in the U.S. Army during World War II. The term means that one feels deprived in relation to selected other groups' feelings of deprivations. Thus, the black soldiers in the U.S. Army who were from the northern part of the United States (where there was less overt discrimination) felt more deprived and more discriminated against than the black soldiers from the South (where there was more overt discrimination). The difference occurred because there was no pretense of equality and freedom in the South, which was not the case in the northern part of the United States. As a result, black soldiers from the North rated higher in "relative deprivation" than the black soldiers from the South.

I have suggested that social policy that is sharing surplus in orientation is likely to generate relative deprivation. To understand this relationship, one needs to examine the French strikes during the mid-1990s. The French working classes (and those in other "conservative" states as Esping-Andersen, 1990, calls them) felt that they were entitled to many benefits, but the French government felt that it could no longer afford to pay those benefits. Reduction of benefits led to nationwide strikes, and the French working classes felt "relatively more deprived" than other workforces. In Germany, the situation is not that much different (see Petty, 1996) from that of France (see Dornbusch, 1997; Petty, 1996; "The politics of unemployment," 1997).

In contrast, I have suggested that marketing-surplus policy leads to diminishing returns. The term "diminishing returns" is borrowed from elementary economics, where increased spending does not show a linear relationship to increased returns. Instead, increased spending may show a rate of return that is disproportional to the increase. Feldstein (1994) documented that U.S. spending on health care shows diminishing returns, and Tanner (1996) did the same for welfare spending. In sum, increased spending does not mean increased benefits. Third parties (as documented in chapter 3) consume the extra spending, and a great deal goes to maintaining bureaucracies. Both von Hayek (1976, 1978) and Schumpeter (1950) would say, "We told you so!" In addition, marketing-surplus policy has been called a form of paternalism (Mead, 1997); it is a form of social policy in which large numbers of people from the middle class are major beneficiaries of state action (Bartik, 1991; Clotfelter, 1991).

Welfare Societies and Welfare States Revisited

In chapter 1, I took the position that the two ideas of welfare societies and welfare states are inseparable and should be treated as a pair of interacting sets. At this point, I would like to point out that most, if not all, of the styles of redistribution discussed in this chapter must be seen as a function of both societal culture and state policy.

A policy is made by the state in a political environment. That form of policy making is also embedded in the cultural environment of a society. Thus, the political environment of policy making and the cultural environment in which the policy is seen as appropriate collective endeavor are inseparable. For example, the opposition of liberal and conservative policy making is embedded in the culture of U.S. society, where a socially constructed reality dictates that these two positions are the only approaches to dealing with problems of vulnerability. As we can see from Table 4-1, preemptive policy making would be culturally alien to Americans. In the case of health care (as outlined in Table 4-9), in the United States, where health care for all citizens is a serious problem (estimates are that between 35 and 45 million people have no health care insurance), a rational person might suggest that the social conflict model or the collective welfare model should be considered as policy alternatives. However, such alternatives would be viewed by many as culturally alien to the United States and consequently would be beyond the realm of possibility. (See the Appendix for suggestions for moving incrementally to a national health care system.)

Assessment of Styles of Redistribution

In a classic work, Suchman (1967) introduced the twin ideas of "theory failure" and "program failure." According to his concept, a given theory calls for a given program structure; one then can assess how or whether that program structure can produce changes in given forms of human behavior. Thus, a given theory may explain why poverty persists or why juveniles commit delinquent acts or why people form dependency on drugs or alcohol. Such a theory may be called a theory of causation.

A theory of causation, in turn, prescribes a program structure. For example, one theory of causation of delinquency (Cloward & Ohlin, 1960) informs us that delinquency occurs because working-class adolescents lack certain opportunities taken for granted by middle-class adolescents. A theory of intervention arising from this theory of causation would call for a program structure in which casework and group work services are available to working class youths, and a series of economic, social, and cultural opportunities are built into these services. Any effort to evaluate would view this program structure as an independent variable and could start with a null hypothesis that this program structure makes no difference in changing working-class delinquencies. If one or two such program structures fail (that is, does not change delinquencies), then it can be seen as a program failure. If a substantial majority of the program structures fail, then that is an indicator of theory failure (that is, the theory of causation is a failure). Suchman also introduced the idea of a "social experiment," in which a unique program based on a given theory can be viewed as an independent variable, the introduction of which to a social context should produce a predicable dependent variable.

Ever since Suchman's (1967) introduction of the ideas of theory failure and program failure, a substantial literature has emerged on the methodology of program evaluation (Bennett & Lumsdaine, 1975; Cook & Campbell, 1979; Rossi & Freeman, 1985, 1993). However, nearly all of these methodological paradigms are based on a multivariate model. Alford (1998) outlined that research and evaluation in the social sciences can be done according to one of the three following paradigms:

1. the "multivariate" paradigm, which is established through data, in which the units of analysis are variables and the observer is neutral, and which results in explanation
2. the "interpretive" paradigm, which is established through observation, in which the unit of analysis is interaction and the observer is a participant, and which results in insight or understanding
3. the "historical" paradigm, which is established through events, in which the units of analysis are events and the observer is a spectator, and which results in a narrative account.

I take the position that policy research or policy analysis is better carried out through historical or interpretive paradigms than through multivariate designs. The only time multivariate designs are appropriate is when there are clear measures of a nation's productivity, dependency ratio, and indicators of the well-being of its population. Thus, the first two chapters of this book were based on a multivariate paradigm; however, theories of redistribution (as outlined in chapters 3 and 4) do not lend themselves to a multivariate paradigm. Suchman's (1967) notion of a "social experiment" often lacks replicability when applied to national policies, and without replicability a policy (which contains many unreplicable interactions or historical events) cannot and must not be thought of as an independent variable.

I illustrate this point through the examples of the New Deal in America and Bismarck's social insurance programs in Germany. The programs had the following characteristics:

- Bismarck's program was pre-emptive policy making, whereas the New Deal was situational.
- Both programs were planned as Keynesian welfare states (although the German programs were instituted before Keynes gave it his blessing).
- The German program tended toward institutional policy making, whereas the U.S. program tended toward residual policy making.
- Both programs were designed to have manifest and latent beneficiaries.

- Germany was designed to be a social security state, and the United States was designed to be a positive state.
- Germany provides a clear example of sharing surplus, and the United States is an example of a marketing-surplus orientation.

None of these policies lends itself to assessment by a multivariate model.

Policy analysis, thus, more easily follows a historical paradigm, as Alford (1998) would call it. The interpretive paradigm also is appropriate at times, because policy making involves many culturally bound interactions that need to be deciphered. Forcing policy analysis to a multivariate design, when the variables are neither theoretically grounded nor uniform in measurement gives an appearance of science but does not offer a clear explanation of cause and effect sequences. (See Chatterjee & Sinclair, in press, for a review of methods of policy.)

Social Policy as Social Experiment

Given the position at the end of the last section of this chapter—that it is not methodologically desirable to do social policy assessment by quasi-experimental multivariate design—an important question remains: Can social policy be seen as a social experiment?

The answer is an overwhelming "yes!" Given this yes, it is important to see the problems inherent in seeing social policies as social experiments. An experiment requires, at least

- that the experimenter knows what the experimental variable (call it "x") is
- that the experimenter can standardize it (that is, x can be introduced in several settings, and it remains identical in all of these settings)
- that the experimenter can obtain one or several measures (called pretest) about at least one setting (where x is supposed to produce a desired end) before the introduction of x)
- that the experimenter can introduce x to this setting after these pretest measures
- that the experimenter can obtain one or more measures (called posttest, which is identical to the pretest used before) about the setting after the introduction of x
- and that a comparison is then made to see whether the posttest is higher (or lower) than the pretest. If the posttest is higher (or lower), then it can be assumed that this change since the pretest is the result of the experimental variable x.

This form is a "historical before-and-after design."

A better experiment takes place when the experimenter can do all of the steps listed above and in addition, can find a second setting almost identical to the first. In this case, the experimenter also gets some pretests and instead of introducing the experimental variable x, introduces a placebo or nothing. A posttest measure then is obtained about this second setting. If the pretest and posttest measures are about the same in the second setting but not so in the first setting, then the experimenter will have reason to believe that the experimental variable x produced the change in the first setting. This form of experiment, in which two identical settings are used but only one is subjected to x is an "elementary quasi-experimental design."

A further refined experiment is possible when the experimenter can obtain a third and a fourth identical setting. The third setting is not given a pretest, subjected to x, and is then given the same posttest as used in the first two settings. The fourth setting, identical initially to the other three, is not subjected to x at all, but is given a posttest measure only. It is important that all pretest and posttest measures be identical and that all pretest measures are administered in time 1 and all posttest measures are administered in time 2. The reason for not administering a pretest in the third setting is to make sure that the text does not influence the setting. The third and fourth settings are thus tested only once, with a posttest. This form of experiment approaches a Solomon-Four-Group experimental design (Campbell & Stanley, 1963; Solomon, 1949).

Most experiments are variations on these designs (see Rossi & Freeman, 1993). However, there appear to be several factors that are easy to use in physics, chemistry, or psychology experiments, but are difficult to use in large-scale social experiments. The first example is when social policy is thought of as the experimental variable x; it is nearly impossible to find two identical nations, one of which experiences a given social policy and the other does not. Second, it is nearly impossible to standardize social policy, so that an experimenter in social policy can claim that the variable x has been administered in two or more settings. Social policies cannot be standardized.

Thus, the option left to most scholars attempting to assess the effects of social policy is to use the historical before-and-after design. Alternatively, he or she can use a posttest-only design, as I did in chapter 2 assessing the effect of socialist versus capitalist economic policies and their impact on human welfare. In posttest-only design, the experimenter can see the effect of the experimental variable x in a setting that has experienced it and then compare it (that is, the posttest measure from the first setting) with that of a second setting that has not experienced x.

Returning to the idea of social policy execution as a social experiment, it seems that historical before-and-after design or posttest-only designs are more appropriate than designs of more advanced true experiments.

References

Alford, R. A. (1998). *The craft of inquiry*. New York: Oxford University Press.

Barry, N. (1990). *Welfare*. Minneapolis: University of Minnesota Press.

Bartik, T. J. (1991). *Who benefits from state and local economic development policies?* Kalamazoo, MI: W. E. Upjohn Institute for Employment Research.

Bennett, C. A., & Lumsdaine, A. A. (1975). *Evaluation and experiment*. New York: Academic Press.

Berger, P. (1986). *The capitalist revolution*. New York: Basic Books.

Blake, J. (1989). *Family size and achievement*. Berkeley: University of California Press.

Blau, P. (1964). *Exchange and power in social life*. New York: John Wiley & Sons.

Buchanan, J. M. (1968). *The demand and supply of public goods*. Chicago: Rand McNally.

Buchanan, J. M. (1969). *Cost and choice: An inquiry into economic theory*. Chicago: Markham.

Campbell, D. T., & Stanley, J. C. (1963). *Experimental and quasi-experimental designs for research*. Chicago: Rand McNally.

Chatterjee, P. (1996). *Approaches to the welfare state*. Washington, DC: NASW Press.

Chatterjee, P., & Sinclair, J. (in press). The impact of social policy. In J. Midgley, M. Tracy, & M. Livermore (Eds.), *The handbook of social policy*. Thousand Oaks, CA: Sage Publications.

Clotfelter, C.T. (1991). *Who benefits?* Durham, NC: Center for the Study of Philanthropy and Volunteerism.

Cloward, R., & Ohlin, L. (1960). *Delinquency and opportunity*. New York: Free Press.

Cook, T. D., & Campbell, D. T. (1979). *Quasi-experimentation, design, and analysis issues for field settings*. Chicago: Rand McNally.

Dornbusch, R. (1997, November 10). State vs. market in Europe. *Business Week*, pp. 4–5.

Dye, T. R. (1995). *Understanding public policy*. Englewood Cliffs, NJ: Prentice Hall.

Edwards, R. (1993). *Rights at work: Employment relations in the post-union era*. Washington, DC: Brookings Institution.

Esping-Anderson, G. (1990). *The three worlds of welfare capitalism*. Princeton, NJ: Princeton University Press.

Feldstein, P. J. (1994). *Health policy issues*. Ann Arbor, MI: AUPHA/Health Administration Press.

Friedman, M. (1962). Capitalism and freedom. Chicago: The University of Chicago Press.

Furniss, N., & Tilton, T. A. (1977). *The case for the welfare state: From social security to social equality.* Bloomington, IN: Indiana University Press.

Gans, H. (1972). The positive functions of poverty. *American Journal of Sociology, 78,* 275–289.

Gould, A. (1993). *Capitalist welfare systems.* London: Longman.

Gould, W. (1993). *Agenda for reform: The future of employment relationships and the law.* Cambridge, MA: MIT Press.

Heilbronner, R. (1961). *The worldly philosophers.* New York: Simon & Schuster.

Hernandez, D. (1993). *America's children: Resources for family, government, and the economy.* New York: Russell Sage Foundation.

Hirschman, A. O. (1980). *Morality and the social sciences: A durable tension.* Memphis, TN: P. K. Seidman.

Hobhouse, L. T. (1911). *Liberalism.* New York: Holt & Co.

Hobhouse, L. T. (1922). *The elements of social justice.* London: G. Allen & Unwin.

Janowitz, M. (1977). *Social control of the welfare state.* Chicago: University of Chicago Press.

Jessop, B. (1994). Post-Fordism and the state. In A. Amin (Ed.), *Post-Fordism: A reader* (pp. 251–279). Oxford, England: Blackwell.

Korpi, W. (1978). *The working class in welfare capitalism.* London: Routledge & Kegan Paul.

Korpi, W. (1983). *The democratic class struggle.* London: Routledge & Kegan Paul.

Korpi, W. (1989). Power, politics, and state autonomy in the development of social citizenship. *American Sociological Review,* 54, 309–328.

Malinowski, B. (1926). *Crime and custom in savage society.* London: Routledge & Kegan Paul.

Mauss, M. (1990). *The gift: The form and reason for exchange in archaic societies.* New York: W. W. Norton.

McClosky, H., & Zaller, J. (1984). *The American ethos: Public attitudes toward capitalism and democracy.* Cambridge, MA: Harvard University Press.

Mead, L. M. (1997). *The new paternalism.* Washington, DC: Brookings Institution.

Melhado, E. M. (1998, April). Economists, public provision, and the market: Changing values in policy debate. *Journal of Health Politics, Policy, and Law, 23,* 215–263.

Merton, R. (1957). *Social theory and social structure.* Glencoe, IL: Free Press.

Mishra, R. (1984). *The welfare state in crisis.* New York: St. Martin's Press.

Moroney, R. M. (1991). *Social policy & social work.* New York: Aldine de Gruyter.

Moroney, R. M., & Krysik, J. (1998). *Social policy and social work: Critical essays on the welfare state.* New York: Aldine de Gruyter.

Moynihan, D. P. (1969). *Maximum feasible misunderstanding.* New York: Free Press.

Murray, C. (1984). *Losing ground: American social policy, 1950–80.* New York: Basic Books.

Parsons, T. (1951). *The social system.* Glencoe, IL: Free Press.

Petty, T. (1996, April 27). Kohl defends plan to reduce social benefits. *The Plain Dealer* (Cleveland), p. 5.

The politics of unemployment: Europe hits a brick wall (1997, April 5). *Economist, 343,* 21–23.

Rimlinger, G. U. (1971). Welfare policy and industrialization in Europe, America, and Russia. New York: John Wiley & Sons.

Rossi, P., & Freeman, H. (1985). *Evaluation: A systematic approach.* Beverly Hills, CA: Sage Publications.

Rossi, P., & Freeman, H. (1993). *Evaluation: A systematic approach.* Newbury Park, CA: Sage Publicatons.

Sapolsky, H. V., & Finkelstein, S. N. (1977). Blood policy revisited: A new look at "the gift relationship." *Public Interest, 46,* 15–27.

Schlesinger, A. M. (1949). *Paths to the present.* New York: Macmillan.

Schlesinger, A. M., Jr. (1986). *The cycles of American history.* Boston: Houghton-Mifflin.

Schumpeter, J. (1950). *Capitalism, socialism, and democracy.* New York: Harper & Row.

Simmel, G. (1902). The number of members as determining the sociological form of the group. *American Journal of Sociology, 8,* 1–46.

Segal, E. A., & Brzuzy, S. (1998). *Social welfare policy: Programs and practice.* Itasca, IL: F. E. Peacock.

Solomon, R. L. (1949). An extension of control group design. *Psychological Bulletin, 46,* 137–150.

Stouffer, S. A. (Ed.) (1949). *The American soldier: Adjustment during army life* (Vol. 1 in Studies in Social Psychology, World War II). Princeton, NJ: Princeton University Press.

Suchman, E. A. (1967). *Evaluative research.* New York: Russell Sage Foundation.

Tanner M. (1996). *The end of welfare: Fighting poverty in the civil society.* Washington, DC: CATO Institute.

Thomas, W. I. (1923). *The unadjusted girl.* Boston: Little, Brown.

Titmuss, R. M. (1959). *Essays on the welfare state.* New Haven, CT: Yale University Press.

Titmuss, R. M. (1960). *The irresponsible society.* London: Fabian Society.

Titmuss, R. M. (1968). *Commitment to welfare.* New York: Pantheon.

Titmuss, R. M. (1971). *The gift relationship.* New York: Pantheon.

Trattner, W. I. (1977). *From poor law to welfare state.* New York: Free Press.

U.S. Bureau of the Census. (1995). Births to unmarried women and teenage mothers. In *Statistical abstract of the United States 1992.* Washington, DC: U.S. Government Printing Office.

van Wormer, K. (1996). *Social welfare: A world view.* Chicago: Nelson-Hall.

von Bertalanffy, L. (1968). *General system theory: Foundations, development, applications*. New York: G. Braziller.

von Hayek, F. A. (1976). *The mirage of social justice*. Chicago: University of Chicago Press.

von Hayek, F. A. (1978). *The constitution of liberty*. Chicago: University of Chicago Press.

Weber, M. (1946). *From Max Weber*. New York: Oxford University Press.

Wilensky, H., & Lebeaux, C. (1958). *Industrial society and social welfare*. New York: Free Press.

Wilson, D. (1979). *The welfare state in Sweden*. London: Heinemann.

5

Styles of Redistribution 2: Boundary Defining and Rationing

The welfare state has formed with certain boundary defining and rationing systems. These systems evolved sometimes by default and other times by design in various cultural systems. The existing format can be replaced by another format, but no welfare state is possible without some form of boundary defining and rationing.

In the preceding chapter, I showed that social policy formulation is a form of prescription for collective behavior and outlined some major paradigms for describing this type of behavior. This chapter outlines how boundary defining is inherent in nearly all forms of group or collective behavior (Coser, 1956; Forsyth, 1990; Hall, 1966; Merton, 1972; Schutz, 1958); consequently, redistribution also is subject to boundary-defining behavior. Boundary defining is done by one or both of two ways: setting social distance between recipients and nonrecipients and by installing rationing devices. The first method involves asking, Is the recipient socially close or distant (social distance) from the mainstream of society? The second method also translates as a question: How much should the recipient get and should the amount received vary inversely with social distance? The second question can be restated as: If the social distance between the recipients and the mainstream is relatively great, does that mean the provisions made for them will be relatively meager and, conversely, if the same social distance is low, will the provisions be generous? Thus, this chapter focuses on outlining two factors: boundary defining, which creates a hierarchy of recipients, and rationing, which limits the amount of redistribution.

Boundary Defining

Social Policy as a Prescription for Behavior

Understanding social policy as a prescription for behavior departs from traditional definitions of social policy. For example, Titmuss (1968) thought of social policy as ritualized moral transactions between those who are able to fend for themselves and those who cannot do so. In contrast, Kahn (1969) saw social policy as a rational exercise in which certain goals have been determined and in which the strategy to achieve them has been delineated. Lasswell (1970) saw social policy as a problem-oriented effort in which scientific theories are used for problem solving. Moroney (1991) and Moroney and Krysik (1998), citing many other scholars of social policy, described social policy essentially as a form of collective behavior that moves along a continuum from moral to rational–scientific ends. Our definition of social policy as the state's prescription for collective behavior emanates from this continuum. However, I add here that two continuua, not one, guide collective behavior to build and manage a surplus.

An example of nonrational ends dictating policy comes from the arena of U.S. foreign policy between 1949 and 1970. Neither a moral nor a rational end governed U.S. behavior toward communist China and Cuba (although the "evil of communism" was the pretense used to explain much of what the United States did). Rather, emotional responses, which can be termed nonrational ends, governed the behavior of the United States. It was a form of group behavior that reflected a collective denial that a large nation (that is, communist China) existed at all.

Another example comes from a domestic policy conflict in the United States in which prolife groups try to deny women the right to have an abortion. They take a moral position that life is valuable and that once it has formed in a woman's womb, it cannot be terminated. The same groups, however, often support capital punishment in their recommendations on corrections policy or are against programs that could make the quality of life better for children. There does not seem to be any cognitive consistency in supporting the prolife position while opposing programs that improve the quality of life for others, yet those morally conflicting ends have found their way into policy on many levels. Psychodynamic theoreticians have long maintained that many parts of human behavior are not guided by rationality or morality but by certain unconscious or primitive defenses (see Robbins, Chatterjee, & Canda, 1998). One such primitive defense is "identification." Freud himself claimed that such primitive identification is responsible for a great deal of group or collective behavior. Social policy being a form of collective behavior, it is influenced by primitive defenses of the dominant group of a society.

Basically, three dimensions of behavior prescription exist and are illustrated in Figure 5-1: a moral dimension, shown at the top left side of the figure; an amoral–rational dimension, shown at the right side of the figure; and a nonrational dimension, shown at the figure's bottom left. The figure combines the moral dimension of Titmuss (1968) with the rational dimension of Kahn (1969). Social policy emanates from one or more of those dimensions. Policy making influenced by the moral dimension is based on

Figure 5-1.

Social Policy as Prescription for Collective Behavior

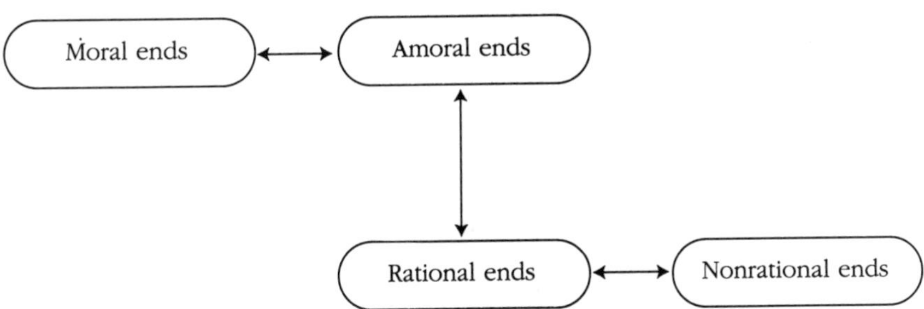

in-group membership and guilt induction; policy making influenced by the amoral–rational dimension is based on reciprocity and expediency; and policy making influenced by the nonrational dimension is based on out-group membership and anxiety generated by out-group members. (Table 5-2 outlines the three dimensions that influence policy making.)

Moral Dimension

In *Mutual Aid* (1902/1955), Kropotkin outlined a classic example of the moral dimension. He claimed that providing humanitarian aid to others in need is universal in all collectivities and that it is human nature to engage in this behavior. Most modern social welfare policy books in England and the United States have been heavily influenced by Kropotkin's position (which was further developed by Titmuss, 1959, 1960). Not sharing the surplus with those who are in need evokes guilt, which is the driving mechanism for behavior.

The "mutuality" (in Mutual Aid), which is the basis of this type of policy making behavior, however, often is interpreted along in-group lines. That is, the person needing assistance is viewed as in or out of such lines of mutuality (Kropotkin, 1902/1955). Sociologists call this interpretation in-group or out-group membership. One common illustration of such in-group or out-group membership is ethnic or tribal identification. When a member of an ethnic or a tribal group is seen as needy of welfare, the group or tribe may see giving that person aid as morally necessary. Not providing aid in such cases is a violation of the definition of mutuality and may generate guilt in other members of the ethnic group or tribe who are in policy-making positions. At other times, citizenship is viewed as the basis of mutuality or in-group behavior. All citizens (and it is better if they are also members of the same tribal or ethnic group as that of the policymakers) are worthy of support or help.

Amoral–Rational Dimension

In this scenario, some form of protection for those in need is sought, or avoidance of some embarrassment or other problem is the reason for social policy (see Oakshott, 1962). This dimension is the classic Bismarckian position, in which either the loyalties of those in need are being bought or the policy is designed to ensure that a needy population is not going to cause a riot or revolution. Roosevelt's New Deal resembled this position: the goal was not to meet the needs of vulnerable populations but to prevent what the vulnerable populations might do. Reciprocity and expediency, not guilt, drove the policy-making behavior. In the amoral–rational dimension, part of the surplus goes to the needy not because of morality, but because such behavior protects the fortunate and the privileged.

Nonrational Dimension

In his classic work, *Group Psychology and the Analysis of the Ego,* Freud (1922) developed the idea that when adults encounter group or community situations, they identify persons in this situation as ego-syntonic (that is, ego-friendly) or ego-dystonic (that is, ego-threatening). In the ego-syntonic situation, people are identified as replacements for either parents or siblings from earlier life; in the ego-dystonic situation, unresolved conflicts or anxieties with family members surface to create problems. Recently, Forsyth (1983) and Stein (1994) used this theory to explain why many apparently nonrational behaviors occur. Behaviorally, neither guilt nor reciprocity is the driving mechanism here; it is what Freudians call transference, which is the formation of a strong like or dislike of a person or a group for unconscious reasons. In collective behavior, the decision to share or not share surplus thus may result from the strong unconscious like or dislike of one group for the demeanor, behavior, or appearance of another.

Two types of identification may occur. Familial identification happens when the person with whom identification occurs represents a family member because of his or her age, demeanor, gender, or other mannerisms. Tribal identification happens when the person with whom identification occurs represents the ethnoracial, ethnolingual, or ethnoreligious group of which one is a member. The original psychodynamic theoreticians assumed that familial and tribal identification are the same, because their clinical observations about this phenomenon took place in ethnically homogenous settings. Modern industrial states often contain diverse ethnic groups, however, some of which often are seen as out-group members.

Members of out-groups who resemble family members in age, gender, or demeanor, may create conflict in the minds of in-group members. This conflict, in turn, calls for maintaining social distance from such individuals; this social distance leads to emotional distance. Thus, the presence or

Figure 5-2.

Two Types of Identification and Their Impact on Social Policy

Tribal identification between policymakers and recipients	Familial identification between policymakers and recipients: Yes	Familial identification between policymakers and recipients: No
Yes	**Moral** (allocation decisions are based on guilt)	**Amoral–Rational** (allocation decisions are based on expediency or reciprocity)
No	**Amoral–Rational** (allocation decisions are based on expediency or reciprocity)	**Nonrational** (allocation decisions are based on anxiety)

absence of familial or tribal identification may generate anxiety or discomfort, which can affect allocation decisions (as illustrated in Figure 5-2).

When members of the policy-making group identify both tribally and familially with members of a target population (that is, those who will receive redistribution), the social policy decisions are likely to have moral overtones (Figure 5-2). When either tribal or familial identification is lacking, then the social policy decisions are likely to be amoral–rational. When no identification exists, the consequent social policy decisions are likely to be nonrational.

Table 5-1 outlines 10 hypothetical situations in which a national culture must decide how to share surplus with either a nondominant group or a group ethnoculturally similar to policymakers. Table 5-2 summarizes the three prescriptions for collective behavior in managing redistribution, and Table 5-3 shows the criteria for entry into and exiting from vulnerable roles.

Table 5-1. Identification and Policy Outcome

NATIONAL CULTURE	DOMINANT GROUPS WHO CONTRIBUTE TO POLICY DECISIONS	GROUPS WHO MAY NEED PART OF SURPLUS	POLICY OVERTONES
South Korea	Korean	Bangladeshi contract laborer	Nonrational or amoral–rational
Germany	German	Turkish contract laborer	Nonrational or amoral–rational
England	White English	Pakistani immigrant	Nonrational or amoral–rational
United States	White American	African American	Nonrational or amoral–rational
Italy	Italian	Albanian immigrant	Nonrational or amoral–rational
South Korea	Korean	Korean	Moral
Germany	German	German	Moral
England	White English	White English	Moral
United States	White American	White American	Moral
Italy	Italian	Italian	Moral

Table 5-2. Three Prescriptions for Managing Surplus

ENDS	DOMAINS	BEHAVIORAL MECHANISM
Moral	Sociological, psychological	Norm of mutual aid Guilt induction Identification
Amoral–rational	Political, economic	Expediency Reciprocity
Nonrational	Sociological, psychological	Exclusion or distancing Absence of identification

From Freud to von Bertalanffy

We have suggested that an important factor influencing redistributionist policymaking is the defense mechanism of positive or negative identification, a Freudian concept. We now suggest that identification (in group or collective settings) is similar to what is called "boundary defining" or "boundary maintenance" in social systems (see Parsons, 1951; Parsons & Bales, 1955) and in general systems theory (von Bertalanffy, 1968). Bales (1955) used this concept to understand group boundaries, Kast and Rosenzweig (1974) and Mintzberg (1993) used it to understand organizational boundaries, and Bacon (1996) and Harvey (1989) used it to understand community boundaries. In psychodynamic theory, the mechanism of identification creates familial and tribal boundaries by dictating who is an "insider" and who is not (that is, an "outsider"). In the fields of macrosociology and anthropology, Merton (1972) showed that the definition of insiders and outsiders performs important group boundary-defining functions. Boundary defining is an important part of human behavior. Policymakers, being human, are subject to boundary-defining behavior, as are their redistributionist policies. The following section outlines how boundary defining is embedded in several structural mechanisms.

Structural Mechanisms for Boundary Defining

Three social mechanisms, both together and independently, create and maintain social boundaries. They are role, stratification, and linguistic themes.

Role as a Boundary-Defining Mechanism

In addition to the roles of citizen, child, and elderly person, people with the following roles may become clients of the welfare state or receive surplus: sick, disabled, mentally ill, former prisoner, addict, unemployed, unskilled, woman, homeless, veteran, and immigrant.

Citizenship Role

As noted earlier, Marshall (1964) and Titmuss (1968) argued that membership in a collectivity should be a sufficient condition to receive any redistribution. They translated "membership in a collectivity" as citizenship in a state, and they argued that citizenship (rather than class) should be a sufficient condition for receiving surplus. This argument also meant that the state should provide certain services itself, such as health care, education, and housing, and that those services should be available to all citizens regardless of class. Kahn and Kamerman (1975) called it the "not for the poor alone" model of the welfare state. Most active-engaged capitalist and active-engaged socialist states have at least a national health service through which basic health care is offered to anyone regardless of class or citizenship (see Esping-Andersen, 1990). Many other active-engaged states also offer pensions for older people who have a work history in the country and income supplements for people who are poor, disabled, chronically ill, and so on. Changing demographic structures, coupled with increased entitlements emanating from citizenship, are turning some of those able and sound welfare states into troubled welfare states (see Figure 1-1).

Citizenship as the only requirement for receiving redistribution is popular among those arguing for equity in most welfare states (see Figure 1-1), whereas those preferring the enhancement of efficiency or a balanced position between equity and efficiency are not so enthusiastic about it (Hill & O'Neill, 1993; Tanner, 1996). It seems that the former group, following in the footsteps of Titmuss (1959, 1960, 1968), defines role boundaries that make receipt of redistribution possible as wide and large as possible, whereas the latter group argues for reduction of those boundaries.

All modern states have legal ways of defining citizenship. Quite often all persons born in the territorial boundaries of a state are citizens by birth. Some states have restrictions on this way of defining citizenship—for example, some states require the parents of a baby born in its territorial limits to be of certain ethnicity or religion—but this trend is declining. In addition, immigrants can acquire citizenship through naturalization. In most modern industrial states, citizenship is obtained (or denied) based on traditions of that state as codified in law.

Often either citizenship or some step toward obtaining it is required before one may participate in a labor market or be a candidate for welfare state benefits. People who have taken those steps may be categorized as "resident alien," "nonresident alien allowed to work temporarily in a given job," or something similar. Thus a series of roles defines the status of noncitizens and, in turn, their eligibility to work or receive benefits. Not all modern states use citizenship as a qualifier for welfare state services, however. For example, several modern industrial states provide access to their national health services for anyone needing it regardless of his or her citizenship status.

Use of citizenship as a condition for labor-force or welfare state participation is a form of rationing. In effect, it reduces the demand for goods and services (the basic packages offered by the welfare state) that are limited in supply. In several wealthy countries with a surplus, a problem arises when domestic workers do not want certain types of jobs. As a result, "guest workers" (as in Germany, the United States, or Korea, for example) may come into the country, legally or illegally, to supply labor. In those cases, the demand-and-supply matrix of a country's labor market conflicts with the country's immigration, labor, or welfare policy. This conflict may result in social policies that are neither moral nor rational and that take on nonrational orientations (see Figure 5-2 and Table 5-1).

Table 5-3. Four Criteria for Entry to and Exit from Vulnerable Roles Requiring Social Policy Response

	DEFINED BY			
ROLE	BIOLOGY	CHRONOLOGY	BEHAVIOR	ASSETS
Child	Yes	Yes	Yes	Maybe
Aged	Yes	Yes	Yes	Maybe
Sick	Yes	No	Yes	Maybe
Sick (mentally)	Maybe	No	Yes	Maybe
Disabled	Yes	No	Yes	Maybe
Disabled (mentally)	Yes	No	Yes	Maybe
Addict	No	No	Yes	Maybe
Unemployed	No	No	Yes	Maybe
Unskilled	No	No	Yes	Maybe
Migrant	No	No	Yes	Maybe
Homeless	No	No	Yes	Yes
Woman	Yes	No	Maybe	Maybe
Soldier	No	No	Yes	No

Child Role

Almost all cultures have a concept of what a child is. In poor countries (as in countries with little surplus) the child role is chronologically much shorter than in rich countries that have a surplus. Even in rich countries, however, stratification contributes to the social construction of child. The higher one's location on the class ladder, the more prolonged is childhood. Conversely, the lower one's position on the class ladder, the less prolonged is childhood. For example, the child role ends at age 17 or 18 for the lower socioeconomic and working classes in rich countries, whereas it does not end until age 22 or older for members of the middle and upper classes.

All rich countries with a surplus attempt to either share or market their surplus in such a way that children can be supported to stay out of the labor market, remain healthy, and get an education. Class and citizenship often shape the success or failure of those efforts. That is, in some rich countries with surplus, poor and noncitizen children (that is, children of some immigrants) do not receive adequate health care or education.

Certain specific issues in relation to the child role need to be pointed out. When the birth rate drops at the higher end of the stratification ladder (as shown in Table 5-4) but not at the lower end, more children will be born in the lower or poverty classes. Because of their placement on the stratification ladder, many of these children are at risk of various problems, including

Table 5-4. Class Positions in Industrial Societies

CLASS	KEY ASSETS	BARGAINS WITH	SOURCE OF INCOME	VULNERABLE WHEN
Upper	capital and knowledge	capacity to employ	capital	industry shifts, capital shifts, human condition
Middle	knowledge and knowledge-able labor	capacity to employ, labor, advise, or manage	salary	knowledge shifts, labor market shifts, human condition
Working	skilled labor	capacity for collective bargaining	wages	obsolescence of skills, labor market shifts, human condition
Lower	unskilled labor	capacity for disruption	wages or welfare state benefits	reduced demand for unskilled labor, human condition

poor education, inadequate health care, increased vulnerability to drug and alcohol abuse, and increased criminal victimization. The children in the middle and upper classes generally are supported by their parents, who obtain the basic necessities of life through the market. The children at the lower end often are supported poorly by their parents or are not supported at all; they require state policy for support.

The child role poses several issues for the state, including issues of child support, child protection, and preparation of children for future participation in society. Child support entails ensuring that children's basic needs are met. At times the state may have to provide support, and at other times the state's family policy or domestic relations policy may require that parents or the family provide support for the child. Child protection may include protecting children from abuse or neglect (sometimes from their own family members); the idea of such protection is relatively new in the industrial states. Child protection also may lead to the construction of a parallel justice system for children, that is, a correctional system that tries to be a surrogate parent to children who committed deviant acts. The technology of child correction often is extremely inadequate, and the lofty goals of child rehabilitation only mean institutionalizing problem children. A large percentage of children so "treated" by the state as surrogate parent are poorly prepared for participation in society.

Aged Role

Similar to the child role, the aged role also poses issues for the state. Such issues involve elderly support, elderly protection, and care for elderly people so they can enjoy the remaining years of their lives. The matter of support for elderly people involves income maintenance policy, the matter of protection involves prevention of abuse, and the matter of care involves either home care or institutionalized care.

Those in the aged role often are targets of support through redistribution. They may receive housing, health care, pensions or other forms of income maintenance. Again, social class and citizenship may affect one's ability to receive redistribution as an aged person. For example, in some countries, including the United States, poor minorities have lower life expectancies and may not live long enough to achieve the aged role. In those cases, state efforts to support the aged reach more people from the upper end of the stratification ladder.

Elderly people from the middle class and upper class are likely to have pensions and retirement benefits from their earlier labor force participation (see Table 5-4). Most of the time their benefits can be purchased from the marketplace. However, in most welfare states both the state and the market support the elderly population (see Cottingham & Ellwood, 1990). One possible reason for this dual support is the labor force participation and political participation of middle- and upper-class elderly people. Because the lower-class population, especially in passive-reluctant welfare states, have lower life expectancies and consequently contribute fewer numbers to the pool of older people, political participation by older middle-, and upper-class people enables policy to be shaped to meet their needs.

However, care and support for elderly people in all industrial societies are reaching crisis situations. Life expectancy in all industrial societies is fairly high for people who have reached age 60—averaging 20 to 24 years beyond that age. Although middle-class people over age 60 may meet their income maintenance needs through their pensions, they almost always take more from social security systems than they put in. The sick role, discussed in the next section, often gets added to the aged role after an individual reaches the age of 70 or 75; the transition of roles leads to escalating health care costs. A great deal of the health care costs for elderly people are incurred in the final two or three years of their lives. In addition, in industrial societies, the elderly population increasingly end up in nursing homes (hospitals in Japan) during the last few years of their lives, a living situation that contributes to the costs of caring for this population. Also, the chances of elder abuse increase substantially when this population becomes fragile, dependent, and vulnerable.

Sick Role

Talcott Parsons (1951) contributed the concept of sick role. Several subsets of this role exist: the temporarily ill (which was the major concern of Parsons), who are expected to get better; the chronically ill, who are not expected to get better; and the mentally ill, about whom knowledge and treatment technologies are inadequate even in rich countries. The temporarily ill may need short-term health care and often can be made into self-sufficient market participants. The chronically ill and the mentally ill more often cannot be cured but must be managed. Depending on their position on the stratification ladder, the quality of their management may vary.

The sick role poses serious problems in all welfare states. In passive-reluctant states, a patchwork exists to respond to the sick role. Those who participate in the labor force can purchase insurance from the marketplace. However, working poor people in secondary labor markets and non-working poor people from the lower socioeconomic classes are often without any health care coverage in passive-reluctant welfare states. In contrast, almost all active-engaged welfare states have some kind of national health services covering their entire population, not just poor people. National health services, however, also have high health care costs, rationing of services, and charges of mismanagement.

Two major questions about the need to respond to the sick role are common in all welfare states:

1. How can the demand for health care be reduced, given that the supply always is limited?
2. What is the most efficient organization for supplying health care?

These questions are discussed later in this book.

An added dimension to the sick role in all industrial societies is the management of the mentally ill role. The term "mentally ill" covers a large spectrum, ranging from those who are unable to operate in society to those who can function in society with help. With regard to those who cannot function in society, state policy must decide whether to provide any care, to provide only custodial care, which will keep them at subsistence levels, or to provide care that keeps them comfortable. The caregiver industry calls for providing comfortable care (and not returning to the "madhouse" tradition of another era), but the cost of comfortable care keeps escalating.

In most, if not all, welfare states there is an increasing tendency to cast the criminal in the sick role. Several social movements have attempted to develop a social definition of "sick" or "mentally ill" roles for criminals of all types (see Liska, 1987). This effort has led to struggles for social policy, because it creates a conflict of social attribution. Should a criminal (as defined by the country's tradition and law) just be punished or punished and rehabilitated? If social policy is to pursue the latter option, then what is the technology for rehabilitation? Also, given limited resources, should rehabilitating criminals have the same priority as education and inoculation of children or pensions for the retiring elderly population? Furthermore, crimes against property and persons are more often committed by people from the lower end of the stratification ladder, and state policy that does not attempt some kind of rehabilitation amounts to a form of class discrimination (see Akers, 1978; Wilson, 1975, 1983, 1997; Wilson & Herrnstein, 1985).

Disabled Role

At least two types of roles exist that are made up of people who are disabled. The first consists of people with physical disability from injury or illness. The second consists of people who are developmentally disabled, who are also known as "mentally retarded." In poor countries they are lifelong dependents on their families. In countries with a surplus, they can become clients of the welfare state, supported by the surplus. Most rich countries have state-funded programs to socially integrate people with disabilities. Here again, class origin may influence how they are managed.

The disabled role in industrial societies may emerge for one or more of the following reasons: an acute sick role leading to disability, which may result from natural causes; an accident or injury not related to work but resulting in disability; a work-related accident or injury leading to disability; and a war- or civil defense–related injury leading to disability. A person with a disability often cannot work or can only participate in the labor force to a limited extent. In addition, work-related injuries often are concentrated among the working and lower classes.

Care for a person with a severe disability may require skilled nurses or nursing homes, which contribute to costs. Often finding caregiving facilities for people with disabilities is problematic, especially if they do not have family resources. Furthermore, managing disability is posing another problem in industrial societies: Who should be faulted or held responsible for this disability? Some members of the legal profession have made determining responsibility a specialty, receiving high compensatory and punitive damages (which are shared by the attorney) for their clients through litigation. Such high awards affect the health professions and insurance industry, among others, and further contribute to cost escalation. Also, some argue that clients never receive the large awards because they are reduced on appeal.

Another category of the disabled consists of people with developmental disabilities, also known as the "mentally handicapped" or "mentally retarded." Like people with mental illnesses, people with developmental disabilities fall along a continuum, from being able to function in society to needing constant care. And state policy options for this group are similar to those for managing people with mental illnesses.

Addict Role

In all societies, some people become dependent on substances such as drugs or alcohol. Their role is that of "addict." In some cultures an addict may be viewed as a person who is sick or disabled, and he or she may attend treatment programs, often at state expense. As with other roles, an addict from the higher end of the class ladder may have greater access to services and welfare state benefits than does someone from the lower end of the stratification ladder.

Several substances can lead to addiction; prominent among them are alcohol and illicit drugs. Social movements in industrial countries have successfully attributed a sick role to the addict, and this effort is comparable to the attribution of the sick role to the criminal. Different addictions are viewed differently: A heroin or cocaine addict may be seen as both criminal and sick, whereas an alcoholic may be seen merely as sick. In most active-engaged welfare states, health services provide treatment for addiction. In passive-reluctant welfare states, alcohol and other addictions, when suffered by people from the middle and upper classes, are seen as health problems, whereas addictions suffered by people from the lower classes are viewed as problems to be handled by the justice system or the penal system (see Wilson, 1997). Social policy toward the addict is influenced, at least in part, by the addict's position on the stratification ladder.

Unemployed Role

Several roles exist among unemployed people, ranging from those who are temporarily unemployed but can re-enter the labor market to those who have become unskilled as a result of changes in the technological base of a society. People may be unskilled and unable to work because they are poor, poorly educated, sick, or developmentally disabled. Some are legal or illegal immigrants, and some are children; these groups form a part of the bottom of the stratification ladder. Given the low value of unskilled labor in wealthy societies and the high cost of turning an unskilled person into a skilled person, the state may opt to distribute surplus to, rather than market surplus to unskilled people. This redistribution may take the form of a grant-in-aid or general relief. In this case, the cost of marketing surplus may be high because the potential future gain from taxing newly skilled workers' incomes may not justify the cost of training them. Controversies exist over whether grants-in-aid to unskilled people should be kept at, below, or slightly above the minimum wage level.

The unemployed role generates several issues for state policy. It calls for income maintenance and in some countries, maintenance of job-related benefits such as health care and contributions to pension funds. Some extremely complex problems emerge in this area, however. For example, as an economy moves from Fordist to post-Fordist, certain job categories become obsolete. For unemployed middle-aged workers (that is, those between ages 40 and 60), this obsolescence creates a crisis because not only their jobs but also that entire category of jobs may be gone forever. In this case, state policy must provide income maintenance as well as training for new jobs. It often is emotionally and psychologically difficult for middle-aged workers who may have been employed in manufacturing jobs to move to service-related jobs or otherwise change careers. Furthermore, the loss of whole job categories is a problem for both the working class and the middle class. State policy may have to confront the fact that although human life expectancy is increasing, the life expectancy of certain job categories is not. As a result, job loss during middle age and the need to re-enter the labor force in a different job category may become common. In those circumstances, the state must coordinate its labor policy with its welfare policy.

Unskilled Role

A person may become unskilled in at least two ways. He or she can be unskilled on entering adulthood, because the family and educational system failed to prepare him or her for labor force participation. Or a person can become unskilled because his or her skills become obsolete in a changing economic environment. When a state develops a policy to serve unskilled people, it usually is biased in favor of people whose skills have become obsolete. This category of unskilled workers, who may be called the "newly unskilled," have capacity for collective bargaining through unions and may also have political representation. Even with the capacity for collective bargaining and political representation, this group may become permanently unemployed as a result of changes in the economy, however. People who are unskilled at the beginning of the adult role often are immigrants or their descendants or members of groups who have been marginalized for a long time. They frequently are not covered by state policy, and social policy toward them ranges from rational to nonrational (see Figure 5-1). The only remedy available to this group is generally the capacity for disruption (see Table 5-4).

Immigrant Role

Immigrant can be another role calling for state intervention. If a person is a legal immigrant under contract to perform jobs that the local working or lower classes would not do, then he or she may receive limited benefits. If a legal immigrant is competing for work that is generally done by native skilled or unskilled labor, then hostilities toward his or her immigrant group may lead to policies denying welfare benefits to that group, ostensibly for lack of citizenship. Finally, illegal immigrants face the worst of all worlds. Often employers in wealthy countries use them for work that no local worker would do, and in rich countries, certain markets (for example, agricultural harvesting, wine making, garment manufacture, and domestic help) have evolved that need and attract both legal and illegal immigrants. Immigrants are often at the very bottom of the stratification ladder, and policies toward them range from amoral–rational to nonrational.

Most industrial societies continue to create a market for unskilled or low-skilled labor, both of which are needed in industry as well as in service-related activities. In the latter, the market for relatively unskilled workers is often the secondary market (that is, a market in which there are no fringe benefits). When an insufficient number of citizen workers fit this category, either because they choose not to take those jobs or the number of native-born people has declined as a result of demographic changes, immigrant workers generally fill these jobs. Passive-reluctant welfare states, for the most part, omit immigrants from any state welfare coverage, and active-engaged welfare states respond to them piecemeal. The problem is that the secondary market in industrial societies has a demand for these workers, but state policy responds to the workers with either disinterest or efforts toward expulsion. Members of this group are no less vulnerable than others in terms of their needs, but they have no capacity for collective bargaining or political representation.

Gender Role

In almost every modern industrial society, the female role (which is a gender-based role) was seen as a vulnerable role (like the child role or the aged role), and social protection is extended to women (Kottak, 1979). However, in most industrial societies, women have acquired the right to participate in the labor force, to vote, and to run for political office. However, women continue to face situations in which they need special protection.

First, some women need protection from their own partners, a situation known as domestic protection. Often the social control agents of the state are lukewarm in their attempts to protect victimized women, and at times the victimized women themselves refuse to take advantage of available protection by not prosecuting their abusers. Second, women are more frequent victims of assaults, muggings, and sexual harassment outside the home. Third, women are often paid less than men even when they do the same work. Fourth, in most welfare states (although not in Sweden) women's claims to social security benefits are often processed as claims of wives or mothers rather than as independent citizens. These circumstances can result from the fact that in many welfare states, the homemaker role is not viewed as labor force participation.

In some industrial societies, there is ambivalence in dealing with guaranteeing equal rights to women. An example of this ambivalence is the Equal Rights Amendment (ERA) to the U.S. Constitution. The ERA was first introduced in the U.S. Congress in 1923 by Alice Paul. The objective was to give women the same protections given to men by the state (see Becker, 1981). Although the ERA passed the House in 1971 and the Senate in 1972, organized opposition contended that formal enactment of the ERA would reduce the protection women receive from traditional institutions such as the family, marriage, and the community (Schlafly, 1977). The opposition prevented the ERA from being ratified by the requisite number of states, and in 1982, the time limit for ratification expired (Mansbridge, 1986).

Homeless Role

The homeless are a newly documented problem in industrial societies, but they are not a new problem. Terms such as "hobo," the "skid-rower," "bum," and other vernacular names have been popular in industrial societies to describe people who makes their homes near a train or bus station, bridge, or viaduct. Homeless people often are addicted to drugs or alcohol, mentally ill, developmentally or physically disabled, or immigrants. Sometimes they are victims of domestic violence or abuse, a situation that is particularly true for women. State policies toward the homeless vary from providing housing to providing tax incentives to voluntary agencies for crisis interventions with the homeless.

Veteran Role

The role of soldier or veteran soldier is a often a consideration for welfare state planning. Most welfare states provide for this role, which is seen as deserving of benefits. Skocpol (1992) documented that the U.S. welfare state really originated with the provision of benefits to the veterans of the Civil War in the 1860s.

Redistribution and Role

Ebaugh (1988) pointed out that roles require rules of entry and exit, which are socially constructed. Thus, entry into a marital role requires some form of pronouncement, ritual, or ceremony, and exit from it also requires at least some form of pronouncement (death or divorce). When certain roles are socially constructed as vulnerable ones that require attention from a state's social policy, they, too, require rules of entry and exit. In modern welfare states, the rules of entry and exit often are codified by law and administered by a rational-bureaucratic organization. One or more of four criteria are used to define entry or exit eligibility: biology, chronology, behavior, and assets. Table 5-3 summarizes how law and bureaucracy operationalize the criteria. In Table 5-3, a "no" answer means that the criterion is not a factor in developing a social policy response. Thus, biology is not a consideration for social policy toward the unskilled and neither is chronology (age). Behavior, however, is a criterion, because the inability of unskilled people to work is a form of behavior, and this behavior needs to be either changed or managed. Furthermore, assets of unskilled people may be a criterion for the state, depending on whether it has a means-tested policy (in which case the possession of assets will be a consideration) or a universalistic policy (in which case possession of assets will not be a consideration).

Boundary Defining by Stratification

Sociologists from Sorokin (1927) to Beeghley (1989) have struggled to understand the concept of social class, which ranges from high (or up) to low (or down) in a hierarchy and which is perhaps the most important form of social stratification that emerges in all industrial societies. Class position is often a single predictor of life conditions and life chances in industrial societies. Table 5-4 summarizes class positions in industrial societies. The fifth column in Table 5-4 lists the vulnerabilities of persons occupying the different class positions. The common vulnerability for members in every class is the human condition, by which I mean conditions such as catastrophic illness, chronic illness, disability, addiction, and accidents and injury, in addition to problems of aging, desertion, or isolation. Even wealthy families may have a mentally retarded child or a daughter who is emotionally isolated. Apart from the problems of the human condition, income-maintenance needs differ by class. The upper class may want support from the state, claiming that its capacity to employ is at stake. Similarly, the middle class may claim that its capacity to advise and manage is at stake, the working class may claim that its capacity for collective bargaining is dysfunctional, and the lower class may claim that there is no demand for its unskilled labor.

Almost all industrial states attempt to respond to the income-maintenance needs of the four class groups (Table 5-4). States range from a sharing-surplus to a marketing-surplus philosophy to meet those needs. They also vary in behavior, as described earlier, from moral to amoral–rational to nonrational. If the state supports the groups from the lower classes, then it is enhancing equity; if it supports the groups from the upper classes, then it is enhancing efficiency (see Figure 1-1). A democratic state tries to do a combination of both. Even in democratic states, however, the balance is often "penny wise and pound foolish" at best. The state's efforts are guided less by concerns for balancing equity and efficiency and more by considerations for who the voters are.

In addition to income-maintenance needs, the state may become concerned about the health, education, housing, safety, and other needs of groups within its political limits. The state's formula for responding to those needs varies. It may direct groups to meet their needs (for health, education, housing, safety, and so forth) at the marketplace and offer anything from no help to grants-in-aid, vouchers, or tax relief. Conversely, the state may produce the needed services under its own auspices and expect those in need to become its clients. Passive-reluctant welfare states (see Figure 1-1) often use grants, vouchers, tax breaks, or a limited (and rationed) package of services on a means-tested basis. In contrast, active-engaged welfare states (again, see Figure 1-1) offer one or more of those grants and services under its own auspices on a universal basis. When the state selects clients for the welfare state based on class, it does so rather explicitly when the clients are from the bottom of the class ladder but more tacitly when they are from the top. There are many examples of such state support to the top echelons of society.

Boundary Defining by Selected Themes

Themes are linguistic templates that offer direction for and set aspirations of human groups. In mercantile cultures, they are also used to create images for or to sell a given product line (for example, "Happiness is your Ford dealer"). Similarly, a real estate developer might use the word "Walden" to sell or popularize a new housing development. In some cases, architects of social policy choose metaphors to make that policy look attractive. Even in those efforts, however, elements of boundary defining and selling ideas across those boundaries exist. Themes are designed for specific audiences in somewhat the same way that market developers and advertisers develop metaphors for different types of actual or potential customers.

Berger and Luckman (1967) pointed out that social realities are constructed by linguistic symbols, which lead to prescription of roles (that is, who should do what in a given situation), which in turn, are structurally supported or not supported by a hierarchy of values. Kluckhohn (1949) established and Rokeach (1970) further developed the idea of hierarchy of values. That is, people differ in their preferences for certain end states (that is, what is desirable). Furthermore, groups (categorized by age, race, social class, or other station in life) also vary in their preferences for end states. Gans (1964) and Banfield (1973) argued that social class is an important determinant of human values. Sontag (1988) pointed out that metaphors chosen by individuals and groups often denote their preferred end states.

The contributions by Banfield (1973), Berger and Luckman (1967), Gans (1964), Kluckhohn (1949), Parsons (1951), Rokeach (1970), Sontag (1988), and Thomas (1923) are the starting point for my premise that in a given cultural system at a given time, selected themes that are popular at that time define styles of redistribution. The selection of the themes is not accidental. Rather, they reflect the preferences and prejudices of the policymakers. Underlying those preferences and prejudices are different hierarchies of values, which in turn, establish different types of social boundaries, thereby denoting how given recipients of redistribution should be treated by society. Some examples of themes follow.

Medical Themes

In *Social Diagnosis* (1917), Mary Richmond pioneered the transfer in American social work of the medical metaphors of diagnosis and treatment to the societal level. Richmond saw society from a biological perspective, and a diagnosis was supposed to yield a judgment of either wellness or illness. In professionalized social work, Gordon Hamilton (1940) built an entire vocabulary for social caseworkers with the words "diagnosis" and "treatment." Erich Fromm (1941, 1955) talked eloquently about "sick" societies creating sick individuals. The Milford Conference report (American Association of Social Workers, 1929) also used the medical metaphor, and Harry Hopkins, the chief architect of the New Deal in the United States used the term "relief" (making an analogy to relief from a situation of illness) to describe the consequences of the disastrous market failure in the United States during the 1930s (Leiby, 1978).

Medical metaphors can create several types of social realities. One is that the entire society is ill and that certain social policies should be used to treat it. Another is that certain population groups are ill (the position of public health agencies and epidemiologists), and they should be either treated or isolated and then treated. When psychodynamic theory was popular, the sick metaphor was commonly applied to people in unskilled and unemployed roles (as outlined in Table 5-3) (see McBroom, 1965). Today, this metaphor is more commonly applied to those in sick (mentally or physically), disabled (mentally or physically), and addict roles. Medical metaphors also legitimize groups who should act as treatment agents in this situation, such as social workers and public health nurses. The treatment agents then become legitimate claimants to state expenditures. Medical metaphors also are extremely useful in marketing surplus, because they stimulate a form of productivity from members of the middle class who serve as caretakers of people suffering from social conditions such as poverty or dysfunctional families (Table 4-10).

Social Problem Theme

The discipline of sociology introduced the theme of a social problem (Merton & Nisbet, 1966). It would appear that the manifest function of a welfare state is to use its surplus to solve social problems. Using a classic text (Merton & Nisbet, 1966) and a modern work (Neubeck, 1991) on social problems, Table 5-5 lists many conditions that seem to qualify as social problems. Neubeck (1991) listed social problems ranging from environmental abuse to health care that Merton and Nisbet (1966) did not include. However, juvenile delinquency did not appear to be a social problem for Neubeck. Divorce and community disorganization did not make his list, either. Urban communities with poverty, crime, delinquency, drug and alcohol abuse, and poor educational opportunities were eminently visible in the United States in 1991, but those problems were not viewed as community disorganization (see MacLeod, 1995; Wilson, 1996). Homelessness did not make the list in

Table 5-5. Comparison of Sociologists' Constructions of Social Problems

MERTON AND NISBET'S VERSION	NEUBECK'S VERSION
MENTAL DISORDERS	MENTAL ILLNESS
Juvenile deliquency	—
Crime	Criminal behavior
Drug addiction	Drug abuse
Alcohol abuse	Alcoholism
Suicide	Suicide
Sexual behavior	—
Population crisis	Population and underdevelopment
Race and ethnic relations	Racism
Family disorganization	Family-related problems
Work and automation	Work
Poverty and disrepute	Economic inequality and poverty
Community disorganization	—
War and disarmament	Militarism and war
—	Environmental abuse
—	Concentration of power
—	Educational opportunities
—	Sexism
—	Ageism
—	Health care

Note: — = Not listed by authors.

Sources: Adapted from the text of Merton, R., & Nisbet, R. (1966). *Contemporary social problems*. New York: Harcourt, Brace, & World; Neubeck, K. J. (1991). *Social problems: A critical approach*. New York: McGraw-Hill.

Table 5-6. Per Capita GDP, Disposable Personal Income, GDP in Chained (1992) Dollars, Disposable Personal Income in Chained (1992) Dollars, and Consumption in Chained (1992) Dollars of U.S. Population, Selected Years, 1960–95

YEAR	PER CAPITA GDP IN DOLLARS	PER CAPITA DISPOSABLE INCOME	PER CAPITA GDP IN CHAINED (1992) DOLLARS	PER CAPITA DISPOSABLE INCOME IN CHAINED (1992) DOLLARS	PER CAPITA CONSUMPTION IN CHAINED (1992) DOLLARS
1960	2,913	2,008	12,512	8,660	7,926
1965	3,700	2,541	14,792	10,292	9,257
1970	5,050	3,545	16,520	12,022	10,717
1975	7,550	5,367	17,896	13,404	11,899
1980	12,226	8,665	20,252	14,813	13,216
1985	17,529	12,587	22,345	16,597	14,954
1990	22,979	16,670	24,559	17,941	16,532
1995	27,541	20,174	25,615	18,757	17,403

SOURCE: U.S. Bureau of the Census. (1996). *Statistical abstract of the United States, 1996* (116th ed.), p. 448. Washington, DC: U.S. Department of Commerce.

either book, nor did problems such as child abuse or domestic violence. According to the lists in Table 5-5, it appears that the number of issues acknowledged as social problems increased substantially between 1966 and 1991.

Table 5-6, however, shows that U.S. prosperity increased substantially at the same time. Between 1960 and 1994, U.S. per capita gross domestic product (GDP) and gross national product almost doubled. The same is true of per capita disposable income and per capita consumption. The table indicates a rather prosperous and wealthy nation, which the United States indeed is. Table 5-7 shows yet another perspective. The percentage of families under the poverty line dropped substantially between 1960 and 1970, and pretty much stayed there. Conversely, the proportion of people under age 19 in the population dropped substantially between 1970 and 1994. In comparison, the proportion of people age 65 or older increased from 9.8 percent in 1970 to 12.7 percent in 1994. The latter trend is also reflected in the median age distribution, which increased from 28.0 in 1970 to 34.0 in 1994. The decline in the proportion of families below the poverty line from 1960 to 1970 can be attributed, at least in part, to the War on Poverty of the 1960s. The percentage subsequently rose only 2.2 percentage points between 1980 and 1994 (during the Reagan–Bush administration). The initial drop between 1960 and 1970 can be attributed to the state's equity (that is,

Table 5-7. Poverty and Age Distribution in U.S. Population, Selected Years, 1960–94

YEAR	% OF FAMILIES BELOW POVERTY LINE	% OF POPULATION AGE 19 OR YOUNGER	% OF POPULATION AGE 65 OR OLDER	MEDIAN AGE OF POPULATION
1960	18.1	—	—	—
1970	10.1	38.3	9.8	28.0
1975	9.7	—	—	—
1980	10.3	32.0	11.3	30.0
1985	11.4	—	—	—
1990	10.7	28.8	12.5	32.8
1994	11.6	28.8	12.7	34.0

NOTES: — = data not available.
SOURCE: U.S. Bureau of Census. (1996). *Statistical abstract of the United States, 1996* (116th ed.), pp. 15 and 476. Washington, DC: U.S. Department of Commerce.

War on Poverty) efforts, but the fact that it stayed relatively low thereafter reflects the state's efficiency efforts.

What are the implications of those trends? Over a 35-year period, the number of recognized social problems increased, the population aged, and the percentage of the population entering the labor force declined. As poverty was reduced, the recognition of other social problems and the demand for their solution increased. At about the same time, the United States moved from a Fordist economy to a post-Fordist economy. In the post-Fordist economy, unskilled jobs and other options for poor people declined, the stigma against illegitimacy diminished, single-parent families were no longer viewed as a social problem, and adolescent pregnancy and parenthood among the lower classes became routine (Wilson, 1997).

A comparable trend occurred in the active-engaged states of Western Europe. Aging populations wanted comfortable retirements, the birth rates dropped, and the state's capacity to tax began to decline. Some of the states became troubled welfare states (see Figure 1-1; see also Evans, 1996a, 1996b; Evans, Paugam, & Prelis, 1995; Hobcraft & Kiernan, 1995). Solving problems began to seem like an elusive dream in the entitlement-oriented, cradle-to-grave welfare states (Atkinson, 1996).

As we approach the 21st century, the theme of social problem solving needs re-examination, for which I offer the following approach:

- The attempt to solve old and new social problems of humankind is a utopian dream. Although it is a noble dream, social problems cannot be solved. Some, such as poverty, addiction, or homelessness, can be reduced. Others, such as aging, illness, and several kinds of dependency, have to be managed. The state, facing a diminishing surplus, needs to find a new formula to manage all social problems, whereby some can be reduced and others will have to be kept from increasing.

- The more prosperous a national culture becomes, the more social problems needing solutions are uncovered, and the demand for "solving" these problems increases. This inclination is probably greater in passive-reluctant states with a marketing-surplus orientation. Schumpeter (1950) observed that such demands occur because of the activities of selected middle-class groups who have a "vested interest in social unrest" (p. 146), because they are the latent beneficiaries of the state's attempt at solving problems (see Table 4-5).
- Managing most social problems can be better accomplished by a family policy, which could monitor such things as adolescent pregnancies (and their possible termination), the capacity of a family to afford a child at any given time, the educational opportunities of children, and so on. The objective of a family policy will be to keep families together, to encourage family planning, to keep parents in families employed in the labor force as much as possible, to help with child care when needed, and to help the family remain socially integrated. In addition, prevention of abuse or neglect of any family member should also be under the policy umbrella. It should be noted that the middle-European welfare states (called "conservative" welfare states by Esping-Andersen, 1990) have such family policies in place (perhaps because of the influence of the Catholic Church), whereas the policies of the Anglo-Saxon countries in general and that of the United States in particular are somewhat antifamily in effect (Esping-Andersen, 1990; Tanner, 1996).

Advocacy and Justice Themes

Two other themes guiding social policy are those of advocacy and justice. At times these themes are used to take sides with vulnerable populations, such as people with mental illness, children, or older people, who may be exploited by predatory groups. In such cases the state sides with a person or a group that is seen as being in a vulnerable role (see Table 5-4) and draws a somewhat protective boundary around them. Advocacy and justice themes often become the foundation of child welfare, mental health, or aging policy. Here the people or group given state protection are seen as highly deserving and in a hierarchy of values are given preference when it comes to deciding whom to protect.

Transaction Themes

Examples of transaction themes in social policy include the New Deal and the Fair Deal in the United States. The first was used in the 1930s during the Great Depression and denoted the beginning of a welfare state in that nation. The second was used after World War II. Scocpol (1992), claimed that the welfare state began in the United States after the Civil War, but she acknowledged that the benefits of this welfare state were reserved only for the veterans of the Civil War and not open to other vulnerable populations. I do not think that the United States after the Civil War was a welfare state, because it was engaged in a very specialized form of reciprocity. This reciprocity began after the Civil War, was centered around pensions and other benefits for those who fought in the Civil War, and ended by the beginning of the 20th century. It should be noted that these benefits did not become the foundation of a welfare state. At about the same time, Bismarck's preemptive social policies were being introduced in Germany, but policymakers in the United States did not take any interest in them until Harry Hopkins, a member of Roosevelt's administration, visited Germany in the 1930s.

The New Deal theme began in 1932 with the pledge of Franklin D. Roosevelt, who, as a presidential nominee, said, "I pledge you, I pledge myself, to a new deal for the American people" (Berkowitz, 1980, 1991). The theme, although intended primarily for the working class, was an inclusive one ("the American people") and attempted to have expansive boundaries that would include nearly everyone who was suffering as a result of the Depression. The theme promised a transaction between the citizens and the state that had not previously existed, and this transaction was to extend the state's protective functions.

The Fair Deal was a promise made by Harry S. Truman as he began his presidency in the late 1940s. He promised a full-employment law; national health insurance; extension of social security to agricultural, domestic, and self-employed workers; public housing; and an increase in minimum wage. Most of those promises were not realized, however. In the United States, the "deal" metaphor is an important one because it fits embedded assumptions of a mercantile culture (Schein, 1992). (A "mercantile culture" refers to a set of learned behaviors in a society in which language associated with sales, marketing, promotion of a product, and consumer sovereignty is important for legitimizing human behavior and exercising social control. Schein gave examples of how for-profit organizations develop a culture of their own. I extend Schein's ideas from the organizational level to the national level.) Both Roosevelt and Truman offered a "deal" to the working classes, the middle classes, and others. The theme covered rather expansive boundaries and covered many roles described in Table 5-3.

Guardianship Theme

This theme forms the basis of social policy in national cultures in which a tradition exists of one social class (usually the upper class; see Table 5-4) behaving as caretakers or guardians of another (usually the lower class). This theme creates a "noblesse oblige" orientation—a view that the lower classes are like dependent children and that they can be a source of social instability unless a small and designated part of the surplus is shared with them. Bismarck's Germany is one clear example of the guardianship theme (see Rimlinger, 1971). Inherent in the guardianship theme may be efforts to pre-empt socialist developments, an objective about which Bismarck was clear (Rimlinger, 1971). I used Bismarck's Germany as an exemplar of pre-emptive social policy in chapter 4 (and Table 4-1).

It has been argued, especially by certain Marxist scholars (Bernstein, 1968; Levine, 1988), that the New Deal, although popularized with transaction themes, was also developed to pre-empt socialist developments in the United States. The argument goes as follows: Roosevelt, despite his sympathies for the masses, was of upper-class origin, was committed to preserving a capitalist democracy, and came from a noblesse oblige–oriented upper echelon of society. Given American culture and its rhetoric of equality, however, transaction metaphors were used because of their better fit with that culture's assumptions.

John Stuart Mill (1900, p. 266) is perhaps the best-known architect of the guardianship theme:

> [T]he lot of the poor, in all things which affect them collectively, should be regulated for them, not by them. They should not be required or encouraged to think for themselves, or give to their own reflection or forecast an influential voice in the determination of their destiny. . . . The rich should be in loco parentis to the poor, guiding and restraining them like children.

The guardianship theme establishes and maintains rather strong and somewhat rigid class boundaries. It does not seem to incorporate the notion that the welfare state may want to promote a form of even limited upward social mobility (see Table 5-4). In contrast, transaction themes imply, at least at the surface level, that the lower economic classes are autonomous actors who are capable of upward social mobility and that at times, upward mobility may be facilitated by the welfare state.

Community as a Theme

The use of the term "community" as a theme is common among the London School writers, such as Titmuss (1959, 1960, 1968, 1974) and Marshall (1964), and with Fabian or communal socialists (see Table 3-2). Even though it is obvious that the modern state cannot be a surrogate community, the use of this theme gives a romantic impression that some *gemeinschaftlich* (community-like) entity will provide certain caregiving functions to at least some of the roles listed in Table 5-4. (Hillary Clinton's "it takes a village" is an example of this kind of theme, a theme she borrowed from the cultures of Western Africa.)

The use of community as a theme may disguise certain types of socialism. Community action, however, is always local action, guided by some form of face-to-face interaction. In contrast, state action is guided by bureaucracies (Weber, 1946). Community action is affective action—sometimes purposive affective action—whereas state action is often prompted by affect-neutral procedures.

A second problem with community as a theme is that state policy may use the standards of one community to set up behavioral requirements or benefit procedures for all communities. In homogeneous societies this approach is not a great problem, but in highly heterogeneous societies, the approach may become a form of oppression. Community as a theme, then, may create false or inappropriate boundaries in social policy.

A potential third problem also exists with using the theme of community, and it is likely in state-sponsored housing. Architects of state-sponsored housing may want to call their efforts "community building," which in reality leads to "ghetto building" (See the appendix, which outlines this continuum between a community and a ghetto). In such cases, coalitions of government bureaucrats, entrepreneurs from the middle class, and other interest groups claim that they are engaged in "community building." When the term "community" is used more as an advertising logo, it serves as camouflage for forcing certain types of housing on poor people, which they did not participate in developing and in which they are not likely to develop any ownership rights.

Community as a theme is popular in social work practice, and it can be used in practice with individuals, when a community is viewed as a reference groups (that is, a group that prescribes the behavior of an individual and with which an individual identifies). It is also appropriate in the practice of community organization and community development. However, it may pose one or all three of the problems discussed when used in the development of state policy.

War as a Theme

A militaristic theme was used in the United States during the Great Society days of Lyndon Johnson; it was called the "War on Poverty." It was used again to develop drug and alcohol policy, as the "War on Drugs" that Richard Nixon declared. The war theme creates solidarity and sounds like a call for national unity. The theme establishes an our-nation-versus-evil-outsiders dichotomy and sends a message that the entire population is expected to lend its support and loyalty. The source of the problem is usually described as outsiders literally "invading" sacred national territories. At times it also is a call for solidarity against treasonous insiders who are creating a market for certain "evil" artifacts. Furthermore, the theme can be used to designate deviant insiders as persons guilty of treason or to justify restrictive changes in laws or policy, "for the good of the war effort."

Dysfunction Themes

A famous example of the dysfunction theme is Daniel P. Moynihan's *The Negro Family: A Case for National Action* (1965). In this monograph, Moynihan outlined why so many social problems existed in the inner-city black communities of the United States, why the black families in American inner cities were dysfunctional, and why well-thought-out national policies were needed to "solve" these problems.

Many scholars, especially black scholars, objected to this monograph (see Billingsley, 1968). They took the position that the monograph "labeled" black families or that the book did not see how they adapted to hostile environments. Social workers moved from looking at the "deficits" of a community to looking at the community's "assets," which could be used to bolster its strength (Robbins et al., 1998). The unpopularity of the dysfunction theme, coupled with the demise of the War on Poverty policies, led to almost no action on black family breakdown in the inner cities of the United States. Murray (1984) argued that U.S. social policy, which was a combination of either benign inaction or a basically antifamily social policy, had made the problem worse.

Perhaps the lesson learned from this example is that dysfunction themes may clearly designate a target population needing some kind of social policy. However, a clear definition of a problem or target population does not mean that the theme will be politically acceptable. The boundaries defined here clearly emerge and are similar to the guardianship theme discussed earlier: "They," who are target of action, are pitted against "us," the sponsors of action. They become the wards, and we emerge as guardians.

Empowerment Themes

Many social workers use the term "empowerment" to describe their activities (Gutierrez & Ortega, 1991; Lee, 1994; Solomon, 1976). The term usually means helping people gain control over their lives. The Great Society programs used the theme (Keating, Rasey, & Krumholz, 1990), and national social policy in the United States during the 1990s has used this theme for public housing development (Silver, 1990).

Management Themes

Management themes have become popular; in some cases, they are replacing the social problem-solving theme. The 20th century began with two very important movements: the scientific charity movement (Trattner, 1979) and the scientific management movement (see Taylor, 1911). The first movement was an industrial society's effort to use science to deal with conditions such as dependency, marginality, and vulnerability. The second was the same society's effort to find scientific ways to enhance profit or make organizations effective, efficient, and productive. Now it seems as though a tacit consensus has emerged that social problem solving is not a useful theme because problems cannot be "solved" like math or scientific problems. Some problems, such as poverty, addiction, and infant mortality, can be reduced. Others, such as aging, developmental disability, or illness, have to be "managed."

Conspiracy Themes

Regulating the Poor, a celebrated work by Piven and Cloward (1971), argued that the state uses labor policy as a way to regulate the flow of labor. In times of economic expansion, programs of poverty relief contract, ensuring a supply of labor. In times of economic hardship, the state placates the poor by giving them public aid. Piven and Cloward's work gives the impression that a "conspiratorial state" exists that regulates labor supply. This "conspiratorial state' has no concern for poor people, makes policy affecting them from a cold and distant position, and manipulates poor people as if they were lifeless beings. However, developing labor force policy is a legitimate state function—it is part of protecting liberty by enforcing contracts and attaining full employment (Table 3-5), and there is nothing duplicitous about this form of behavior on the part of the state.

Rationing

A basic axiom in elementary economics is that consequences result when the demand for certain goods or services does not equal the supply. Economists use this axiom, at least in part, to develop theories of pricing. Sociologists and social psychologists who are proponents of exchange theory use this axiom to understand actions of individual people and groups. Almost universally, surplus in rich societies is not shared by determining how much surplus exists and how it can be divided into target populations. Rather, it is determined by a social construction both of the target populations' need and of how the surplus can meet that need. This social construction of need is "demand," and the portion of the surplus used by the state to meet this demand is "supply." The result is rationing. The effects of such rationing can be seen in the national health services of England, Denmark, the Netherlands, and other Western European countries. In a way, such rationing also is present in nearly every HMO in the United States. In both cases, either the nation or the organization promises to meet all the health needs of people who are their members in exchange for a fixed amount of taxes or health insurance premiums. In health care delivery, the national health service or the HMO is expected to provide almost unlimited care. If we apply the word "fixed" to supply, and "unlimited" to demand, then we see a condition in which fixed supply faces unlimited demand. The result is some kind of rationing of services to reduce demand.

Rationing is achieved sometimes by design and sometimes by default. For example, creating a long waiting list discourages certain users. Certain forms of treatment options may not be offered, or a health practitioner may need a committee to approve certain procedures. Chatterjee (1996); Coulton, Rosenberg, and Yankey (1981); and Lipsky (1980) have documented numerous rationing devices in the welfare state.

My central point, however, is not just about rationing health care within the welfare state. It is that all welfare state services—income supplements, pensions, child allowances, health care, housing, and even education—face the demand-and-supply matrix.

Social Policy and Other Policies

Social policy decisions also need to be synchronized with other policies, such as those governing labor, housing, education, health, fiscal matters, corrections, and immigration. All those policies are involved in using surplus. Minimum wage, child labor laws, parental leave, the right to collective bargaining, exposure to hazardous materials, and work-related injuries, for example, all relate to labor policy yet have an effect on social policy. Similarly, matters such as whether immigrants should be allowed to work may fall under immigration policy, but they affect labor and social policy. Social policy thus has tributaries from almost all other policy spheres.

Summary

Given the existence of surplus, social policy has been defined as a form of behavior prescription for dispensing surplus. The psychological underpinning of the decision makers who create social policy that prescribes the behavior ranges from moral to amoral–rational to nonrational. Class, citizenship role, and other roles are factors that influence the dispensation of surplus. Although the purpose of directing surplus to various groups is to solve social problems, those problems are easier to manage than to solve. Again, two ways exist to manage social problems: sharing surplus and marketing surplus. Each management philosophy carries its own consequences.

References

Akers, R. J. (1978). *Deviant behavior.* Belmont, CA: Wadsworth.

Atkinson, A. B. (1996). *Incomes and the welfare state: Essays in Britain and Europe.* Cambridge, England: Cambridge University Press.

American Association of Social Workers. (1929). *Social casework: Generic and specific—A report of the Milford Conference.* New York: American Association of Social Workers.

Bacon, J. (1996). *Life lines.* New York: Oxford University Press.

Bales, R. F. (1955). How people interact in conferences. *Scientific American, 192*(3), 31–35.

Banfield, E. (1973). *The unheavenly city.* Boston: Little, Brown.

Barlett, D. L., & Steele, J. B. (1998, November 9). Corporate Welfare. *Time,* pp. 36–54.

Becker, S. D. (1981). *Origin of the Equal Rights Amendment.* Westport, CT: Greenwood Press.

Beeghley, L. (1989). *The structure of social stratification in the United States.* Boston: Allyn & Bacon.

Berger, P., & Luckman, T. (1967). *The social construction of reality.* New York: Doubleday.

Berkowitz, E. (1980). *Creating the welfare state: The political economy of twentieth century reform.* New York: Praeger.

Berkowitz, E. (1991). *America's welfare state: From Roosevelt to Reagan.* Baltimore: Johns Hopkins University Press.

Bernstein, B. J. (1968). The New Deal: The conservative achievements of liberal reform. In B. J. Bernstein (Ed.), *Towards a new past: Dissenting essays in American history* (pp. 263–288). New York: Pantheon.

Billingsley, A. (1968). *Black families in white America.* Englewood-Cliffs, NJ: Prentice Hall.

Chatterjee, P. (1996). *Approaches to the welfare state.* Washington, DC: NASW Press.

Coser, L. (1956). *The functions of social conflict.* New York: Free Press.

Cottingham, P., & Ellwood, D. T. (1990). *Welfare policy for the 1990s.* Cambridge, MA: Harvard University Press.

Coulton, C. J., Rosenberg, M. L., & Yankey, J. (1981). Scarcity and the rationing of services. *Public Welfare, 39*(3), 15–21.

Ebaugh, H. (1988). *Becoming an EX: The process of the role exit.* Chicago: University of Chicago.

Esping-Andersen, G. (1990). *The three worlds of welfare capitalism*. Princeton, NJ: Princeton University Press.

Evans, M. (1996a). *Families on the dole in Britain, France, and Germany.* London: London School of Economics and Political Science.

Evans, M. (1996b). *Means-testing the unemployed in Britain, France, and Germany.* London: London School of Economics and Political Science.

Evans, M., Paugam, S., & Prelis, J. A. (1995). *Chunnel vision: Poverty, social exclusion, and the debate on social welfare in France and Britain.* London: London School of Economics and Political Science.

Forsyth, D. (1983). *Introduction to group dynamics*. Monterey, CA: Brooks/Cole.

Forsyth, D. (1990). *Group dynamics.* Newbury Park, CA: Sage Publications.

Freud, S. (1922). *Group psychology and the analysis of the ego.* London: Hogarth.

Fromm, E. (1941). *Escape from freedom*. New York: Farrar & Rinehart.

Fromm, E. (1955). *The sane society*. New York: Rinehart.

Gans, H. (1964). *The urban villagers.* New York: Free Press.

Gutierrez, L. M., & Ortega, R. (1991). Developing methods to empower Latinos: The importance of groups. *Social Work with Groups, 14*(2), 23–43.

Hall, E. T. (1966). *The hidden dimension.* New York: Doubleday.

Hamilton, G. (1940). *Theory and practice of social casework.* New York: Columbia University Press.

Harvey, D. L. (1989). *Potter addition.* New York: Aldine de Gruyter.

Hill, M. A., & O'Neill, J. (1993). *Underclass behaviors in the United States.* New York: Baruch College of the City University of New York.

Hobcraft, J., & Kiernan, K. (1995). *Becoming a parent in Europe.* London: London School of Economics and Political Science.

Kahn, A. (1969). *Theory and practice of social planning.* New York: Russell Sage Foundation.

Kahn, A., & Kamerman, S. B. (1975). *Not for the poor alone: European social services.* Philadelphia: Temple University Press.

Kast, F. E., & Rosenzweig, J. E. (1974). *Organization and management: A systems approach.* New York: McGraw-Hill.

Keating, W. D., Rasey, K. P., & Krumholz, N. (1990). Community development corporations in the United States: Their role in housing and urban redevelopment. In W. VanVliet & J. Van Weesep (Eds.), *Government and housing* (pp. 206–218). Newbury Park, CA: Sage Publications.

Kluckhohn, C. (1949). *Mirror for man.* New York: McGraw-Hill.

Kropotkin, P. (1955). *Mutual aid.* Boston: Porter Sargent. (Original work published 1902)

Lasswell, H. (1970). The emerging conception of the policy sciences. *Policy Sciences,* pp. 3–14.

Lee, J. (1994). *The empowerment approach to social work practice.* New York: Columbia University Press.

Leiby, J. (1978). *A history of social welfare and social work in the United States.* New York: Columbia University Press.

Levine, R. (1988). *Class struggle and the New Deal.* Lawrence: University Press of Kansas.

Lipsky, M. (1980). *Street-level bureaucracy: Dilemmas of the individual in public services.* New York: Russell Sage Foundation.

Liska, A. E. (1987). *Perspectives on deviance.* Englewood Cliffs, NJ: Prentice Hall.

MacLeod, J. (1995). *Ain't no makin' it: Aspirations and attainment in a low-income neighborhood.* Boulder, CO: Westview Press.

Mansbridge, J. (1986). Why we lost the ERA. Chicago: University of Chicago Press.

Marshall, T. H. (1964). *Class, citizenship, and social development.* New York: Anchor Books.

McBroom, E. (1965). Helping AFDC families: A comparative study. *Social Service Review, 39,* 390–398.

Merton, R. K. (1972). Insiders and outsiders: A chapter in the sociology of knowledge. *American Journal of Sociology, 78,* 9–47.

Merton, R., & Nisbet, R. (1966). *Contemporary social problems.* New York: Harcourt, Brace, & World.

Mill, J. S. (1900). *Principles of political economy.* New York: Colonial Press.

Mintzberg, H. (1993). *Structure in fives.* Englewood Cliffs, NJ: Prentice Hall.

Moroney, R. M. (1991). *Social policy and social work.* New York: Aldine de Gruyter.

Moroney, R. M., & Krysik, J. (1998). *Social policy and social work.* New York: Aldine de Gruyter.

Moynihan, D. P. (1965). *The Negro family: A case for national action.* Washington, DC: U.S. Department of Labor, Office of Policy Planning and Research.

Murray, C. (1984). *Losing ground: American social policy, 1950–80.* New York: Basic Books.

Neubeck, K. J. (1991). *Social problems: A critical approach.* New York: McGraw-Hill.

Oakshott, M. (1962). *Rationalism in politics and other essays.* London: Methuen.

Parsons, T. (1951). The social system. Glencoe, IL: Free Press.

Parsons, T., & Bales, R. F. (1955). *Family, socialization and interaction process.* Glencoe, IL: Free Press.

Piven, F. F., & Cloward, R. (1971). *Regulating the poor.* New York: Pantheon.

Richmond, M. E. (1917). *Social diagnosis.* New York: Russell Sage Foundation.

Rimlinger, G. (1971). *Welfare policy and industrialization in Europe, America, and Russia.* New York: John Wiley & Sons.

Robbins, S., Chatterjee, P., & Canda, E. (1998). *Contemporary human behavior theory.* Boston: Allyn & Bacon.

Rokeach, M. (1970). *The open and the closed mind.* New York: Basic Books.

Schein, E. (1992). *Organizational culture and leadership.* San Francisco: Jossey-Bass.

Schlafly, P. (1977). *The power of the positive woman.* New Rochelle, NY: Arlington House.

Schutz, W. C. (1958). *FIRO: A three-dimensional theory of interpersonal behavior.* New York: Rinehart.

Schumpeter, J. (1950). *Capitalism, socialim, and democracy.* New York: Harper Torch books.

Silver, H. (1990). Privatization, self-help, and public housing—Home ownership in the United States. In W. VanVliet & J. Van Weesep (Eds.), *Government and housing* (pp. 123–140). Newbury Park, CA: Sage Publications.

Skocpol, T. (1992). *Protecting soldiers and mothers.* Cambridge, MA: Harvard University Press.

Solomon, B. (1976). *Black empowerment: Social work in oppressed communities.* New York: Columbia University Press.

Sontag, S. (1988). *AIDS and its metaphors.* New York: Farrar, Straus, Giroux.

Sorokin, P. (1927). *Social mobility.* New York: Harper.

Stein, H. (1994). *Listening deeply.* Boulder, CO: Westview Press.

Tanner, M. (1996). *The end of welfare: Fighting poverty in the civil society.* Washington, DC: CATO Institute.

Taylor, F. W. (1911). *The principles of scientific management.* New York: Harper Torch books.

Thomas, W. I. (1923). *The unadjusted girl.* Boston: Little, Brown.

Titmuss, R. M. (1959). *Essays on the welfare state.* New Haven, CT: Yale University Press.

Titmuss, R. M. (1960). *The irresponsible society.* London: Fabian Society.

Titmuss, R. M. (1968). *Commitment to welfare.* New York: Pantheon.

Titmuss R. M. (1974). *Social policy: An introduction.* New York: Pantheon.

Trattner, W. I. (1979). *From poor law to welfare state: A history of social welfare in America.* New York: Free Press.

U.S. Bureau of the Census. (1996). *Statistical abstract of the United States, 1996* (116th ed.). Washington, DC: U.S. Department of Commerce.

von Bertalanffy, L. (1968). *General systems theory.* New York: Brazilliar.

Weber, M. (1946). *From Max Weber.* New York: Oxford University Press.

Wilson, J. Q. (1975). *Thinking about crime.* New York: Basic Books.

Wilson, J. Q. (1983). *Crime and public policy.* San Francisco: ICS Press.

Wilson, J. Q. (1997). *Moral judgment.* New York: Basic Books.

Wilson, J. Q., & Herrnstein, R. J. (1985). *Crime & human nature.* New York: Simon & Schuster.

Wilson, W. J. (1996). *When work disappears: The world of new urban poor.* New York: Alfred A. Knopf.

6

Lessons Learned in the 20th Century

The welfare state is a fine innovation. However, the experiences from the 20th century have taught us that a new paradigm is needed to secure its place in history. One such paradigm can be the continuum between sharing surplus and marketing surplus, and a well-positioned welfare state should rate somewhere in the middle of the continuum.

The welfare state is unquestionably one of the noblest accomplishments of the 20th century. This century has seen two devastating world wars, a holocaust, nuclear explosions over two highly populated cities, many famines, and many bloody regional wars. It also has seen the end of European colonialism, the collapse of the Communist empire, the demise of apartheid, and the triumph of free market–oriented capitalism.

The entire concept of the welfare state meant a shift from private charity to organized protection by the state. Throughout history, many states have existed in which either the state or the aristocracy gave charity to less fortunate populations. To establish built-in protection at the state level for those populations was indeed a major—and noble—accomplishment. The welfare state has been called "a system of full employment" (Beveridge, 1945); "mature politics" (Eulau, 1962); state-sponsored investment to stimulate consumption, because business has failed to do so (Keynes, 1936, as cited by Heilbronner, 1961, pp. 239–242); the socialist triumph (Schumpeter, 1950); and the rights due to citizenship (Titmuss, 1959). This chapter acknowledges that the welfare state is a major accomplishment of humanity, identifies the elements of this noble accomplishment that remain problematic, and suggests options for correcting them.

To start, one should note that noble as the welfare state is, it is only available in the First World and, in a diminished capacity, in the Second World. For the most part, there are no welfare states in the Third World. It has already been observed that the ability of a state to have a welfare state is heavily dependent on that state's position in a world hierarchy (Chatterjee,

1996). Thus, one problem with the welfare state is its lack of worldwide availability. As we observed in chapter 1, this lack is a result of low productivity in the Third World countries. The problem in Third World countries essentially is one of economic and social development; once economic development occurs, the welfare state becomes possible. A school of thought called "dependency theory" (see Frank, 1969; Furtado, 1970; Lenski, Lenski, & Nolan, 1991; Wallerstein, 1974) argued that the First World countries are rich today because they exploited the Third World countries and that consequently, a redistribution from the First World to the Third World is warranted. I do not think that such a global redistribution is likely to happen, however. It is therefore important to take into account the views of modernization theorists (see Eisenstadt, 1966; Inkeles & Smith, 1974; Parsons, 1971; Rostow, 1962; Skocpol, 1979), who suggested that increased productivity, along with certain types of cultural change (see Midgley, 1995), is needed before organized social protection plans can be developed in the Third World.

The welfare states generate another problem: By providing social protection to their citizens, most of whom may be counted among the local working and middle classes, they create a class boundary between citizens and immigrants. In most modern First World countries, a labor market exists for immigrants from the Second and Third World. Often the immigrants are ineligible for welfare state benefits or are eligible only for limited benefits. In the ever-expanding global economy, some system needs to be worked out so that the immigrant laborers also are covered by a social protection plan.

With these observations about the welfare state in a world system, we now outline the major lessons learned during the 20th century.

Lessons Learned in General

1. *Industrialization is a sufficient condition for the evolution of the welfare state.* During the 20th century, two types of industrialization were observed: capitalist industrialization in the First World and socialist industrialization in the Second World. Both types produced welfare states.

2. *The welfare state relies on one or more styles of redistribution. In practice, it seeks equity.* In chapters 1 and 2, I showed that this axiom is extremely useful. However, a welfare state is not possible when the wealth-generating capacity in its society is weak.

3. *Capitalist industrialism is a better developer of efficiency than is socialist industrialism. Any form of industrialism is a better developer of efficiency than is a preindustrial economy.* For example, one can compare the development of Afghanistan (a Third World country) with that of Turkmenistan and Tajikistan (Second World countries) during the 20th century. The first

country has never been subjected to industrialization of any type, whereas the latter two have been subjected to socialist industrialization. The three countries are ethnolingually somewhat similar and can be assumed to have started from a somewhat similar cultural base. By the 1990s, Kazakstan and Turkmenistan were far ahead of Afghanistan in productivity, welfare state development, and human development index (HDI) ratings. The same holds true for South Korea (a Third World country subjected to capitalist industrialism) and North Korea (a Second World country subjected to socialist industrialism) as well as East Germany (a First World country subjected to socialist industrialism) and West Germany (a First World country subjected to capitalist industrialism). In all these natural experiments, capitalist industrialism was a superior developer of efficiency. The capitalist countries also generate high human development index (HDI) ratings.

4. *Capitalist industrial societies almost invariably create a society with a class hierarchy* (see Table 5-4). *Class-related politics (in which the political strength of the working class may be a crucial question) and the way in which a national culture prioritizes its vulnerable roles* (see Table 5-3) *are factors that influence redistribution.* It does not seem possible that redistribution efforts ever can be freed from political interests. In this regard, sharing surplus (Table 4-10) is a weaker form of social policy, because state policy directs allocations to the political winners first and to the political losers second, if at all. In contrast, marketing surplus is a stronger social policy for the following reasons: One, it does not get the state tied up with heavy entitlements. Second, it fuses the interests of poor people with those of groups from the middle class who are in the poverty business.

5. *A popular trend in the welfare states of the First World, especially in the active-engaged states, has been to promise benefits on the basis of citizenship.* Furthermore, those benefits have been promised as entitlements. Entitlements created difficult conditions in rich First World countries, such as France, Germany, Belgium, and other European First World countries. These difficulties included increasing dependency ratios (see chapter 2), diminishing ability to tax (because the tax rates were already much higher in active-engaged states), and an increasing sense of unfairness among those whose benefits were to be changed. Even left-leaning governments in Great Britain, France, and Germany during the last few years of the 20th century were facing shortages of resources and were looking at possibilities of budget cuts. Helmut Kohl, a leader of substantial stature in Germany, had to admit openly that serious cuts were needed in social welfare (Petty, 1996).

One of the major architects of the entitlement policy was the Fabian socialist Richard M. Titmuss (1959, 1968) in Great Britain and the communal socialists on the European continent (see chapter 3 and Tables 3-2 and 3-3).

Given the problems experienced from universal and citizenship-oriented redistribution, policymakers should explore a reciprocity-oriented benefit structure. L.T. Hobhouse (1911, 1921) proposed this type of policy structure; its application, however, would raise questions about how to manage vulnerable populations who are not part of a reciprocity network. At the end of chapter 7, I propose a plan for dealing with those possibilities.

6. *Regardless of whether redistributionist policies are based on citizenship (and role) or reciprocity (and role), they are distributions resulting from past activities.* As such, they become a part of the state's cost centers. A welfare state also needs to be seriously interested in currently vulnerable populations who are likely to become assets in the future, such as children. Although support for those populations may be part of the state's current cost centers, it can be viewed as an investment in the future. Awareness of this issue has grown, but the future welfare state needs to be more aware of the temporal dimension (present versus future orientation). One way of accomplishing that investment is to prioritize the child role (Table 5-3) as the first claimant of redistribution. A look at the record shows that passive-reluctant welfare states are the worst offenders in this regard. The United States and Japan are far more generous in their provisions for their elderly population, including wealthy elderly people, and are miserly in their provisions for children (Achenbaum, 1993; Battin, 1994).

7. *A two-tiered system of redistribution is clearly visible in most welfare states. What can be appropriately redistributed through these two tiers and who should be the targets of it has not been settled.* For example, many First World countries have instituted a national health service, which may provide basic health care either to people at the bottom of the stratification ladder or to everyone regardless of his or her position on that ladder. The state is the provider in this tier. People needing health care services not readily available through the state-sponsored tier can obtain it from the other, market-driven tier. Often the people using the market-driven tier are from the middle class or higher and use both tiers. In contrast, people from the working class on down use only the state-sponsored tier. Similar issues exist in education and housing. Altough ambivalence can be expressed about this system because it creates one tier for everyone, including the poor, and another tier that excludes the poor, this may be the only system that creates the widest possible redistribution in a market-driven society.

8. *Welfare states' redistributionist policies have not dealt well with indigenous populations.* For example, the Native American groups of North America, the Aboriginal groups of Australia, the Eskimos of North America, and the Maoris of New Zealand are examples of special cultural populations. They are not part of the mainstream stratification system described in Table 5-4. They

lived very differently until their land and other resources were annexed by Europeans. Some of these groups live in specially designated communities, which are variously called "reservations" or "special areas." The Titmuss (1959) solution was to call them citizens of the nation-state. The new solution may entail calling them either "wards of the state" or "citizens." Wards of the state may become citizens, at which time they become part of the reciprocity system described earlier. If they remain wards of the state, however, then their community membership should guide their identity, and their claim for protection should be directed to their individual communities and not to the state. In the latter case, the state can deal only with the communal governments of the wards of the state. The reason for the proposed change is that it is not fair to require culturally different groups to participate in the reciprocity system of an industrial culture.

9. *All people should be encouraged to participate in an asset-building program.* One of the experiences of the 20th century has been the formation of an "underclass" that has no assets. Instead of giving this group entitlements, society should encourage its members to develop assets. People who have assets will have incentive to preserve them, eventually (it is hoped) eliminating the need for dependency on the welfare state.

10. *A great mistake may have been made in removing stigma and other social controls from illegitimacy. In many settings, the inability to control illegitimacy has led to social conditions in which that behavior is routine.* Every effort should be made to develop social control over self-indulgent child bearing and absence of reciprocity with society.

A sad case study emerges when one reviews the conditions of the black underclass communities of the United States. The term "underclass" is attributed to Ken Auletta (1982), although Gunner Myrdal (1944) originally coined the phrase. Whether it is a polite term is debatable, but I think it is appropriate because it describes a population group at the bottom of the class hierarchy shown in Table 5-4. This population is, at best, economically underemployed because its members are unskilled (Table 5-3) and are often in the secondary market. Today that community has a sense of entitlement and feels that the state has an obligation to maintain them and their children (Hill & O'Neill, 1993; Tanner, 1996). Three sets of decisions in these communities—reproductive decisions, family decisions, and decisions related to labor force attachment—are important concerns for welfare policy.

Reproductive Decisions

Increased welfare spending seems to correlate with increased illegitimate births (Bernstam, 1988; Hill & O'Neill, 1993; Ozawa, 1989; Rosenzweig, 1996; Tanner, 1996; U.S. Bureau of the Census, 1996). In contrast, decreased welfare spending seems to reduce illegitimacy (Rector, 1995; Tanner, 1996). Illegitimacy has become commonplace in the black underclass population (Frazier, 1979; Gutman, 1975).

Family Decisions

Increased welfare spending contributes to family abandonment, demasculinization of male family members, and the absence of male role models in black underclass families (Garfinkle & McLanahan, 1986; Moffitt, 1992). The antifamily policies in the United States where only single women with children can receive benefits contributes to the problem.

Labor Force Attachment Decisions

Rational choice theory (Hechter, 1987) holds that if welfare payments are equal to or higher than the wage that is available to members of the underclass, then no incentive to work exists. This proposition has been found to be empirically true (Tienda & Stier, 1991). Most members of the underclass lack the skills to enter even low-level jobs. To be more specific, skills are missing in two areas: performance skills—the ability to do a job—and social skills—the attitudes and work habits that make holding a job possible (see Bane & Ellwood, 1983; Brandon, 1995; Deere, Murphy, & Welch, 1995; O'Neill, Bassi, & Wolf, 1987).

The conditions described above contribute to diminishing returns from welfare spending. The U.S. welfare state, a passive-reluctant state with marketing-surplus policy, has reached that state of diminishing returns.

11. *During the 20th century, several international bodies asked only Third World countries to develop population-control policies. China, a Second World country, developed a population policy that criminalized having children over a certain number.* Having a population policy in the First World countries can be thought of as a violation of citizenship rights. Yet a new social policy on population control will be needed in the future. Unplanned families by poor populations only contribute to their "capacity for disruption," (see Table 5-4), lower the HDI level, and increase human suffering to a level that even the best welfare state cannot alleviate. Granted, even the thought of population control may lead to legal battles, constitutional battles, and human rights problems in the First World countries. Strict policy, however, will be needed to discourage having children without the benefit of marriage (see item 10) and marrying without revealing a source of income. In fact, liberal first-trimester abortion policies may be encouraged and made available on demand throughout the First World.

12. *During the 20th century, no First World country contemplated a demographic policy.* However, some Third World countries, such as Malaysia and

Singapore, which were in the process of capitalist industrialization developed demographic policies. In those two countries the native middle class were marrying later in life (in their late twenties or thirties—late by Third World standards) and having fewer children than other population groups in an around those countries. (See, for example, Alatas, 1997; Government of Malaysia, 1992; Leete, 1996; Peletz, 1996; Sloane, 1998; Wazir-Jahan, 1992.) The leaders of both countries became concerned that this trend might lead to population imbalance and enacted tax incentives to encourage the middle class to marry earlier and have more children. However, in those countries it is often the parents' responsibility to find mates for their young adult children. Consequently, it was not that difficult for the state to assume a parental function by encouraging young people from the middle class to marry and have children. In the First World countries, such a policy would be difficult to carry out, but such a policy may become necessary. For example, in France the birth rate among the middle class is already very low.

My main point is that a demographic policy can monitor whether the bottom echelon of a society (as shown in Table 5-5) is growing faster than the middle. If that circumstance is taking place, then a demographic policy can put corrective measures in place: offer tax relief or tax incentives to the middle class to bring their birth rate to an adequate level.

13. *During the 20th century, policies have been extremely incomplete in their approach to the roles of child and unskilled* (see Table 5-3). *That is, in many cases no investment has been made in children, children's education, and preparing children for becoming skilled adults (and, perhaps, skilled parents).* This lack of investment definitely has been a problem in the United States but is emerging as a problem in some parts of Europe as well. At times, the problem occurs because immigrant populations from the Third World have been marginalized, and their children are thus poorly prepared to become part of the labor force (see Soysal, 1996).

14. *The following items have emerged as redistribution needs for various roles (see Table 5-4): income maintenance, health care, housing, and education.* Income-maintenance needs of people in various roles (Table 5-4) and classes (Table 5-5) are a major concern of the state, as are the availability of health care and housing. Education and employment, as well as their availability, are additional concerns. A further concern is whether and to what extent the state should become or remain a major employer.

Lessons on the Functions of the State

15. *During the 1970s, George and Wilding (1976) proposed four orientations to the state as a redistribution agent (Table 3-1). It seems that this typology*

should have shown six, not four, orientations (Table 3-2). Furthermore, by the end of the century three of George and Wilding's six orientations have been either discredited or discarded, leaving basically three orientations (Table 3-3).

16. *The 20th century has seen the extension of the functions of the state. Of the many original functions (see Table 3-5), the protection function has taken on extended meanings, evolving from protection against external and internal predators to protection against ignorance, ill health, and poverty.* This extension, however, has resulted in two tiers: a first tier, generally managed by the state, and a second tier, generally managed by the market. In most cases, the artifacts in the second tier are superior to those in the first. Equality and justice themes have been introduced to legitimize the new functions of the state. In reality, however, equality and justice have been less relevant to the new functions than protection has.

Like the protection function, the regulation function also took on many forms: regulation of food, medicine, industry, banks and financial institutions, labor and collective bargaining efforts, currency stability, and the movement of capital across international borders. In fact, the regulation function has been tied to the state's protection function, because if the basic protection functions are not met—protection from internal and external threats—and extended—protection from poverty, ill health, illiteracy, and so forth—the regulation function alone would not produce the stability necessary for generating and maintaining a surplus.

Lessons on Styles of Redistribution

17. *Redistribution clearly has emerged as a special form of group behavior.* Earlier, redistribution had been seen only as an ideological prescription. In the 20th century, the growth of knowledge about group behavior led to the recognition that all social policies are forms of group behavior. Several models of this behavior exist, and approximately ten types of group behavior apply to the development of social welfare policy (also called redistribution in this context).

18. *Pre-emptive social policy is preferable to situational social policy because it is likely to avert a great deal of human suffering.* This argument derives from rational choice theory: Preventing damage is always preferable to repairing it. However, pre-emptive social policies have a tendency to become sharing-surplus policy, and I have outlined the problems inherent in that policy in chapter 4 (see Table 4-10).

19. *The work of Joseph Schumpeter (1950) (a rival of John M. Keynes) led to the development of an alternative to the model of redistribution that Keynes*

proposed. The Schumpeterians stressed the importance of reciprocity between the poor or other recipients of welfare and the managers of the state. This new model also stressed private, market-driven approaches to dealing with various forms of human suffering. In chapter 3, I showed how Hobhouse (1911, 1921) also had emphasized this idea.

20. *During the latter half of the 20th century, analyzing welfare policy in terms of the dichotomy "residual versus institutional" evolved and remained popular.*

21. *Both Milton Friedman (1962) and Richard M. Titmuss (1959, 1968) developed models for social policy after the 1950s.* Titmuss remained popular among European policymakers and among social workers in many countries. In contrast, passive-reluctant states were sympathetic to Friedman's version of social policy. The two scholars could be seen as attempting to optimize two different sets of ends: Friedman was optimizing the pursuit of liberty and choice, whereas Titmuss was optimizing equality and justice. Friedman's policies are gaining in popularity.

22. *The concept of manifest and latent beneficiaries (introduced in chapter 4) makes it clear that many types of social policies have both intended and unintended beneficiaries; impact analysis cannot be carried out without knowledge of this factor.* Many debates emerged during this century about how to assess the impact of social policy (Rossi & Freeman, 1993; Suchman, 1967). One important step in impact analysis is the deciphering of the goal of a policy or a program (Cameron & Whetten, 1983; Mager, 1972; Price, 1968, 1972). Often it is assumed that social policies have clearly designated targets.

23. *Furniss and Tilton (1977) described three possible types of state redistribution: the positive state, which provides basic protection functions; the social security state, which provides extended protection functions; and the social welfare state, which provides comprehensive protection functions.*

24. *Esping-Andersen (1990) proposed three types of welfare state regimes: conservative (for example, middle European countries); liberal (such as Anglo-Saxon democracies); and social-democratic (such as Scandinavian countries).* He also used a concept from Marx, commodification, to describe the welfare state and introduced a new concept, *decommodification,* which refers to the ability of a group to live independently of the market structure. Esping-Andersen argued that the liberal states are lowest in decommodification, the conservative states are moderate in decommodification, and the social-democratic states are highest in decommodification. Furthermore, he found an inverse relationship between decommodification and stratification (as described in Table 5-4) in the First World countries.

25. *Schlesinger (1949) and Schlesinger (1986) introduced a typology, liberals versus conservatives, which became a standard tool for analyzing redistribution efforts in certain disciplines.* Liberalism was seen as preoccupation with public issues, with emphases on equality and justice, whereas conservatism was seen as a commitment to private property and privacy issues, with emphases on the free market and the profit motive. Furthermore, liberals seemed to believe that increased spending on social programs would help solve social problems (as well as that social problems have social solutions), whereas the conservatives seemed to believe that the answers to social problems lay in reduced spending and increased commitment to personal responsibility.

26. *Melhado (1998) outlined three models of redistribution: the economic efficiency model, the social conflict model, and the collective welfare model.* Similarly to Esping-Andersen (1990), he argued that the economic efficiency model is based on high commodification.

Sharing Surplus and Marketing Surplus Revisited

This book proposes three new models: pre-emptive versus situational, manifest beneficiaries versus latent beneficiaries, and sharing surplus versus marketing surplus. I discussed the first two in earlier chapters. The third one, I feel, explores a dimension not previously covered in the analysis of social policy.

A story has it that President Truman once asked for policy advice and was told by his economic advisers that on the one hand, he could do this, and on the other, he could do that (Heilbronner, 1962). Truman reportedly answered that he needed a one-handed economist! Truman, who needed policy guidance, wanted clear information about what goals could be set and what policies would get him there. It is my contention that the continuum between sharing surplus and marketing surplus would have solved Truman's dilemma, at least in social welfare policy. This mode of analysis was developed after reviewing the spectrum of social policies that have emerged during the 20th century.

Sharing surplus, a form of social policy prevalent in most of continental Europe (which Esping-Andersen, 1990, would refer to as "conservative" countries) leads to more and more entitlements. Marketing surplus, a form of social policy in which both marginalized populations and their custodians are beneficiaries, is present in some liberal (as Esping-Andersen would call them) countries, and specifically in the United States. It is also present, to some extent, in Britain. The Scandinavian countries, high both in entitlements and in using the middle class as custodian of the unfortunate populations, fall somewhere in the middle, but closer to the sharing-surplus countries.

None of the pure forms are desirable, I would advise President Truman (or anyone else). Unadulterated sharing of surplus leads to relative deprivation, as evidenced by the huge strikes and turmoil in Europe during the late 1990s. It is high on equity but prevents the state from making decisions that facilitate efficiency. Eventually, sharing surplus begins to suffocate productivity. Unadulterated marketing surplus, however, leads to diminishing returns. This form of social policy has many latent beneficiaries, one of which is the middle class, whose political interests become fused with those of certain unfortunate populations. This reason in itself is a reason for diminishing returns because the custodians of welfare are politically powerful and force the state to spend more and more. The result is diminishing returns (see Feldstein, 1994; Rector & Lauber, 1995).

I would further advise Truman that balancing equity and efficiency is desirable; to that end, the United States needs a policy of social control of the professions and the mercantile interests; however; to accomplish those ends, the country needs policy somewhat to the left of marketing surplus. The United States, a passive-reluctant welfare state that has pursued mostly marketing-surplus social policy, has the world's second-highest HDI, has work available for anyone who wants it, and has boosted the confidence of capital holders and organized labor to almost an all-time high. Truman probably would be proud to see that some of the promises of his Fair Deal have been met. Conversely, nations that have pursued a sharing-surplus orientation are locked in public battles over their diminished capacity to deliver what they promised, are experiencing the decreasing confidence of key business groups, and have working classes who are unhappy because there are certain jobs they will not do and because their perks are drying up.

Vulnerable populations remain: Vast Third World populations have no social protection. Many people in the Second World are poorly covered by their social protection plans because the plans cannot deliver what they promise. Even in the First World countries, some groups have no protection. A major challenge is how to extend social protection to the First World populations not covered by welfare state plans. My solution is that it should not be done with welfare. Instead, social protection should be extended by helping those population groups engage in market participation and through population-planning efforts.

Lessons on Themes

Themes set directions and define boundaries; they also mislead. The evidence of these functions is revealed as we review the most commonly used themes in social welfare:

1. *The biological metaphor of illness (that is, "sick society") has been prominent and creates a tendency to medicalize.*
2. *The social problem–solving metaphor is unrealistic.* Many problems cannot be "solved" but must be "managed" instead.
3. "Equality" and "justice" themes are common in social policy formulation. All welfare policy, essentially, is created for social stability and to give social protection. Middle-class values and visions, in essence, guide most welfare state democracies. Guardianship themes, however, are clearly present in settings that have a noblesse oblige tradition. In settings with a liberal tradition (as Esping-Andersen, 1990, and Rimlinger, 1971, view them), equality and justice themes prevail. The use of guardianship themes seems more honest than the use of equality and justice themes.

References

Achenbaum, W. A. (1993). Generational relations in the historical context. In V. Bengston & W. A. Achenbaum (Eds.), *The changing contract across generations* (pp. 114–132). Hawthorne, NY: Aldine de Gruyter.

Alatas, F. S. (1997). *Democracy and authoritanism in Indonesia and Malaysia.* New York: St. Martin's Press.

Auletta, K. (1982). *The underclass.* New York: Random House.

Bane, M. J., & Ellwood, D. (1983). *The dynamics of dependence.* Washington, DC: U.S. Department of Health and Human Services.

Battin, M. (1994). A truce in the age wars? Intergenerational justice and the prudential lifespan solution in health care. In T. R. Marmor, T. M. Smeeding, & V. L. Greene (Eds.), *Economic security and intergenerational justice* (pp. 133–153). Washington, DC: Urban Institute Press.

Bernstam, M. (1988). *Malthus and the evolution of the welfare state: An essay on the second invisible hand* (Working paper E–88–41, 42). Palo Alto, CA: Hoover Institution.

Beveridge, W. H. (1945). *Full employment in a free society.* New York: W. W. Norton.

Brandon, P. (1995). *Jobs taken by mothers moving from welfare to work and the effects of minimum wages on this transition.* Washington, DC: Employment Policies Institute.

Cameron, K., & Whetten, D. A. (1983). *Organizational effectiveness.* New York: Academic Press.

Chatterjee, P. (1996). *Approaches to the welfare state.* Washington, DC: NASW Press.

Deere, D., Murphy, K., & Welch, F. (1995). Sense and nonsense on the minimum wage. *Regulation 18*(1), 47–56.

Eisenstadt, S. N. (1966). *Modernization*. Englewood-Cliffs, NJ: Prentice Hall.

Esping-Andersen, G. (1990). *The three worlds of welfare capitalism*. Princeton, NJ: Princeton University Press.

Eulau, H. (1962). The American welfare state. In J. S. Rouchek (Ed.), *Contemporary political ideologies* (pp. 415–431). Patterson, NJ: Littlefield.

Feldstein, P. J. (1994). *Health policy issues*. Ann Arbor, MI: AUPHA/Health Administration Press.

Frank, A. G. (1969). *Capitalism and underdevelopment in Latin America*. New York: Monthly Review Press.

Frazier, E. F. (1979). *The Negro family in the United States*. New York: Free Press.

Friedman, M. (1962). *Capitalism and freedom*. Chicago: University of Chicago Press.

Furniss, N., & Tilton, T. A. (1977). *The case for the welfare state: From social security to social equality*. Bloomington: Indiana University Press.

Furtado, C. (1970). *Economic development of Latin America*. Cambridge, England: Cambridge University Press.

Garfinkel, I., & McLanahan, S. (1986). *Single mothers and their children*. Washington, DC: Urban Institute.

George, V., & Wilding, P. (1976). *Ideology and social welfare*. London: Routledge.

Government of Malaysia. (1992). *Improvements and developments in the public service*. Kuala Lumpur: National Print Department.

Gutman, H. (1975). *The black family in slavery and freedom*. New York: Pantheon.

Heilbronner, R. L. (1961). *The worldly philosophers*. New York: Simon & Schuster.

Hill, M. A., & O'Neill, J. (1993). *Underclass behaviors in the United States*. New York: Baruch College of the City University of New York.

Hobhouse, L. T. (1911). *Liberalism*. London: Williams & Norgate.

Hobhouse, L. T. (1921). *The elements of social justice*. London: Allen & Unwin.

Inkeles, A., & Smith, D. (1974). *Becoming modern*. Cambridge, MA: Harvard University Press.

Leete, R. (1996). *Malaysia's demographic transition*. Kuala Lumpur: Oxford University Press.

Lenski, G., Lenski, J., & Nolan, P. (1991). *Human societies: An introduction to macrosociology*. New York: McGraw-Hill.

Mager, R. F. (1972). *Goal analysis*. Belmont, CA: Lear Siegler.

Melhado, E. M. (1998, April). Economists, public provision, and the market: Changing values in policy debate. *Journal of Health Politics, Policy, and Law, 23*, 215–263.

Midgley, J. (1995). *Social development.* Thousand Oaks, CA: Sage Publications.

Moffitt, R. (1992, March). Incentive effects of the U.S. welfare system: A review. *Journal of Economic Literature, 30*(1), 1–6.

Myrdal, G. (1944). *An American dilemma.* New York: Harper.

O'Neill, J., Bassi, L., & Wolf, D. (1987). The duration of welfare spells. *Review of Economics and Statistics, 69,* 241–249.

Ozawa, M. (1989). Welfare policies and illegitimate birth rates among adolescents: Analysis of state-by-state data. *Social Work Research & Abstracts, 25*(1), 5–11.

Parsons, T. (1971). *The system of modern societies.* Englewood Cliffs, NJ: Prentice-Hall.

Peletz, M. G. (1996). *Reason and passion.* Berkeley: University of California Press.

Petty, T. (1996, April 27). Kohl defends plan to reduce benefits. *Plain Dealer* (Clevelend), p. 5

Price, J. (1968). *Organizational effectiveness.* Homewood, IL: Irwin.

Price, J. (1972). The study of organizational effectiveness. *Sociological Quarterly, 13,* 3–15.

Rector, R. (1995). The impact of New Jersey's family cap on out-of-wedlock births and abortions. In M. Tanner (Ed.), *The end of welfare: Fighting poverty in the civil society* (pp. 82–83). Washington, DC: CATO Institute.

Rector, R., & Lauber, W. (1995). *America's failed $5.4 trillion war on poverty.* Washington, DC: Heritage Foundation.

Rimlinger, G. (1971). *Welfare policy and industrialization in Europe, America, and Russia.* New York: John Wiley & Sons.

Rosenzweig, M. (1996). *Parental support and AFDC support of young adult women.* Paper presented at a meeting of the National Academy of Sciences, Washington, DC.

Rossi, P., & Freeman, H. (1993). *Evaluation: A systematic approach.* Newbury Park, CA: Sage Publications.

Rostow, W. W. (1962). *The process of economic growth.* New York: W. W. Norton.

Schlesinger, A. M. (1949). *Paths to the present.* New York: Macmillan.

Schlesinger, A. M., Jr. (1986). *The cycles of American history.* Boston: Houghton-Mifflin.

Schumpeter, J. (1950). *Capitalism, socialism, and democracy.* New York: Harper & Row.

Skocpol, T. (1979). *States and social revolutions.* Cambridge, England: Cambridge University Press.

Sloane, P. (1998). *Islam, modernity, and entrepreneurship among the Malays.* New York: St. Martin's Press.

Soysal, Y. (1996). *Limits of citizenship.* Chicago: University of Chicago Press.

Suchman, E. A. (1967). *Evaluative research.* New York: Russell Sage Foundation.

Tanner, M. (1996). *The end of welfare: Fighting poverty in the civil society.* Washington, DC: CATO Institute.

Tienda, M., & Stier, H. (1991). Joblessness and shiftlessness: Labor force activity in Chicago's inner city. In C. Jencks & P. Peterson (Eds.), *The urban underclass* (pp. 135–154). Washington, DC: Brookings Institution.

Titmuss, R. M. (1959). *Essays on the welfare state.* New Haven, CT: Yale University Press.

Titmuss, R. M. (1968). *Commitment to welfare.* New York: Pantheon.

U.S. Bureau of the Census. (1996). Out-of-wedlock births vs. welfare spending: 1995. In M. Tanner (Ed.), *The end of welfare: Fighting poverty in the civil society* (p. 7). Washington, DC: CATO Institute.

Wallerstein, I. (1974). *The modern world system: Capitalist agriculture and the origins of the European world economy in the 16th century.* New York: Academic Press.

Wazir-Jahan, B. K. (1992). *Women and culture: Between Malay Adat and Islam.* Boulder, Co.: Westview Press.

7

Repackaging the Welfare State

> The future paradigm of the welfare state should be based, for the most part, on reciprocity rather than entitlement. The vision of such a state should come from Hobhouse and not Titmuss.

It is appropriate at this time to ask, What are the reasons for the world-wide crisis in the welfare state? How can this crisis be averted, or should it be averted? One convenient way to analyze an organization or a rational bureaucracy is to ask, What are the goals of this organization? Does it have multiple goals or a single goal (Price, 1968, 1972)? Is there a discrepancy between its stated goals and pursued goals (Etzioni, 1964; Mintzberg, 1993)? With these questions in mind, this chapter shows how the welfare state is caught in the pursuit of multiple and sometimes contradictory goals and highlight the discrepancies between its stated goals and the goals it actually pursues.

Barry (1990) and George and Wilding (1976) have labored at length to show how scholars from Adam Smith to John Rawls have had differing visions for the welfare state. Nearly all of them wanted to facilitate one or more of the following ends: freedom, or liberty; justice; equality; and community. The stated goal for the welfare state was to pursue one or more of those ends.

As I have argued throughout this book, however, the actual goal of the welfare state was basically one of protection. At first, the state protected itself and its citizens from outside invaders and within-state criminals. Protection was extended in the postsurplus states to include protection from poverty, ill health, ignorance, homelessness, and abuse. The extended protection goals are seen in policies providing income maintenance, health care, education, housing, and protective services. In the pursuit of extending protection, theme after theme was added to make the simple concept of protection look good and politically appropriate. The themes were loaded with ideas about freedom, liberty, justice, equality, and the like, because these ideas serve as sacred invocations to justify almost any action in Western societies. In sum, the actual goal that the welfare states pursued had more to do with protection than with anything else.

Profit Centers and Cost Centers

Like any other rational bureaucracy, a state can be seen as having cost centers and profit centers. We argue that a state's cost centers cannot (and should not) operate without parity with its profit centers. A lack of parity is precisely what is happening worldwide, both in active-engaged and in passive-reluctant states.

From a function-specific perspective, the modern state's major profit centers are the warfare state and the mercantile state. The warfare state allows the development of a market for the sale of weapons and other war-related artifacts to client states (some in the Third World). This market exists even when the state is not at war. The activities of the warfare state can lead to economic gain for key industries; this gain, in turn, contributes to the state's capacity for taxation. Similarly, the mercantile state encourages key industries and enforces antitrust laws. Even though the mercantile state cannot always fully control all mercantile behaviors within its borders, the behavior of the mercantile state often enhances the state's capacity to tax.

The modern state's major cost centers are the welfare state and the correctional state. In contrast to the warfare and mercantile states, the correctional state and the welfare state do not generate products that could be sold for a profit. The tax base provided by the warfare state and the mercantile state support the welfare state and the correctional state. The profit centers of the state encourage a wealth-building function, whereas the cost centers serve a wealth-reducing function. The only part of the welfare state that contributes to investment in the future is its education and job-training centers. Following the tradition of Schumpeter (1950), the following sections elaborate on what the welfare state is not and what the welfare state is.

What the Welfare State Is Not

The welfare state is not a revolutionary device. It does not call for any fundamental social change in the present social and economic order. At times, it may contribute to some forms of incremental change, but it is basically not an agent for fundamental social change. Rather, it is an agent of the dominant groups in society. The welfare state is not a wealth-redistribution device. Wealth redistribution may take place only after catastrophic events, such as war, major changes in the economy, or revolution. In contrast, the welfare state is an income-transfer device.

The welfare state is not a radical income-transfer device. Given that it is an income transfer device, the income supplements and other in-kind services that the welfare state provides often compare with only the lower level income and services available in the market.

The welfare state is not a vehicle for attaining utopia. Throughout history, people have generated many visions of utopia. Some forms of utopia are attainable in heaven, others after a glorious revolution, and yet others after years of psychotherapy. Eulau (1962) specifically noted that the welfare state is not a utopia but a political compromise that replaced organized charity of an earlier era (that is, voluntary giving of small amounts to supports recipients at the subsistence level). Earlier Schumpeter (1950) had been more emphatic in his position that the welfare state is a bourgeoisie accomplishment and in no way resembled the utopian dreams of communal socialism. The events at the end of the 20th century—only capitalist economies were supporting the welfare state—further support Schumpeter's contention: The welfare state is not a reflection of the dream of communal socialism. Rather it is a device to further support capitalist economies, and it is enabled in alliance with bourgeoisie professions from the middle class.

The welfare state is not a facilitator for attaining either equality or freedom. The attainment of equality and freedom of the working and lower classes was one of the stated goals of the welfare state (Barry, 1990; George & Wilding, 1976). The idea of equality, however, was never made explicit. One may ask, Who is to be equal with whom? Will welfare recipients be equal to market participants? To these questions, the answer is likely to be a resounding no. For the most part, those who fail to participate in the market become clients of the welfare state, who seldom attain equality with market participants. A small contribution to equality can be seen in one area, however: the provision of pensions to older people who retire after many years of market participation. Pension recipients reap benefits from both worlds, the state and the market.

Freedom, or liberty, is hardly attained from welfare state benefits, unless one argues that metaphorically, freedom from poverty or freedom from ill health are the same as protection from poverty or protection from ill health. I argue against the "freedom from" idea because even successful market participants are never really free from becoming poor or falling ill. When successful at the marketplace, however, they are closer to freedom in all its dictionary meanings. Furthermore, dimensions of freedom exist that the welfare state can never cover, such as the freedom to self-actualize. The capitalist welfare states, by their very nature, can pursue neither too much equality, which may destroy the incentive for wealth building, nor too little equality, which may erode the foundations of a democracy.

The welfare state is not an execution of a socialist blueprint. The socialist blueprint called for "to each according to his need" and discouraged entrepreneurship and the market economy. Instead, welfare state benefits, when they flow toward the bottom of the stratification ladder, are designed to prevent social disruption; when they go to the top of the stratification ladder, the benefits promote "the capacity to employ" (see Table 2-4). I propose that the welfare state, in essence, is one of the foundations of capitalist democracy.

The welfare state is not capable of "curing" most social problems. Some social problems, such as aging, disabilities, and mental retardation, cannot be cured or solved by the welfare state. They can be ameliorated, and their occurrence in certain population groups within a given society can perhaps be changed. Other social problems, such as addiction, perhaps cannot be changed without examining how some of the largest drug and alcohol markets are created and how the demand for those substances can be reduced in wealthy countries. Certain metaphors, such as the War on Poverty, represent quixotic ventures against unwinnable wars. Realistically, "the poor will always be with us," and the welfare state can create opportunities whereby poverty reduction, rather than poverty eradication, is possible.

The welfare state is not capable of managing "the revolution in rising expectations." The capitalist market system has created artifacts, services, and consumer goods that are among the best in the world. It is not always possible for the welfare state to make top-of-the-line goods and services available to its clients, including health care and legal services. One can always purchase better legal and health care services in the market than those that are available through the state. Acceptance of this axiom may mean acknowledging that there should be a two-tiered system of providing certain goods and services (a system already in operation in most welfare states) and that the two tiers should make no pretense about being equal. They are not and they cannot be. This axiom exemplifies why the welfare state cannot enhance equality.

The welfare state is not possible without simultaneous wealth building. The welfare state depends first on the ability to create a surplus and then on the ability to maintain it. This surplus, in turn, has several components: taxes on the accumulated capital of the upper class and the corporations, the high income of the middle and working classes (by world standards), and the seasonal income of poor people. For the most part, the welfare state depends on the ability to transfer income from the middle and the working classes (Chatterjee, 1996; Tullock, 1983). It follows that activities that make this income transfer possible need to be supported and perhaps improved. Without expanding the tax base, the only alternative is to reduce welfare state benefits. Expanding the tax base, in turn, has at least two components: (1) economic development in the capitalist tradition (Berger, 1986; Chatterjee, 1996) and (2) a demographic structure in which more cohorts enter the labor market (who can then be taxed) and fewer people enter the client role of the welfare state.

The welfare state is not now, nor can it ever be, without a class bias. Welfare state policies originate either from the upper classes or from the middle classes; in this view, corporations are extensions of upper- and middle-class interests. All welfare policies introduced to date reflect either upper-class (in Germany and Japan, for example) or middle-class (as in Britain, Sweden, and the United States) biases. These biases may appear in the selection of welfare state clients, the way they are treated, and the benefit structures they are offered. In nearly all welfare states, the lower classes often neither contribute to wealth building nor constitute the preferred clients of the welfare state. Stratification (see Table 5-4) thus contributes to social policy and is a factor in the benefit structure of the welfare state. This axiom explains why moral to rational orientations exist (see Figure 5-2) in policymaking for the upper, middle, and working classes and why nonrational policymaking exists toward the lower classes and immigrants, who come in at the bottom of a stratification ladder.

The welfare state is not a good device for reducing poverty. Market participation, especially participation in a capitalist market structure, is an important means of reducing poverty. Again, capitalism has reduced poverty wherever it has been present. Schumpeter (1950) observed long ago that the presence of capitalism eliminates abject poverty or absolute poverty. However, relative poverty cannot be eliminated—only the poverty floor or definition of poverty can be changed. The welfare state does just that in the First World capitalist societies.

What the Welfare State Is

The welfare state is a device to support the existing state. This proposition is a complement to the idea that the welfare state is not a revolutionary device. The welfare state, regardless of who designed it, is a device to support and strengthen the existing state. In this regard, welfare states can be described with a term from general systems theory: equifinality, which means that the final product is the same despite different origins. The final products, capitalist welfare states, have some differences among them, but they are similar when compared with how noncapitalist systems manage welfare functions. Some authors, such as Piven and Cloward (1971, 1977, 1982) have observed that the state coordinates its labor policy with its welfare policy and uses the welfare policy to support the labor market. Rimlinger (1971) also took this position. That coordination, however, does not mean that sinister motives should be attributed to the state, nor does it mean that the state is manipulating the unfortunate poor. It is natural for the state to defend its present structure and integrity, and coordination of labor policy and welfare policy contributes to that defense.

The welfare state is a device to protect certain vulnerable populations (see Table 5-4). For the most part, current welfare state policies range from mostly universal to mostly means-tested. The more universal the social policy, the more dignity it affords the recipients, but the less the ability the state has to control costs (Chatterjee, 1996). If future policy is made so that welfare expenditures can be seen as an investment in the future, then an alternative way of developing social policy exists. In this investment-oriented social policy, all the roles in Table 5-4 can be seen as either capable or not capable of contributing to society in the future. Supporting people who are capable of contributing in the future may be considered an investment, whereas supporting those who are not can be seen as the routine, required costs of a social contract. The following story highlights this proposition.

John D. Rockefeller, after becoming immensely wealthy, took interest in the conditions of poverty in India and in parts of the United States. After substantial deliberation he learned that all his wealth would not alleviate poverty in either country. He gave up the idea of alleviating poverty for a while, went to Chicago, and founded the University of Chicago. Later, with his son John D. Rockefeller, Jr., he also founded The Rockefeller Foundation, a body devoted to philanthropy in selected causes.

The modern welfare state also can use the lesson Rockefeller learned: The state cannot alleviate poverty and thus must have a set and means-tested contribution for helping those who are incapable of market participation. Investing in education (especially of children), however, is an investment in the future and is likely to enhance market participation.

The welfare state is a device for protecting some vulnerable people while giving them dignity. Welfare states often create a list of recipients who are entitled to welfare state benefits (see Table 5-4). Such entitlements give dignity to individual recipients but contribute to escalating costs for the state.

The welfare state is sometimes a device that simultaneously channels benefit packages to certain vulnerable populations and certain industries. I have referred to this multifunctional action as "marketing surplus" (Table 4-10). Although the long-term economic efficiencies of marketing surplus are not yet clear, the short- and long-term political efficiencies are. Marketing-surplus policy creates large numbers of political supporters for the welfare state because the supporters' industries partly depend on state spending.

The welfare state always depends on its profit centers to keep it viable. At any given time, welfare state expenditures depend on what it can transfer from the workforce. Consequently, groups of people who are workforce participants generate wealth, and the state's capacity to tax them supports its profit centers. The state's profit centers, in turn, support the welfare state. It is therefore quite appropriate for the state to engage in behavior that will keep its profit centers active. This behavior may require supporting the upper class, the middle class, and corporations (Table 5-5) at times so that they can retain their "capacity to employ." A large proportion of the state's revenues emanate from the capacity to employ.

The welfare state depends on a demographic structure in which the ratio of persons entering and staying in the labor force must far exceed that of persons dependent on welfare state allocations. This axiom requires a demographic structure in which the birth rate creates continuous cohorts entering the labor force every year as well as an age distribution that is not top-heavy (that is, the number of people over age 65 does not equal or exceed those under age 65). Class-specific birth rates may contribute to a problem here: If the birth rate of the middle and working classes drops while the birth rate of the lower classes remains level or increases, then the state's capacity to tax is in jeopardy. Birth rates patterns such as these will create a lopsided age distribution and strain the ability of the welfare state to provide benefits.

Being dependent on a profit center, the welfare state is somewhat obligated to cater to producers of wealth. Producers of wealth are people with capital and people who are in the labor market. People with capital need some courting to avoid capital flight. People who have knowledge or skills also need some courting so that they have either a moral or a rational view of the state's transfer efforts.

The welfare state is a poor facilitator of justice. We have observed above that market participation is a better facilitator of justice. The entire concept of juvenile justice was introduced to rehabilitate problem children, but it has become a device to manage problem children from the poverty classes. Problem children from the privileged classes, who can be represented by attorneys procured from the market, get better treatment at the hands of the justice system than do poor problem children. Adult middle- and upper-class offenders also receive "superior justice" when represented by attorneys obtained from the marketplace. In contrast offenders from the lower class, who are often represented by public defenders (paid by the state), receive "inferior justice." Although no justice may be worse than poor or inferior justice, the welfare state, at best, can deliver only poor or inferior justice.

The welfare state is a poor surrogate. Having a surplus leads to the emergence of a surrogate state, which means that the state takes on the role of surrogate parent (as in child welfare), surrogate adult child (as in care of elderly people), surrogate mentor (as in job-skills training), or surrogate family member (as in caring for people with illness or disability). Surrogacy was engineered to provide certain protection functions, which expanded with the growth of surplus. The state is not equipped to provide family functions.

The welfare state is a manager of social problems. In chapter 5 and earlier in this chapter, I observed that the welfare state cannot cure most social problems. Instead, the theme of the state as a manager of social problems is more appropriate.

Increasing welfare state spending may lead to diminishing returns. Basic economic theory holds that in certain ventures, there are three stages of return on investment: (1) higher investment yields higher returns, (2) higher investment yields progressively fixed returns, and (3) higher investment yields progressively lower (that is, diminishing) returns. To some extent, this principle applies to welfare state spending. With regard to the welfare state's protection functions, it may be true that higher investment yields higher returns. However, for functions such as providing equality, liberty, justice, or surrogate family, the welfare state's returns are not proportional to investment.

The welfare state is understood differently by different academic disciplines. The discipline of social work, for example, often supports increased welfare state spending. The discipline of economics, however, is interested in understanding how a collectivity engages in the wealth-building process and what effects state redistribution efforts may have. Other disciplines have viewpoints between these two positions. Given this situation, human knowledge building about the welfare state has been fragmented instead of cumulative.

Paradigm Lost in the Welfare State

As we approach the 21st century, the welfare state almost everywhere seems to be in trouble and in need of a paradigm change. It is in trouble because its foundations—including a surplus built by industrialization, a stable demographic structure, and a relative absence of inflation—are shifting. (See chapters 1 and 2 for a discussion of the foundation of the welfare state.) The state needs a paradigm change because the traditional paradigm—at least in the United States—of "let-us-blame-the-conservatives-who-are-against-it" versus "let-us-blame-the-liberals-who-are-for-it" needs an overhaul. Academic disciplines such as social work and interest groups such as labor unions blame conservatives, and other academic disciplines such as business economics, and managers of industries, commerce, and finance blame liberals (see Table 4-8).

If we start with the premise that a civil society needs to provide a social safety net for its young, aged, and other dependent members, then obviously we want to retain the welfare state. Rather, we need to retain what we have come to understand as welfare state functions. However, we also need to retain the foundations that built the welfare state. Thus, we need a paradigm that allows both goals to be accomplished simultaneously.

Toward a New Paradigm

To start, we need social workers who understand and appreciate the principles of economics, macrosociology, and political science. We also need economists who are sympathetic to the need for maintaining welfare functions. We need to break through the traditional disciplinary boundaries of social work, sociology, economics, and other disciplines. Returning to the idea of paradigm change, the following list itemizes the points of departure from the existing paradigm.

- Social workers, under the influence of the London School (that is, George & Wilding, 1976; Marshall, 1964; Titmuss, 1968) suggested that social policy emerges from the values and ideologies of a society (see also Tropman, 1989). This idea is blatantly wrong. Social policy in favor of nonmarket distribution (that is, social welfare) emerges from affluence. Affluence worldwide comes from economic prosperity brought about by industrialization (see Chatterjee, 1996; Esping-Andersen, 1990; Rimlinger, 1971; Schumpeter, 1950; Wilensky, 1975). More specifically, capitalist industrialization is a better vehicle to produce affluence than socialist industrialization (Berger, 1986; Chatterjee, 1996). Given affluence in a nation, ideology is more a justification than a reason for social welfare (Chatterjee, 1996).
- Ideology and values justify who should receive nonmarket distribution. They do not cause social welfare to develop; they are only a means of selecting and ordering the priorities of nonmarket distribution.
- It is important that advocates for nonmarket distribution not only argue that needy people should receive nonmarket distribution but also show some sophistication about the basis of economic productivity and the resources from which nonmarket distributions should take place. Simply stating that "it is sad that there are needy people in rich countries" is not good advocacy. It is better advocacy to show how support for the needy as well as continued wealth building can be accomplished simultaneously. In other words, movement is needed from a guilt-inducing and simplistic orientation to a budget-conscious, continued-prosperity orientation.
- Social policy—specifically, social welfare policy—should be clearly separated from socialism. Again, the main architects of the dominant paradigm of social welfare were Fabian and communal socialists (see Table 3-2), and their vision became the vision of social welfare (see also Pinker, 1979). This vision is still popular in Anglo-American social work. A point of departure from the existing paradigm would be to acknowledge that socialism is not a good wealth-building agent (Berger, 1986) and that its efforts toward nonmarket distribution may even be a problem for the state. The problems with maintaining social welfare programs in

Cuba, Russia, and most of the countries influenced by the former Soviet Union illustrate this point.

- State spending as a solution to all social problems is a mindset of the traditional paradigm. This mindset originated from the New Deal and became popular in many rich countries. It is true that the modern state is a powerful actor in the economic and political arena and that it can have an important role in human welfare. However, increased and continued spending by the state to achieve social welfare ends has its limits. Even with continued and escalated spending, limits exist to what it can accomplish. It cannot be a replacement for the family, a mentor in the community, or a healing agent, no matter how much money it spends. As we depart from the "allocate more funds for social programs" mindset of the traditional paradigm, we need to understand and acknowledge what the state can do well on its own as well as understand that the state can only be a source of support to existing families and communities, not a replacement for them.
- A point of departure must clearly acknowledge the complexity of human nature. The existing paradigm does not accommodate the role of incentives in human behavior. Perhaps this oversight results from the surrogate state's tendency to reduce incentives (such as those for entrepreneurship, self-sufficiency, and voluntary action), whereas the absence of a surrogate state tends to increase them. A new paradigm must incorporate ways for a helping process to increase the self-sufficiency of the recipients of welfare state redistribution.
- Another point of departure must acknowledge that there are limits to the professionalization of help-givers. Most professions develop from a form of collective bargaining to protect themselves and to draw a boundary around their knowledge structure. However, the professions' public argument generally is that their professionalization would lead to better protection of the public. Likewise, the current mode of professionalization in health care and social welfare has occurred under the pretense of protecting the public, whereas in reality it has protected the professionals themselves and ensured them a secure place in the market. Contrary to popular belief, professionals do not police themselves, and increased professionalization contributes to escalating costs. A new paradigm must not start with an existing commitment to the position that all health and welfare functions must be carried out only by card-carrying professionals. A new paradigm must explore a new form of division of labor in which a clear understanding exists about what roles need professionalization and what roles can be filled by nonprofessionals or paraprofessionals.

- Titmuss (1968) argued that citizenship, rather than social position, should be sufficient reason for being a client of the welfare state. That position was also strongly supported by Marshall (1964). As we approach the 21st century, citizenship-based welfare policies have become an insufficient means for alleviating human misery. Many countries are host to immigrant laborers, contract laborers, "guest" laborers, and other travelers who can find themselves vulnerable in a place where they are not citizens. In the passive-reluctant states, citizenship by itself does not qualify a person to receive all welfare state benefits. For example, health care benefits in those countries have very little to do with citizenship. In most active-engaged welfare states, however, citizenship entitles an individual to a wider range of benefits, of which health care may be one. However, immigrant laborers are often not protected by most safety nets (although in some active-engaged states they can obtain health care).

  A new paradigm should include the provision that people legally engaged in the labor market, even if they are not citizens, should be eligible for welfare state benefits. Translated into moral philosophy, this paradigm says those engaged in reciprocity with the state—that is those legally providing labor to a market within a society are entitled to compensation now and a package of benefits also—should be protected by the safety net provided by the state.

- The traditional paradigm, at least in North American settings, views liberals as supporting social welfare spending and conservatives as opposing it. Although this characterization is partially true, it has become a misleading way of framing social welfare. If we substitute "labor" for "liberals," and "capital" for "conservatives," then the revised position would look like this: Labor groups often support social welfare, whereas capital-holding groups oppose it.

  The real issue behind the debate is that increased social welfare may drive up labor costs, which in turn may increase the costs of a product, leading to reduced profit; in contrast, decreased social welfare reduces labor costs and thus increases profit. In all settings, however, it is in the interest of capital holders to keep labor happy and placated, so that there is no labor trouble and labor more easily becomes productive labor. Bismarck (who was no liberal by any measure) understood this principle, and the goal of his pioneering efforts to build a social welfare program was to keep labor loyal and placated. The point of departure here is that it is in the interest of capital to keep labor placated, so that it can become productive, and that it is in the interest of labor to keep capital locally contained so that jobs are available, and there is no capital flight. A new paradigm would provide a middle ground in which there is no capital flight and no labor trouble.

- The new paradigm must move away from a social problem–solving theme to a social problem–managing theme. I have argued consistently in this book that most social problems cannot be solved. Some can be reduced, and others have to be managed. Management of welfare functions is possible if the objectives are clearly defined and are not allowed to become too lofty (for example, aiming to "cure" all delinquency, "reverse" aging, or declare "war" on poverty). Realistic objectives may include finding employment for the unemployed, making older people comfortable in their own environment, socially integrating disabled people, and helping the unskilled to build labor force attachment. Thus the welfare state needs to move closer to the principles of management by objective, or better yet, management by definable and attainable objectives.

Repackaging the Welfare State

Given the need for paradigm change, how should the basic package be structured? The mission statement directing the repackaged welfare state should rest on the following axiom:

> from each according to his or her productivity, with an ongoing concern for incentives for further productivity, and to each according to his or her basic needs, modified by his or her means to meet them and the state's capacity to transfer.

Translated into objectives, *productivity* can be defined as one's income and *incentives* for further productivity, as a taxation-and-transfer policy that allows the producers of wealth to retain a satisfactory share of what they have produced. *Basic needs* are survival and safety needs, as postulated by Maslow (1968, 1969). Survival needs are income, food, health care, housing, and a capacity to enter the marketplace (that is, education). *Safety needs* are protection from predators of all varieties. All recipients receiving these items through social policy must be means tested. The *state's capacity to transfer* means the absence of any tax revolt from the payers of transfer, coupled with the political legitimacy of a transfer plan. Furthermore, the state's capacity to transfer (that is, the welfare state budget) may also be limited to a fixed ratio of the state's budget.

Legitimization: Not Titmuss but Hobhouse

Any major commitment to a new paradigm needs one or more source of legitimization (Berger & Luckman, 1966; Friedman, 1982). We suggest that the source of legitimization of the repackaged welfare state be Max Weber, not Karl Marx. The new welfare state must be cognizant of Weber's contention that certain types of cultures are conducive to wealth-building, and it should maintain policies that encourage wealth-building activities. Those activities include a commitment not only to a somewhat regulated free market economy but also to the basic human family and the work culture it promotes. As a result, Titmuss and his Fabian socialist dreams should be discarded as a source of legitimization for the welfare state. Instead, the work of Hobhouse (1911, 1921) (see chapter 3) should be used to legitimize the welfare state. A welfare state based on Hobhouse would require a change in redistribution policy from universal entitlements based on citizenship (Titmuss,1968) to particularistic allotments based on reciprocity (Hobhouse). The repackaged welfare state would have a two-tiered system: a top tier for those who are engaged in a reciprocity system, and a means-tested bottom tier for the unskilled or others who receive transfer payments from the state. The top tier should be asset-building for participants—that is, participants in the top tier should be able to build assets through participation. The bottom tier, a below–minimum wage package, should serve poor people.

The repackaged welfare state rests on the ontological assumption that in the affairs of the state, there are few gift relationships. Almost all relationships are exchange relationships. It assumes that human nature is basically Hobbesian and not Marxian. The welfare state becomes possible only when a nation builds a surplus. The dispensation of that surplus must balance the need for providing social protection in a civil society and the need to continue generating a surplus.

References

Barry, N. (1990). *Welfare*. Minneapolis: University of Minnesota Press.

Berger, P. (1986). *The capitalist revolution*. New York: Basic Books.

Berger, P., & Luckman, T. (1966). *The social construction of reality*. Garden City, NY: Doubleday.

Chatterjee, P. (1996). *Approaches to the welfare state*. Washington, DC: NASW Press.

Esping-Andersen, G. (1990). *The three worlds of welfare capitalism*. Princeton, NJ: Princeton University Press.

Etzioni, A. (1964). *Modern organizations*. Englewood-Cliffs, NJ: Prentice Hall.

Eulau, H. (1962). The American welfare state Neither ideology nor welfare. In J. S. Roucek (Ed.), *Contemporary political ideologies* (pp. 415–431). Paterson, NJ: Littlefield, Adams.

Friedman, K. (1982). *Legitimation of social rights and the western welfare state.* Chapel Hill: University of North Carolina Press.

George, V., & Wilding, P. (1976). *Ideology and social welfare.* London: Routledge.

Hobhouse, L. T. (1911). *Liberalism.* London: Williams & Norgate.

Hobhouse, L. T. (1921). *The elements of social justice.* London: Allen & Unwin.

Marshall, T. H. (1964). *Class, citizenship, and social development.* New York: Doubleday.

Maslow, A. H. (1968). *Toward a psychology of being.* New York: Van Nostrand.

Maslow, A. H. (1969). The further reaches of human nature. *Journal of Transpersonal Psychology, 1*(1), 1–9.

Mintzberg, H. (1993). *Structure in fives.* Englewood-Cliffs, NJ: Prentice Hall.

Pinker, R. (1979). *The idea of welfare.* London: Heinemann.

Piven, F. F., & Cloward, R. (1971). *Regulating the poor.* New York: Pantheon.

Piven, F. F., & Cloward, R. (1977). *Poor people's movements: Why they succeed, how they fail.* New York: Pantheon.

Piven, F. F., & Cloward, R. (1982). *The new class war.* New York: Pantheon.

Price, J. (1968). *Organizational effectiveness.* Homewood, IL: Irwin.

Price, J. (1972). The study of organizational effectiveness. *Sociological Quarterly, 13,* 3–15.

Rimlinger, G. (1971). *Welfare policy and industrialization in Europe, America, and Russia.* New York: John Wiley & Sons.

Schumpeter, J. (1950). *Capitalism, socialism, and democracy.* New York: Harper & Row.

Titmuss, R. M. (1968). *Commitment to welfare.* New York: Pantheon.

Tropman, J. E. (1989). *American values and social welfare.* Englewood-Cliffs, NJ: Prentice Hall.

Tullock, G. (1983). *Welfare for the well-to-do.* Dallas: Fisher Institute.

Wilensky, H. (1975). *The welfare state and equality.* Berkeley: University of California Press.

Postscript

Throughout this book, I have argued against any form of socialism, state or communal, as a basis for the modern welfare state. However, that does not mean that I am advocating for the return of laissez faire capitalism. I have made it amply clear that I am advocating for a **regulated** form of capitalism, a form in which state intervention is needed in business practice, banking, currency management, protection of food and medicine, control of inflation or deflation, and reduction of the marginalization of various populations.

Appendix

Program Ideas for the Repackaged Welfare State

Given the objectives developed in this book, the following recommendations are worth considering for the repackaging of the welfare state.

Income Maintenance

Income-maintenance programs should be consolidated under one single department of the state; those programs could include social security and other payments to role occupants from Table 5-4. All income-maintenance programs can be two-tiered: a means-tested basic tier and an additional, asset-building tier to which all labor force participants contribute money toward retirement benefits (similar to the Chilean plan of asset allocation). The basic tier will set an income floor for everybody, which should be below the minimum wage level to create an incentive for market participation. Special supplements may be made available to basic income maintenance for veterans, disabled people, or others in Table 5-4.

Health Care

Health care, like income maintenance, should be consolidated into a two-tiered system. The bottom tier would be a basic (survival and prevention) tier and would be available to all members of society, including guest workers and migrants. This tier would be under state supervision. The second tier would be market driven and could include a hierarchy of services, depending on the ability of a person to purchase such services.

In the United States, where there is no national health care, it may be possible to convert the existing Department of Veterans Affairs system into a community care system for both veterans and the inner-city poor. The system could then be incrementally made into an equivalent of a national health service. With this structure, people higher on the class ladder may get better health care, but that is already the case in market-guided societies. The above plan would not change that; it would, however, make the rationale for redistribution clearer.

In Europe the two-tiered system should be considered. It already is in existence in some parts of Europe. In such a system, all basic health care may be provided by the bottom tier, and forms of optional health care may be managed by the top tier. This proposal is not likely to be popular in many parts of Europe, where a "groupthink" ("a strong concurrence-seeking tendency [in group behavior] that interferes with effective group decision making" [Forsyth, 1983, p. 487]) exists that all forms of health care are owed to citizens. Another term for such groupthink is a "culture of entitlements." I have already argued that such a culture of entitlement emerges from a sharing-surplus orientation.

Education

Education, like income and health care, should be two-tiered. The basic tier for education should lead to high school and community college or polytechnic level and should be available to all children within a territory. A market-driven second tier, from primary school to the university level, should be encouraged. Those opting for the second tier should receive tax relief. Given that education is a key to creating cultural capital (Bourdieu, 1977), the state cannot be trusted with a monopoly over education.

In this area, the U.S. model may be useful. Most rich countries other than the United States claim that they have free education from cradle to grave. The reality is that they allow only a select population, mostly chosen through a combination of merit and social class, to attain higher education. The United States, a "laggard" in health care (Wilensky, 1975), is an innovator in education. The emergence of "red brick" universities in Britain and other parts of Europe is an effort to copy the U.S. approach.

Although the United States has a two-tiered model in higher education (that is, state- and market driven, which results in public and private higher education) that is highly successful, its secondary and elementary educational systems need overhauling. The following recommendations present a method for overhauling these systems:

- Parents choosing (accredited) private education should be allowed tax relief. The amount of such relief should not exceed the prorated amount of tax they would pay for supporting local public schools. Currently, wealthy parents can afford to pay private school tuition and taxes for public schools, but middle-class and working-class parents who choose private education cannot. A better policy would be to offer all parents a choice: Pay taxes and send their children to public schools or pay tuition and send their children to private schools.

- The formula for supporting public schools should be changed from support by local property taxes to support by state-based education tax, some or all of which could be written off for parents sending their children to private schools. The federal government could then match the amount of state support on the basis of a formula.
- Every school should have a community board, made up of parents and other selected local citizens. A primary reason that it is nearly impossible to acquire an education in low-income neighborhood schools is the lack of a community culture that fosters a climate of learning. The absence of such a culture manifests itself in the unsafe environment in which education takes place; the inability of parents and community elders to support homework and other activities; and the assumption of politically active parents and community elders that more spending for schools will solve all problems, when in fact, more spending with the present structure will produce diminishing returns. The responsibility of the community boards would be to facilitate the development of a culture of learning, with the support of the state's protection function, if necessary.

Housing

The state should not be in the housing business. More often than not, state-erected housing units create ghettos rather than communities. (Table A-1 provides a continuum of differences between ghettos and communities.) Instead, it should create a tax policy encouraging private parties to build and acquire housing on an asset-acquisition plan. Ownership should be encouraged and supported by tax and lending policy. Housing policy should encourage community building rather than simply the construction of spatial units. In effect, housing should be privatized, and the state's regulatory and taxation powers should be used to make housing available to all social groups.

Drug Policy

The objective of drug policy should be to reduce availability of problem drugs (that is, reduce supply) and to reduce demand (that is, reduce need). Related objectives should be to reduce criminalization of addicts, so they can

Table A-1. Contrast between Ghettos and Communities

GHETTOS	COMMUNITIES
People are **forced** to live in ghettos.	People **choose** to live in communities.
People are more frequently **renters.**	People are more frequently **owners**.
There is **little community control** over the behavior of children, adolescents, and adults.	There is **community control** over the behavior of children, adolescents, or adults.
Role models are **inappropriate** for crime-free, violence-free market participation.	*Role models* are **appropriate** for crime-free, violence-free market participation.
Asset acquisition is **difficult.**	*Asset acquisition* is **possible and supported** by community norms.
Housing codes are **hard to enforce.**	*Housing codes* are **enforced**
Local merchants are **exploitative,** carrying inferior merchandise.	*Local merchants* are **solicitous** and carry good quality merchandise.
Public transportation is **inadequate** to sources of employment and *public roads* are **poor**.	*Public transportation* to employment sources is **good** or *public roads* are **good.**

SOURCE: This continuum was developed by the author specifically for inclusion in this book. However, intellectual foundations for this table can be found in the following works: Chatterjee, P. (1967). Neighborhoods by choice or compulsion: A focus for settlement policy. *Social Work, 12*(3), 96–101; Gans, H. (1962). *The urban villagers*. New York: Free Press; MacLeod, J. (1995). *Ain't no makin' it*. Boulder, CO: Westview Press; Marris, P., & Rein, M. (1972). *Dilemmas of social reform: Poverty and community action in the United States*. London: Routledge & Kegan Paul; Rainwater, L. (1970). *Behind ghetto walls: Black families in a federal slum*. Chicago: Aldine; Rein, M. (1983). *Social policy: Issues of choice and change*. Armonk, NY: M. E. Sharpe; Rein, M., Esping-Andersen, G., & Rainwater, L. (Eds.). (1987). Stagnation and renewal in social policy. Armonk, NY: M. E. Sharpe; Wilson, W. J. (1987). *The truly disadvantaged*. Chicago: University of Chicago Press; Wilson, W. J. (1995). *When work disappears: The world of the new urban poor*. New York: Alfred A. Knopf; Wirth, L. (1928). *The ghetto*. Chicago: University of Chicago Press.

be helped to become socially integrated; increased criminalization of drug sellers and pushers, so this behavior has high negative sanction, and to reduce the cost of policing and health services, so these resources can be better used elsewhere. The objective of reducing supply can be accomplished by adopting a policy that severely polices the manufacture or import of problems drugs. The objective of reducing demand, especially demand for illegally manufactured or imported street drugs, can be accopmplished by allowing local addicts to use legally manufactured pure drugs under strict medical supervision and at minimal cost. If demand can be reduced in this way, criminal behavior of addicts directed at paying for illegal and impure drugs also is reduced.

Some countries in Europe (for example, the Netherlands) have opted for the reduced-demand type of policy, and they seem reasonably successful in managing the problems emerging from drug addiction–related behavior. (I have argued that all a state can do is manage such problems.) Furthermore, the type of policy followed by governments such as that of the Netherlands reduces policing expenditures by the state and reduces criminal behavior by addicts. Thus, a possible solution to the drug problem in the United States may lie in eliminating a high-demand market for drugs, maintaining the stigma against drug abuse, and bringing addicts under a medical–social program, through which they can take drugs under controlled conditions (Evans & Berent, 1992).

In some passive-reluctant welfare states, such as the United States, a policing approach with battle themes is popular. Such an approach, which attempts to reduce supply but ignores the high demand for it, is again the result of a marketing-surplus orientation in which the manifest beneficiaries are select groups who may become victims of drug abuse, but the latent beneficiaries are members of the middle and working classes for whom policing and treatment jobs are created.

Role of the Social Work Profession

The profession of social work can have an important role in a welfare state built under the new paradigm in this book. Earlier in this book we have suggested that this profession has developed two basic solutions to the problems of vulnerability that merit welfare state intervention. The two basic solutions are "resocialization" (of the poor and the vulnerable) and "redistribution" (to the poor and the vulnerable). The profession originated, in most industrial countries, as one that resocialized immigrants (through settlement houses), poor people (through skills training), soldiers coming back from a war (through counseling and skills training), and other persons on the fringes to become active social participants. This profession also has justly argued for certain kinds of redistribution (for example, for workers injured in industrial accidents, children without opportunities, and marginal workers without skills) and should continue to do so. As we approach the 21st century, however, the profession seems engaged less and less in arguing for redistribution and resocialization. Graduate social workers do not work in resocialization activities anymore because they are now busy being "treatment agents" in the medical model. The future of the social work profession under our new paradigm rests on its ability to undertake and further develop the resocialization functions it has been abandoning.

References

Bourdieu, P. (1977). *Outline of a theory of practice.* London: Cambridge University Press.

Chatterjee, P. (1967). Neighborhoods by choice or compulsion: A focus for settlement policy. *Social Work, 12*(3), 96–101.

Evams. R. L., & Berent, I. M. (1992). *Drug legalization.* La Salle, IL: Open Court.

Forsyth, D. R. (1983). *An introduction to group dynamics.* Monterey, CA: Brooks/Cole.

Gans, H. (1962). *The urban villagers.* New York: Free Press.

MacLeod, J. (1995). *Ain't no makin' it.* Boulder, CO: Westview Press.

Marris, P., & Rein, M. (1972). *Dilemmas of social reform: Poverty and community action in the United States.* London: Routledge & Kegan Paul.

Rainwater, L. (1970). *Behind ghetto walls: Black families in a federal slum.* Chicago: Aldine.

Rein, M. (1983). *Social policy: Issues of choice and change.* Armonk, NY: M. E. Sharpe.

Rein, M., Esping-Andersen, G., & Rainwater, L. (Eds.). (1987). Stagnation and renewal in social policy. Armonk, NY: M. E. Sharpe.

Wilensky, H. L. (1975). *The welfare state and equality.* Berkeley: University of California Press.

Wilson, W. J. (1987). *The truly disadvantaged.* Chicago: University of Chicago Press.

Wilson, W. J. (1995). *When work disappears: The world of the new urban poor.* New York: Alfred A. Knopf.

Wirth, L. (1928). *The ghetto.* Chicago: University of Chicago Press.

GLOSSARY

Acceptable deviant. A recipient who is in a socially unacceptable role (such as a person who is poor because of a physical disability) but whose deviance can be tolerated.

Alienated labor. The process resulting from the conflict between the human need to find meaning and creativity in one's work and an economic ideology that converts work or labor into only an economic exchange. Also, human labor sold as a commodity without any meaningful attachment to the products generated by that labor.

Allocations. The transfer of goods or services in cash, cash equivalent, or in-kind; transfers that go directly to the recipient or to a third party who provides certain goods and services to the recipient.

Anarchism. Belief in the formation of natural communities as a way to achieve a just society.

Anticollectivism. A typology of the welfare state in which redistribution is seen as unwelcome, liberty and individualism are supported, the free market is seen as the organizing principle of society, and the state is thought to facilitate the operation of the free market. It views capitalism as self-regulating, supports a market economy, and is hostile to the ideal of a welfare state.

Cash transfer. A transfer in the form of a check or money, a tax credit or tax deduction, or vouchers redeemable for a set of named goods and services.

NOTE: I wish to thank Barbara Wester for her help in developing this glossary.

Centric transfer. A transfer from one party or group to another through a central collection or clearing agent.

Collectivism. The commitment to collective interest. *See also* **anti-collectivism** and **reluctant collectivism.**

Commodification. The process by which goods and services are commodified in a market society. The concept can apply to the assignment of commodified values to individuals or groups.

Communal socialism. A form of socialism practiced in the community rather than in the state.

Comprehensive social welfare. The transfer of several items to a given person or population at one time, perhaps through the same agent.

Comprehensive transfer. A transfer administered by one set of offices or agencies.

Conflict. A hostile encounter or struggle, which originates in an existing order, either within or between persons, roles, or groups, as a result of actual or perceived differences in the possession of status, resources, or opportunities. *See also* **knowledge-base conflict.**

Cultural capital. A composite of linguistic, aesthetic, normative, and behavioral preferences in a given situation and knowledge; it originates from the familiarity of higher social classes with such preferences.

Decommodification. The ability of a society to liberate its members from going to work as a prerequisite to earning a living. When decommodification of a given item (such as food, health care, or housing) occurs, it is provided to the members of society without cost to its members.

Demand and supply matrix. A theory that income derived from a wage–labor exchange depends on the productivity of labor. Labor and commodities produced with labor are valued according to their demand in the marketplace. When demand and supply are balanced, that is, when there is perfect competition and individuals and groups maximize their choices under the circumstances, market equilibrium exists.

Demographic analysis. The identification and precise measurement of the influences that underlie population changes.

Dependency ratio. The ratio of benefits paid to recipients to the number of persons taxed from the labor force to provide this unit of benefit.

Differentiated welfare state. A welfare state that is relatively autonomous and that emerges as a response to the demand side of the economy.

Direct transfer. A transaction between a recipient and a centric agent; includes groups and organizations employed by the transfer agent to provide services.

Diversified transfer. A transfer administered by many sets of agencies and offices.

Economic alienation. Marxian theory explaining how humanity becomes alienated from human labor. Certain socioeconomic conditions, legitimized by accompanying ideologies, transform labor into a commodity to be sold in the marketplace.

Economic welfare. A person's well-being as a function of that person's income, holdings, tax status, and other financial resources.

Elites. Groups at the top of the social-class hierarchy of an industrialized society.

Elitism. Autocracy of the elites.

Exchange system. A two-way transaction in which one party provides goods or services to another and is recompensed for doing so.

Exchange theory. The idea that all interactions between persons, groups, communities, organizations, and nations are transactions. All transactions are exchanges guided by conscious rationality; many involve material resources, information, role, attractiveness, and the ability to commit violence, and may be even or uneven. Uneven exchanges lead to power imbalances.

Fabianism. A typology of the welfare state within which redistribution is welcomed incrementally and freedom and fellowship are supported, as are purposeful government action and regulated markets as the organizing principle of society. It recommends that the state build institutions to deal with market failure on a planned basis; views capitalism as generating and perpetuating most inequalities; and supports a mixed economy and state-supported and -administered social services, which incrementally move the state toward a total welfare state. A form of socialism popular in Britain from the 1890s onward.

First World. The rich, capitalistic, industrialized and (mostly) white nations of North America, Western Europe, Australia, and Japan that are based on the traditions of a market economy and individualism.

Fordism. An economic system whose basic idea is derived from Henry Ford's mass manufacturing of automobiles on an assembly line coupled with Frederick Taylor's "scientific management" of the assembly line. Its attributes include mass-produced and homogenized products, assembly-line technology, time management, quota-per-time-unit productivity, homogenized workers' skills, unionization, and a market for homogenized products and services. *See also* **post-Fordism.**

Human development index (HDI). A composite measure of human development containing indicators representing three equally weighted dimensions for human development: longevity, knowledge, and income.

Ideology. A system of thought that prescribes the relationship among and between people and their culturally produced artifacts or services.

Ideology of capitalism. A system of thought that assumes that human needs can be understood only as individual needs, not as needs of the members of the community.

Ideology of laissez-faire. The idea that laboring poor people should be left alone, as should rich people.

Ideology of social Darwinism. The idea that only the "fit" or the "able" species, capable of adaptation to the environment, survive.

Ideology of socialism. A system of thought that assumes that human needs can be understood as being on a continuum between individual needs and the needs of the community.

Ideology of utilitarianism. The belief in the maximal happiness of the maximal number.

Income transfer. A transfer that occurs when part of the income of those who are in the marketplace is transferred to those who are not or when part of the income of all people is transferred to those who are relatively privileged.

Indexed transfer. A transfer that is capped so as not to exceed a lifestyle attainable by earning a minimum wage or some other standard.

Indirect transfer. Third-party payments; a transaction between independent providers who are reimbursed by a transfer agent and a recipient.

Industrial society. A society whose economic sector produces mostly secondary goods (manufacturing and processing), the occupational slope of which leads to skilled labor and engineering and management skills to oversee skilled labor, which is dependent on energy to convert raw materials into secondary goods, and which requires capital and skilled labor.

Industrialization. A technological process involving large-scale manufacturing of goods by machines.

In-kind transfer. A transfer in which a commodity or a service is provided to the recipient instead of cash with which the recipient could purchase it in the marketplace.

Institutional social welfare. A form of social welfare in which planned intervention structures are established to manage vulnerable populations. It assumes that social welfare is the first line of defense against calamities.

Integrated welfare state. A welfare state that is responsive to both demand and supply and in which welfare expenditures are indexed to the spending capacity of the state and the purchasing capacity of the currency.

Involuntary payer. The taxpayer, who pays money, in the form of taxes, that provides income to the state to pay for social and other services.

Item-focused social welfare. Social welfare that is focused on one item at a time and in which transfers of only one item at a time take place.

Knowledge-base conflict. Conflict stemming from groups' differences in knowledge structure and the interests generated from those structures.

Labor force replacement ratio. A ratio calculated as the population under age 15 divided by one-third of the present population ages 15 to 59.

Labor market. A market where labor is exchanged for a salary or wages. *See also* **primary labor market** and **secondary labor market.**

Laissez-faire. *See* **ideology of laissez-faire.**

Liaison elite. Appointed rulers from the mother country and their agents, usually local elites from the colonized country.

Liberal tradition. A tradition in which the community and state intervene to support marginal and vulnerable groups.

Limits of transfer. The rationing of income, goods, or services to recipients.

Market exchange. A transaction governed by rules of supply and demand.

Marxism. A typology of the welfare state within which redistribution is immediately welcomed, freedom and collectivism are supported, free markets are viewed as the source of all evil, and in which the state is the main or only player in a controlled market. It views capitalism as an alien ideology that corrupts all humans and supports a planned economy; the welfare state is a socialist state.

Means-tested transfer. A transfer available only to those of specific social position or economic status.

Medicalization. The definition of individual somatic, aesthetic, psychological, and interpersonal problems as well as social problems as problems that can be dealt with the medical metaphors of diagnosis and treatment.

Membership. The concept that a recipient is entitled to certain goods or services by virtue of his or her belonging to a specific group, such as a church or a state.

Micro-level conflict. A conflict within or between persons, roles, and small groups.

Modernization theory. A theory that the problems of Third World nations result from the values, attitudes, and behavior of the people in those countries. Modernization (resocialization) of Third World countries with the values, information, and institutions of the First World countries would lead to industrialization and the development of wealth.

Monopoly capital. A situation in which the owners of capital (that is, the upper class and its agents, who are mostly from the upper middle class) are always in pursuit of further capital accumulation by gaining a monopoly in the marketplace.

Neutral transfer. A transfer situation that cannot be identified as either progressive or regressive.

Noncentric transfer. The absence of a central agent in the transfer situation.

Noneconomic welfare. A person's well-being based on biological, spiritual, emotional, or normative conditions.

Occupational slope. A hierarchy of socially recognized groups, each of which has attained certain levels of skills or education, can have a group identity, can engage in collective bargaining, and can outline their membership requirements.

Political alienation. A Marxian theory portraying the human need to escape the demand for loyalty and the pretentious promise of a political system. Those at the bottom of a stratification ladder surrender their labor and life to serve the interests of those above.

Post-Fordism. An economic system the attributes of which include the individualized and specialized production of products, small and diversified technological processes, output management, total-quality-per-product productivity, diversified and flexible workers' skills, ineffective unionization, and a market for specialized products and services.

Postindustrial society. A society whose economic sector depends on service and information (that is, trade, finance, health, research, insurance, and recreation) and the occupational slope of which leads to knowledge and information processing. It depends on knowledge and information to produce services and requires capital and knowledge.

Postmodernism. A school of thought that assumes that cultural occurrences are bound by language and specific to given localities and are not necessarily a part of either universal or unilinear patterns of development.

Preindustrial society. A society the economic sector of which is extractive (that is, based on agriculture, mining, fishing, and timber) and whose occupational slope leads to farming, mining, and fishing. It depends on the availability of raw materials and requires expanses of land and relatively unskilled labor.

Primary labor market. A labor market where workers have job security, fringe benefits, and career ladders. *See also* **secondary labor market.**

Privatization. The shift of production and transfer activities from the state to private entrepreneurs.

Progressive social welfare. A form of social welfare in which transfers are made from well-to-do people or groups to those who are not or from those who are successful in the marketplace to those who are not.

Progressive transfer. A transfer between a well-to-do person or group and a person or group of modest means.

Proletariat. Marxian term for the poor and the powerless.

Protected entrepreneurs. Powerful individuals and corporations who, having failed in the marketplace, ask for and receive large amounts of transfer from the state.

Provider. A person, group, or organization that has important skills and that provides important in-kind services to a recipient.

Public–private payers. Individuals and nonprofit organizations whose voluntary donations are combined with matching public funds collected by the state acting as a transfer agent.

Rational choice theory. A theory that states that an important function of any cultural group is production and assumes that there are likely to be persons who may avoid any role in the production of public goods. The problem for the state is who, if anyone, should be allowed to avoid this role in the production of public goods.

Reciprocity network. A system in which workers provide productive labor during some time of their life and are protected when they can no longer provide that labor.

Regressive social welfare. A form of social welfare in which transfer flows either uniformly from everyone to the privileged and the successful in the marketplace or from the less privileged and those not engaged in market exchange to those who are.

Regressive transfer. A transfer from a person or group of modest means to a well-to-do person or group.

Reluctant collectivism. A typology of the welfare state within which redistribution is selectively tolerated and liberty and pragmatism are supported. It views somewhat regulated markets as the organizing principle of society and believes that the state should leave the free market alone but remedy the effects of market failure. It also believes that capitalism, although not self-regulating, is nevertheless the best foundation for society, and it supports a mixed economy and privatization of social welfare, sometimes with state support.

Residual social welfare. Social welfare policy based on the assumption that social welfare policy applies only to those who cannot be supported by family or market systems; it has no planned intervention structure in place to manage the vulnerable populations.

Second World. Countries that are neither rich nor poor and that are located in Eastern Europe, Central and Northern Asia, and Cuba. They are or were socialist, are selectively industrial, and are based on the traditions of a planned economy and collectivism.

Secondary labor market. A labor market where workers do not have job security, fringe benefits, or career ladders. *See also* **primary labor market.**

Social welfare. A transfer system through which goods and services are allocated to individuals and groups through a given unit of social organization, such as the family, the church, the guild, the state, or the corporate group, under a set of rules and with a set of reciprocal roles. *See also* **comprehensive social welfare, institutional social welfare, item-focused social welfare, progressive social welfare, regressive social welfare,** and **residual social welfare.**

Social welfare policy. The ensemble of concrete plans by which social welfare is implemented. At times, some of these plans my be in conflict with each other.

Socialism. *See* **ideology of socialism.**

Structural functionalism. A theory that all societies or national cultures must perform certain key functions to survive as cultural entities. Those functions are universal regardless of where the society is located. However, the macrostructures that perform the functions may take different shapes in different cultures.

Syndicalism. The belief that incremental and selective violence against dominant groups is a way to bring about a better and just society, in which ownership and control of industries would rest in the hands of workers' unions rather than the state.

Theory. *See* **exchange theory, modernization theory,** and **rational choice theory.**

Third-party payment system. A system in which the transfer agent pays the provider to render services to the recipient.

Third World. Mostly nonwhite, poor, preindustrial, and developing societies located in Africa, southern and Southeast Asia, and South America that are often nationalistic, selectively industrial to preindustrial, and based on a mixed economy and regional loyalties.

Transfer. *See* **cash transfer, centric transfer, comprehensive transfer, direct transfer, diversified transfer, income transfer, indirect transfer,**

in-kind transfer, means-tested transfer, neutral transfer, noncentric transfer, progressive transfer, regressive transfer, universal transfer, and **zero transfer.**

Transgenerational poor. A group of poor people in the First World, mostly in the United States, who remain poor generation after generation, trapped in a "culture of poverty." The term "transgenerational poor" and "culture of poverty" were popularized by Oscar Lewis (1966). Such groups as transgenerational poor people are now appearing in Europe as well, especially among certain immigrant groups.

Universal transfer. A transfer in the form of a basic floor of income and services to all in a society regardless of social position or economic status.

Utilitarianism. *See* **ideology of utilitarianism.**

Utopia. An unattainable community in which every rule, artifact, and human relationship is perfect. The term was popularized by Saint Thomas More.

Value-orientation analysis. A theory that human values are enduring beliefs that a specific mode of conduct or end-state of existence is personally or socially preferable to an opposite or converse mode of conduct or end-state of existence.

Value system. An enduring organization of beliefs concerning preferable modes of conduct or end-states of existence along a continuum of relative importance.

Voluntary payer. A payer who voluntarily gives through private contributions.

Welfare community. The community as a second-line provider of transfers to persons in need.

Welfare state. The state as a provider of transfers to persons in need. *See also* **differentiated welfare state, integrated welfare state.**

Zero transfer. No transfer.

Reference

Lewis, O. (1966). The culture of poverty. *Scientific American, 215,* 19–25.

Index

D

E

I

J

K

L

M

N

O

P

R

S

T

U

V

W

Z

About the Author

Pranab Chatterjee, MSW, PhD, LISW, received his undergraduate education at Viswa-Bharati University in West Bengal, India. He subsequently earned a master's degree in social work from the University of Tennessee and master's and doctoral degrees from the University of Chicago. He has worked in various settlement houses, community centers, and local community organizations in Chicago and in Cleveland. Currently, he is professor of social work at Case Western Reserve University, Cleveland, Ohio. He is also a bilingual poet and has published several volumes of poetry.

His earlier book, *Approaches to the Welfare State* (1996), also was published by NASW Press.

Repackaging the Welfare State

Cover design by The Watermark Design Office.

Composed by Electronic Quill in Garamond and Bauer Bodoni.

Printed by Graphic Communications, Inc.

(Order form on reverse side)

ORDER FORM

	Title	Item #	NASW Member Price	Non-member Price	Total
__	Repackaging the Welfare State	3045	$26.35	$32.95	________
__	Approaches to the Welfare State	2626	$27.95	$34.95	________
__	Current Controversies in Social Work Ethics	3002	$6.80	$8.50	________
__	The Legal Environment of Social Work	2359	$27.95	$34.95	________
__	Social Policy Reform, Research, Practice	2790	$31.15	$38.95	________
__	Social Work Speaks	2731	$29.55	$36.95	________
				Subtotal	________
			+ 10% postage and handling		________
				Total	________

❐ I've enclosed my check or money order for $ ____________.

❐ Please charge my ❐ NASW Visa* ❐ Other Visa ❐ MasterCard

________________________________ ________________

Credit Card Number Expiration Date

Signature ____

**Use of this card generates funds in support of the social work profession.*

Name ____

Address ____

City ____________________ State/Province ______________

Country ____________________ Zip ______________

Phone ____________________ E-mail ______________

NASW Member # (if applicable) ______________________

(Please make checks payable to NASW Press. Prices are subject to change.)

NASW PRESS

P. O. Box 431
Annapolis JCT, MD 20701
USA

Credit card orders call
1-800-227-3590
(In the Metro Wash., DC, area, call 301-317-8688)
Or fax your order to 301-206-7989
Or order online at http://www.naswpress.org

Visit our Web site at http://www.naswpress.org.

RWSbin